MW00990763

Pairing with the Masters

A Definitive Guide to Food and Wine

Pairing with the Masters

A Definitive Guide to Food and Wine

Certified Master Chef

Ken Arnone

Master of Wine

Jennifer Simonetti-Bryan

Australia • Brazil • Japan • Korea • Mexico • Singapore • Spain • United King[illegible]

Pairing with the Masters: A Definitive Guide to Food and Wine
Ken Arnone & Jennifer Simonetti-Bryan

Vice President, Editorial: Dave Garza
Director of Learning Solutions: Sandy Clark
Senior Acquisitions Editor: Jim Gish
Managing Editor: Larry Main
Product Manager: Nicole Calisi
Editorial Assistant: Sarah Timm
Vice President, Marketing: Jennifer Baker
Marketing Director: Wendy Mapstone
Senior Marketing Manager: Kristin McNary
Associate Marketing Manager: Jonathan Sheehan
Production Director: Wendy Troeger
Senior Content Project Manager: Glenn Castle
Senior Art Director: Bethany Casey Kirchmayer
Cover Design: Bethany Casey Kirchmayer
Cover Photography: Jim Smith Photography
Interior Design: Judi Orozco Publishing Services
Technology Project Manager: Chris Catalina

Library of Congress Control Number: 2012934798

ISBN-13: 978-1-111-54384-6
ISBN-10: 1-111-54384-4

Delmar
5 Maxwell Drive
Clifton Park, NY 12065-2919
USA

Cengage Learning is a leading provider of customized learning solutions with office locations around the globe, including Singapore, the United Kingdom, Australia, Mexico, Brazil, and Japan. Locate your local office at:
international.cengage.com/region

Cengage Learning products are represented in Canada by Nelson Education, Ltd.

To learn more about Delmar, visit **www.cengage.com/delmar**
Purchase any of our products at your local college store or at our preferred online store **www.cengagebrain.com**

Printed in the United States of America
1 2 3 4 5 6 7 15 14 13 12

Contents

Key Features

CULINARY PRIMER

The ultimate culinary fast-track, the Culinary Primer chapter is crucial to understanding the fundamentals of cooking techniques and how each influence the flavor and texture of a dish. It clearly and quickly illustrates the impact of ingredients and technique on food and wine pairings.

WINE PRIMER

The Wine Primer chapter offers readers a shortcut for wine fundamentals. It provides helpful tips, practical charts, instruction on how to taste for specific components in wine, and how they impact pairings.

Wine Components Summary for White Wines

Wine Components	Low	Medium	High
Aromatic Intensity	Chardonnay Champagne Orvieto Muscadet	Pinot Grigio Chenin Blanc*	Muscat/ Moscato Gewürtraminer Sauvignon Blanc Riesling
Body	Sauvignon Blanc* Riesling	Pinot Grigio Albariño Chenin Blanc*	Chardonnay* Viognier Gewürtraminer
Acid	Chardonnay* Viognier Gewürtraminer Fino Sherry	Pinot Grigio Soave/Arneis Grüner Veltliner	Brut Champagne Riesling Sauvignon Blanc
Sweetness	Gewurztraminer* Pinot Gris*	Riesling*	Moscato Sauternes

1 MAIN INGREDIENT X 3 PREPARATIONS = 3 DIFFERENT FOOD AND WINE PAIRINGS

Each main ingredient is prepared using different techniques and/or ingredients to show its range of flavor intensity, richness, and texture. These variations yield separate and unique wine pairings and tasting experiences. The "1 Main Ingredient × 3 Preparations = 3 Different Food and Wine Pairings" structure is the perfect learning tool for the enthusiast, culinary student, and trade professional.

SHRIMP TEMPURA WITH SOY DIPPING SAUCE

Yield: 10 portions
Cooking Method: Deep-Fry

Ingredients	Amounts - US	Volume	Metric
For the Shrimp Tempura			
Shrimp, 16/20, peeled, deveined, stretched	1 ½ lbs.	30 each	680 grams
Flour, all-purpose	5 ¾ oz.	1 ¼ cups	164 grams
Cornstarch	¾ oz.	3 Tbl.	20 grams
Baking powder		1 tsp.	
Salt, kosher		½ tsp.	
Seltzer water, well chilled	10 fl. oz.	1 ¼ cups	300 ml
Sesame oil		¾ tsp.	
For the Soy Dipping Sauce Yield: 16 oz.			
Dashi	8 fl. oz.	1 cup	240 ml
Soy sauce	2 ½ fl. oz.	¼ cup, plus 1 Tbl.	75 ml
Mirin	1 fl. oz.	2 Tbl.	30 ml
Daikon, grated finely	1 ½ oz.	¼ cup	42 grams
Scallions, thin sliced, bias cut	⅝ oz.	⅓ cup	18 grams
For the Dashi Broth Yield: 32 oz.			
Water	32 fl. oz.	1 qt.	1 L
Kombu, (dried kelp)		6 in. square	
Bonito flakes		½ cup	

Lightly score the underside of the shrimp with a knife.

Shrimp are naturally arched in the center and the object is to straighten them out. Using your fingers apply ge[ntle] pressure to shrimp while moving to opposite ends s[...] begins to straighten.

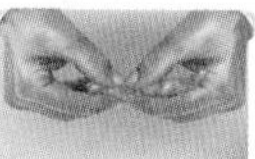

Continue to apply pressure from head to tail so that the shrimp is now completely straight. This is often referred to as 'massaging' the shrimp.

SHRIMP

There are several species of shrimp available on the market today, for example, black tiger, white, brown, and pink. It is important to note that there are taste and quality differences among these products. When available, fresh wild-caught shrimp are preferred.

SHRIMP AND SCALLOP CEVICHE

Yield: 10 portions
Cooking Method: Cure

Ingredients	Amounts - US	Volume	Metric
For the Ceviche			
Shrimp, 16/20, peeled, deveined	20 oz.	32 each	566 grams
Sea scallops, 10/20, heel removed, medium dice	12 oz.	10 each	340 grams
Extra virgin olive oil	2 fl. oz.	¼ cup	60 ml
Lime juice, fresh	6 fl. oz.	¾ cup	180 ml
Lemon juice, fresh	6 fl. oz.	¾ cup	180 ml
Tomato, small dice	8 oz.	1 ½ cup	255 grams
European cucumber, small dice	4 ½ oz.	1 cup	128 grams
Red onion, brunoise	2 oz.	½ cup	56 grams
Scallions, sliced thin, bias cut	1 oz.	½ cup	28 grams
Jalapeño pepper, seeded, minced	¾ oz.	2 Tbl.	20 grams
Cilantro, chopped		1 ½ Tbl.	
Salt, kosher		½ tsp.	
Black pepper, fresh ground		¼ tsp.	
For the Dressing Yield: 12 oz.			
	3 fl. oz.	⅓ cup	90 ml
	3 fl. oz.	⅓ cup	90 ml
	1 fl. oz.	2 Tbl.	30 ml
		½ tsp.	
		2 dashes	
	6 fl. oz.	¾ cup	180 ml
		½ tsp.	
		¼ tsp.	

[...] South American countries and is the national dish of Peru. This [...] town to town, using fish or shellfish that can be raw, seared, or [ty]pically diced and is "cooked/cured" in an acidic marinade, such [a]nd is mixed with a variety of local ingredients such as onions, [...]lo, corn, spicy peppers, and herbs.

SHRIMP SCAMPI

Yield: 10 portions
Cooking Method: Sauté

Ingredients	Amounts - US	Volume	Metric
Shrimp, 16/20, peeled and deveined	1 ½ lb.	30 each	680 grams
Extra virgin olive oil	3 fl. oz.	6 Tbl.	90 ml
Butter, unsalted, cubed	3 oz.	6 Tbl.	85 grams
Garlic, sliced	¾ oz.	2 ½ Tbl.	20 grams
White wine, Chardonnay	4 fl. oz.	½ cup	120 ml
Lemon juice, fresh	1 ½ fl. oz.	3 Tbl.	45 ml
Italian parsley, chopped	¼ oz.	2 Tbl.	8 grams
Crushed red pepper		¼ tsp.	
Lemon zest, fine		½ tsp.	
Salt, sea		½ tsp.	
Black pepper, fresh ground		¼ tsp.	
Baguette, bias cut ¼-inch thick		10 each	
Extra virgin olive oil	1 ½ fl. oz.	3 Tbl.	45 ml

Scampi

1. Brush the baguette slices on both sides with extra virgin olive oil.
2. Grill on both sides until lightly toasted; reserve the crostini for plating.
3. Preheat a large sauté pan over medium heat. Work in batches so that you do not overcrowd the pan and drop the heat. The amount of shrimp you cook in each batch is determined by the size of the pan. *Adjust the amount of oil and butter for each batch.*
4. Add the oil and half the butter to the pan and then a single layer of shrimp.
5. Once the shrimp has sautéed for approximately 1 minute, add the garlic and mix well, ensuring that the shrimp are turned to cook evenly.
6. When the shrimp are cooked three-quarters of the way and the garlic is light brown, add the wine and reduce by half. Add the lemon juice, parsley, crushed red pepper, lemon zest, salt, and pepper; mix well to combine. At this point the shrimp will be cooked and slightly opaque in the center.
7. Turn off the heat and add the remaining butter; swirl the pan to emulsify into the sauce.
8. Place the shrimp scampi on top of the grilled crostini and top with the remaining garlic butter sauce.

The term *scampi* actually refers to *a prawn* in Italian and has become known as the method of preparation listed above.

FOOD AND WINE PAIRING SUMMARY PAGE

Every recipe has a "Wine Pairing Summary Page." This summary details tested wines that are perfect pairings and ones to avoid (and why!). Each is summarized in a chart and marked for fast, easy, and repeated access to save the reader time.

WINE SELECTED with Poached Salmon with Sauce Hollandaise

Wine: Pewsey Vale Dry Riesling ($15)
Origin: Eden Valley, South Australia, Australia

Taste and Texture Comparisons

Dish: Rich, Bold Flavor, Slight Acidity
Wine: Light-Bodied, Strong Lime Aromas, High Acidity, Floral Notes

Rieslings from Eden Valley, Australia, are more akin to those of Austria than of Germany. They are generally dry, light-bodied, racy in their acidity, with strong notes of lime.

Why This Is a Good Pairing

- ***Matching*** – Salmon has a bold flavor, as does the wine. Despite the contrasting textures and weights of the dish and the wine, their flavor intensities match and so one does not overpower the other.
- ***Complementing*** – There is a bridge between the lemon in the sauce and the citrus lime notes in the wine.
- ***Contrasting*** – The flavor of the salmon contrasts with the wine, making the flavors of both stand out.
- ***Cleansing*** – Eden Valley Rieslings are known for intense acidity. The acid cuts through the richness of the salmon and the Hollandaise sauce. Additionally, the acid makes the flavors of the salmon and the sauce pop.

Wines That Didn't Work

NV Brut Champagne (blend) – The acidity is high enough for a cleansing reaction, but the flavor of the champagne is not intense enough to balance the wine with the dish. In the end, the dish covers the wine.

California Chardonnay – We tried a moderately oaked Sonoma Chardonnay, thinking the butter in the Hollandaise would complement the wine's soft buttery notes, but it makes the dish taste heavy and oily.

Alternative: Nuits-St.-Georges Burgundy—Pinot Noir is known to pair well with salmon. Pinot Noir in Burgundy has soft, red berry fruit aromas that are augmented by the salmon. Similar to the Riesling, its high acidity cuts through the richness in the Poached Salmon with Sauce Hollandaise, making the dish more refreshing.

We also tried a few New World Pinot Noirs that did not work as well as the Burgundy. The fruit of the wine is heightened, and although the dish works with the Riesling, the intense fruitiness of the New World Pinot Noirs covers the flavor of the salmon.

SUMMARY	Pewsey Vale Eden Valley Dry Riesling	Nuits-St.-Georges, Burgundy, Pinot Noir	NV Brut Champagne	Oaked California Chardonnay
Matching	+	+		
Complementing	+			
Contrasting	+	+		
Compounding				(–)
Complexing				
Cleansing	+	+	+	
Covering			(–)	
Clashing				

RECIPES MEASURED IN U.S. AMOUNTS, VOLUMES, AND METRIC EQUIVALENTS

Each recipe's ingredients are offered in U.S. standard quantities (i.e., ounces), volume (i.e., cups, tablespoons, teaspoons) and metric equivalents (i.e., grams, milliliters). These measurements offer flexibility for the user based on knowledge, environment, and preference.

SHRIMP RAVIOLI WITH TOMATO COULIS

Yield: 50 ravioli

Ingredients	Amounts - US	Volume	Metric
For the Ravioli			
Basic Pasta Dough		see recipe	
Egg wash, for sealing the ravioli		as needed	
For the Ravioli Filling			
Ricotta Impasta	10 oz.	1 ½ cups	284 grams
Shrimp, seared, chopped	10 oz.	1 ¼ cups	284 grams
Fontina cheese, grated	2 oz.	1 cup	56 grams
Tarragon, chopped		1 Tbl.	
Lemon zest, blanched		1 ½ tsp.	
Roasted garlic, paste		¾ tsp.	

WINE AND DISH "TASTE AND TEXTURE COMPARISONS"

These snapshot, easy-to-read descriptions are designed to help the reader compare and contrast the dish and the wine components directly and side by side for effortless learning.

WINE AND CHEF NOTES, ALTERNATIVES, AND TIPS

Notes offer the reader helpful and interesting tips and facts on a variety of wine and culinary topics from both authors—a Certified Master Chef and a Master of Wine.

Button mushrooms are grown in sterilized manure and should be washed prior to use; however, they are sensitive to moisture, absorb water, and oxidize easily. Just prior to use: wash, drain, and dry mushrooms well before cutting and cooking.

This is a traditional Italian dish; cacciatore means "in the style of the hunter."

Pinotage is the flagship grape of South Africa. It has a few different styles, and this one falls closer to the "coffee camp" with obvious oak influence. It is aged in 80% medium-toast French barrels and 20% heavy-toast American barrels.

APPENDIXES

The Appendixes include quick charts that can be used as reference tools when applying food and wine pairing for any occasion.

Appendix A
Recipes by Wine

GRAPE/BLEND	WINE	MAIN PROTEIN/ INGREDIENT	RECIPE TITLE	PAGE
Sparkling	Agrapart & Fils 7 Crus	Lobster	Lobster Thermidor	74
Sparkling	Charles Heidsieck Brut Réserve	Ravioli	Shrimp Ravioli with Tomato Coulis	223
Sparkling	Domaine Carneros Sparkling Rosé	Crab	Jumbo Lump Crab with Cocktail Sauce	37
Sparkling	Moët et Chandon Nectar Imperial Demi-Sec	Strawberry	Strawberry Shortcake	282
Sparkling	Piper-Heidsieck Brut	Shrimp	Shrimp Tempura with Soy Dipping Sauce	53
Sparkling	Pommery Brut Rosé	Chocolate	Chocolate Soufflé	290
Sparkling	Veuve Clicquot Yellow Label Brut	Salmon	Gravlax	98
Albariño	Burgans Albariño	Ravioli	Cheese Ravioli with Asparagus	215
Arneis	Valdinera Roero Arneis	Halibut	Poached Halibut with Fennel and Orange Slaw	82
Chardonnay	Au Bon Climat Chardonnay	Beef Tenderloin	Beef Tartare	158
Chardonnay	Chateau St. Jean Chardonnay	Mezze Rigatoni	Mezze Rigatoni Salad with Roasted Butternut Squash	239
Chardonnay	Christian Moreau Chablis	Chicken Legs	Buttermilk Fried Chicken	122
Chardonnay	Gloria Ferrer Chardonnay	Chicken Breast	Chicken Breast Stuffed with Spinach and Gruyère	119
Chardonnay	Olivier Leflaive Puligny-Montrachet	Lobster	Lobster Bisque	71
Chardonnay	Penfolds Bin 311 Chardonnay	Shrimp	Shrimp Scampi	56
Chardonnay	Sequoia Grove Chardonnay	Scallops	Sautéed Sea Scallops with Truffle Goat Cheese Sauce	62

About the Authors

Chef Ken Arnone has achieved the highest level of certification in his craft, Certified Master Chef (65 in the US) and Global Master Chef (300 worldwide). His culinary expertise was honed at the Culinary Institute of America, Cuisine Actuelle, The Salish Lodge, and the New York Marriott Marquis as he traversed across the country.

Chef Arnone is currently bringing his passion for food to restaurateurs, hotels, private clubs, and corporations via consulting. His vast knowledge base, attention to detail, and creative style have attracted many prominent clients, including Colavita, Granite City Food and Brewery, Darden Restaurant Group, GRS Restaurant Group, Marriott International, and Renaissance Hotels. Chef Arnone has skillfully executed Food and Wine events for over 15 years. He recently launched Pesto Diavolo, a fiery spread and dip that is available retail as well as on the web.

Master of Wine **Jennifer Simonetti-Bryan** holds the world's top wine title, judges in international wine competitions around the world, and has trained thousands of professionals in the industry.

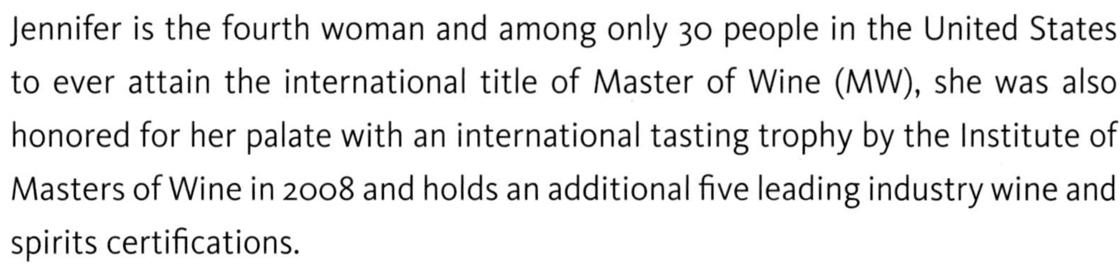

Jennifer is the fourth woman and among only 30 people in the United States to ever attain the international title of Master of Wine (MW), she was also honored for her palate with an international tasting trophy by the Institute of Masters of Wine in 2008 and holds an additional five leading industry wine and spirits certifications.

With an energetic and dynamic personality, Jennifer Simonetti-Bryan has hosted seminars with famous Food Network stars such as Rachael Ray, Bobby Flay, Tyler Florence, Mario Batali, and Jacques Pépin. She is also the author of *The One Minute Wine Master* and host of several wine and spirits courses for The Great Courses.

Ms. Simonetti-Bryan is a frequent guest on national television including NBC's *Today Show*, Fox Business, Fox News, Bloomberg TV, as well as national radio and local news across the country. Additionally, for her expertise she has been featured in *Fortune*, *O The Oprah Magazine*, *Businessweek*, *Everyday with Rachel Ray, Reuters, Gotham, Wine Enthusiast*, and *Wine & Spirits Magazine*.

Acknowledgments

We would like to thank the following for participating in our testing process: Arlington Wine & Liquor, Cape Classics, Colavita, Dreyfus Ashby, Emile Henry, Kobrand Wines and Spirits, Lauber Imports, Masi Agricola, Palm Bay International, Polaner Selections, Rémy Cointreau USA, Riedel USA, Stock Yards, The Country Vintner, Villeroy & Bach, Wine Australia, and Wines of South Africa.

Special thanks to Jim Smith for his photographic skills and positive attitude as well as to Renee Leber for her input and the culinary student perspective.

Most importantly, we would like to thank Christopher, Sharon, Ty, Trevor, Elizabeth, Michele, Michelle, and our families for their support.

1
Introduction

METHODOLOGY, LAYOUT AND HELPFUL HINTS

As a Certified Master Chef and Master of Wine, we are both incredibly passionate about food and wine pairing and share a dedication for precision. It is important to us that our book contributes to the wisdom and perspective on the topic of food and wine as well as fuels enthusiasm for food and wine pairing.

Our objective is clear—to create a definitive guide to food and wine pairing that is easy to read, easy to learn from, and that has principles that are quick to apply.

Master of Wine Jennifer Simonetti-Bryan and Certified Master Chef Ken Arnone.

Master of Wine Meets Certified Master Chef

There are only 65 certified master chefs in the United States and only 31 masters of wine. Given that there are so few of us, you would think we'd pair up all the time. This partnership is the first we have seen of this sort, but we're sure it won't be the last.

Our vision is that this book will empower you to take control and make more confident pairing decisions. There are more than 280 pairings from which to learn in this book. We know it will open your eyes to the possibilities you can create and help you unlock your greatest potential.

METHODOLOGY

Our Approach

When discussing or studying food and wine pairings, too often a food and wine pairing is evaluated by comparing only one specific dish with one specific wine. For this book we took another approach—we purposely change the preparation of the recipes to see how a different technique or ingredient impacts the wine pairing.

There are three recipes per main ingredient. For example, the three recipes for scallops are:

1. Grilled Sea Scallops with Extra Virgin Olive Oil
2. Sautéed Sea Scallops with Truffle Goat Cheese Sauce
3. Prosciutto-Wrapped Sea Scallops with Basil-Walnut Pesto

Although the recipes have the same base main ingredient, the varied techniques and ingredients within each recipe alter the wine pairings dramatically.

We did this to yield information that will help you in several ways. It will help you understand how different techniques impact wines you might pair with a main ingredient. It also teaches you how to decide on a preparation technique that will make a dish more likely to pair well with a specific wine you want to enjoy.

Scallops prepared three different ways illustrates a range of weights, textures, and flavors.

Perfect Pairings and Why

Pairing with the Masters clearly identifies the specific wine that pairs best with a specific recipe and why.

We could have created a simple list of wines that should pair well with a main ingredient. However, we believe that extensive taste testing and an explanation as to why a pairing worked is necessary to truly understand food and wine pairings.

To demonstrate, consider the statement, "Scallops pair well with Sauvignon Blanc, Chardonnay, and Pinot Noir." Does this mean no matter how you prepare the scallop it will always go with one of these wines? Do we mean all Sauvignon Blancs, Chardonnays, and Pinot Noirs pair well?

We provide answers to questions like these and more with each main ingredient. For example, as you will see with the three scallop recipes, we explain how a Sauvignon Blanc paired beautifully with the Grilled Sea Scallops with Extra Virgin Olive Oil, yet was too acidic and stripped the flavor of the Sautéed Sea Scallops with Truffle Goat Cheese Sauce. The Sautéed Scallops with the Truffle Goat Cheese Sauce was complemented much better with an oaked Chardonnay. Additionally, while two white wines worked with the first two dishes, the Prosciutto-Wrapped Sea Scallops with Basil-Walnut Pesto overpowered the whites and called for a Pinot Noir.

Explanations of Why Pairings Work or Don't

Showing a specific food and wine pairing is good, but it didn't seem enough to simply say what were perfect pairings and why. This is why we explain why one or two wines go well with a specific dish, and we also explain why two to three others did not pair well.

As each main ingredient showcases three recipes, we explain why a specific wine worked as well as how it reacted with the other two recipes. For example, in our three chicken leg recipes a Chablis paired well with Buttermilk Fried Chicken, but was terrible with the Chicken Cacciatore and was overpowered by the Tandoori Chicken.

We felt these explorations and observations were necessary to give a more well-rounded explanation and complete picture of food and wine pairing.

Recipe and Wine Selection

You will notice a variety of recipes in this book, from classical to traditional to mainstream. They are intended to help you to easily understand the flavor profiles and apply the concepts learned. The more innovative recipes provide guidance for more challenging pairings.

The primary focus was to find a food and wine pairing that was magical. We tested more than *600 food and wine combinations* and each dish was tasted with on average 8 to 14 wines. Each of the recipes and wine selections was also tasted several times to truly understand the dynamics of the pairing.

LAYOUT

Food and Wine Pairing Page

Each recipe has a food and wine pairing page which discusses the wine that was ultimately selected with a specific recipe. Also included on this page is information about that wine, the wine's flavor profile in direct comparison to the dish, reasons why the pairing works, examples of wines that don't work, and a summary grid.

Chapter Summaries

Each chapter has a summary section where we indicate the main ingredient, the three recipes, cooking method, and the selected wines. We also draw conclusions based on our analysis per main ingredient and break it down using three main themes:

1. Main ingredient tendencies
2. Specific techniques that changed the pairing
3. Specific ingredients that changed the pairing

These are the three main reasons that drive and guide a food and wine pairing.

The first theme lists the main ingredient's general tendencies which indicate the types of cooking methods or wines they gravitate towards as well as potential wine range. For example, crab's light weight and texture is suitable for light- to medium-bodied wines.

The second theme identifies how the technique in preparing the dish impacts the pairing versus the others. For example, grilling creates more intense flavors than poaching and the flavor as a result of the grilling can complement mineral notes in wines.

The third theme points out where specific ingredients were significant in changing the pairing. For example, the cardamom and thyme in the duck jus with the Sous Vide Duck recipe complements the earthy and herbal notes in the Côtes du Rhône Rouge.

Although there are no set formulas in food and wine pairing, the understanding you will gain from this book and your own personal experiences will set you up for successful wine selections.

Symbols Used in This Book

This symbol introduces a useful tip or explanation.

This symbol introduces a comment from **Jennifer Simonetti-Bryan, MW.** These are explanations, tips, and stories to keep in mind regarding the wine, the dish, or the pairing.

This symbol introduces a comment from **Chef Ken Arnone, CMC**. These are explanations, tips, and stories to keep in mind regarding the dish, the wine, or the pairing.

HELPFUL HINTS

Types of Pairings

Food and wine pairings can be categorized into three main groups:

- ***One-Way Pairings:*** These pairings either make the wine shine or the food shine, but not both. Although these pairings can be quite good, this wasn't our target.
- ***Two-Way Pairings:*** These pairings make both the food and wine shine.
- ***Three-Way Pairings:*** These pairings not only make both the food and the wine shine, but they also create an additional magical element.

Our goal was to identify and replicate two-way and three-way pairings. This way, everyone wins. However, don't write off one-way pairings, as there may be a situation where you really want either your food or your wine to shine individually.

Matching and the Seven Cs of Pairing

When you taste food and wine together, a variety of reactions unfold on your palate. We found the following eight reactions most prevalent in the success or failure of pairings. I recommend removing this—it seems obvious as its the title. You will see these listed in the wine pairing section with each recipe.

1. ***Matching*** – When a dish and a wine are comparable in weight, texture, or structure, we call that matching. For example, the full-bodied Merlot from St. Emilion is evenly matched with the rich, full weight of the Gorgonzola Dolcelatte-Topped Beef Tournedos. Pairings in which the dish and wine match are less likely to result in one overpowering the other.
2. ***Complementing*** – When a dish and a wine share a common flavor, this common flavor creates a bridge between the dish and the wine that is complementary. For example, if the wine has aromas reminiscent of rosemary (such as many red wines from the Rhône Valley), this can build a bridge to a dish that has rosemary. Pairings that have complementary flavors have a better chance of being two-way pairings.
3. ***Contrasting*** – When a flavor, texture, or structure in the wine draws out a distinct and different or opposite flavor, texture, or structure in the dish (or vice versa), this results in a positive reaction. For example, in many meat dishes, the savory flavor of the meat makes the flavors of the fruit in the wine pop, making the flavor of both the wine and the dish stand out more.

4. ***Compounding*** – This reaction can be positive or negative. Compounding happens when there is a flavor, texture, or structure in common between the wine and the dish and that common flavor is amplified. For example, there are wines that have a green, herbaceous note to them and, when combined with some dishes with these green notes, they compound in a negative way (Green + Green = Green^2). A positive example would be the compounding of the red berry flavors of the Brachetto d'Acqui with Strawberries and Champagne Sabayon.
5. ***Complexing*** – This reaction happens when you taste more layers of flavors as a result of the pairing. The whole is greater than the sum of the parts. The opposite of stripping flavor, complexing generally happens when there is contrasting of flavors. This reaction can make the wine (or the food) taste more expensive than it is.
6. ***Cleansing*** – Cleansing happens when the acidity of the wine cuts through the fat of the dish. For example, the crisp high acid of dry champagne cuts through Shrimp Tempura, creating a refreshing, cleansing sensation (it can also make you feel like you are eating food that is lower in fat). However, cleansing can cause a negative reaction when it strips the flavor of the dish or the wine.
7. ***Covering*** – When a dish or a wine overpowers the other, this is generally a negative reaction. For example, when pairing a delicate white fish with a rich, full-bodied red wine, all you would taste is the red wine. You would lose the flavor of the fish because it would be overpowered by the wine.
8. ***Clashing*** – Clashing occurs when contrasting flavors, textures, or structures are negative or create a new negative flavor, texture, or structure. For example, have you ever drunk orange juice immediately after brushing your teeth? That's a good example of clashing flavors. An example from the book would be a Gewürztraminer with the Grilled Pork Tenderloin with Caramelized Apple Compote. The floral notes (rose) in the wine clash with the grilled pork and apple flavors in the dish.

How Personal Preference Impacts Pairing Perception

Personal preferences and palate differences have a tremendous impact on the perception of a food and wine pairing. For example, we hosted a tasting in Washington, D.C., where we paired Kung Pao Shrimp with a Barolo, Gewürztraminer, and Champagne. We did this to demonstrate wines that worked and did not work.

With the Barolo we were showing that the spice and salt in the dish exacerbate the intense tannins in the wine (in other words, a less than pleasant pairing). When we asked the group who preferred the Barolo versus the two other wines with the Kung Pao Shrimp, a few people raised their hands. When one of them was asked why, he said, "Well, I just love Barolo."

If you love Barolo (or any other wine, for that matter), your palate is going to gravitate towards that wine. It is natural for your palate to recognize a wine that's familiar to you and that you really enjoy.

Understand too that just because you enjoy a wine with a dish we have said "didn't work" doesn't mean you are wrong. It could very well mean your personal preference is for that wine and it doesn't really matter what you eat with it. That's okay—drink it to your heart's content. Having said this, the dish you are pairing your favorite wine with may not be showing it off to its best advantage.

Our intention in this book is to help you understand the flavor attributes and dynamics of food and wine pairings. Our goal is to remain as objective as possible and to establish repeatable two-way and three-way pairings where both the wine and the dish are enhanced and shine together.

2
Culinary Primer

The culinary primer will provide you with a basic understanding of how ingredients and cooking techniques impact a food and wine pairing. All ingredients will gravitate towards specific methods and techniques based on their characteristics. Components such as spices, herbs, vegetables, sauces, etc. also impact the flavor profile and dynamics of a dish. The ingredients and techniques used will truly guide you to the best food and wine pairing.

PASSION

Cook with a passion for food! Allow your passion to lead you through the recipe, which should serve as a guideline for the dish. Sometimes people cook straight from a recipe and in a formulaic way. You control the outcome on the plate and must think as well as use your knowledge and experience to impact the outcome.

Don't make cooking clinical!

CULINARY BASICS

The majority of the recipes in this book represent traditional/classical dishes and their flavor profiles. These recipes and notes will guide you through a complete understanding of preparation, execution, and the basis for establishing successful food and wine pairings. It is important for you to keep in mind that it is easier to adjust the flavor of a dish than it is to choose a different wine.

Ingredients

Raw ingredients are the building blocks of a dish. Starting with the highest-quality ingredients available is the beginning of creating great food. When possible, taste ingredients before purchasing to ensure that they are of a superior quality.

It is my preference to purchase organic, antibiotic-free, hormone-free, free-range, grass-fed and/or local ingredients when possible. These foods are simply healthier and often have a richer and more pure flavor than the alternative.

Flavor Dynamics and Balance

Whether you are cooking one of the classics or creating your own recipe, successful dishes rely on balanced flavor dynamics: rich/acidic, rich/sweet/acidic, sweet/sour, sweet/salty, etc. Understanding these dynamics and the role of each ingredient is important to arrive at a balanced dish. It is relatively common to find a dish that has too many ingredients/components or conflicting flavor profiles such as sweet/sour/salty. Sweet and sour harmonize on your palette, but the introduction of salt can throw off that balance.

Cooking Techniques and Execution

Holding true to the basic techniques of cooking is very important for the success of a dish. You must have a complete knowledge of the basic techniques: poach, sauté, roast, grill, broil, stew, braise, pan-fry, deep-fry, and so on. For example, starting to sauté in a cold pan will never yield the same results as starting with a properly preheated pan. This is because the main ingredient will not brown properly, which impacts flavor, and will more than likely stick to the pan.

Seasoning

Proper *seasoning* determines how the taste of a dish is perceived. We salt foods to bring out their natural flavor, not to taste the salt. Although most recipes call for a specific amount of seasoning, this is a guideline. *You should always taste while cooking and before serving.* There are many variables that impact the amount of seasoning required for a specific dish: moisture level in a product, pre-seasoned components such as stock and sauces, processed ingredients, cook time, and final yield.

Use the technique of slow "stage" seasoning throughout the cooking process so that you don't add too much seasoning in the beginning or feel that you are adding too much at the end. One exception to this rule would be a stock or dish that will reduce/cook over a long period of time, where seasoning early may result in a salty final product. Stage seasoning also allows flavors to develop and marry during the cooking process.

HOW CUT AND INGREDIENTS IMPACT PAIRINGS

The nature of a specific protein, the ingredients used, the cooking method, and how all of this impacts taste are key components to successful food and wine pairings. This is because each ingredient and technique has specific characteristics that determine the final flavor profile of a dish. For example, a poached salmon and a grilled salmon will have very different flavor attributes and each will react differently with a wine.

Most protein cuts of beef, pork, lamb, venison, etc. can be classified in two ways: those that are less exercised and those that are more exercised.

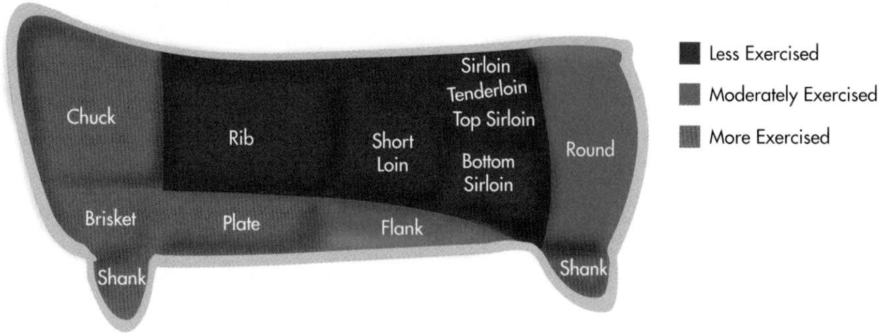

- ***Less Exercised:*** These cuts are naturally tender, have varying amounts of intramuscular fat, are typically marketed in portion cuts, and can be cooked relatively quickly (e.g., poach, saute, grill, broil, stir-fry, pan-fry and deep-fry).
- ***Moderately Exercised:*** These cuts are exposed to some degree of exercise, have varying amounts of intramuscular fat, and can be cooked with either dry or moist heat (e.g., flank steak can be grilled or braised).
- ***More Exercised:*** These cuts come from the more exercised parts of the animal, are inherently tougher, require longer cook times, and often benefit from slow, moist heat such as braising and stewing.

HOW COOKING TECHNIQUE IMPACTS PAIRING

The various cooking techniques and their attributes have a definitive impact on the flavor profile of a dish. The type of heat and cooking medium—dry/moist heat, stock, amount of fat in the dish, and how the sauce is derived—directly influence the flavor profile and thus the wine pairing.

The flavor scale below details the basic range in flavors for each cooking technique.

Flavor Scale: How Technique Impacts Flavor Intensity

Flavor Intensity	Mild				Intense
Technique	1	2	3	4	5
Shallow Poach	X	X			
Deep Poach		X	X		
Sous Vide		X	X		
Stir-Fry		X	X	X	
Pan-Fry/ Deep-Fry			X	X	
Sauté			X	X	
Roast				X	X
Grill				X	X
Braise				X	X
Stew				X	X

This flavor scale is a general guideline and depicts typical flavor profiles derived from these techniques. There are always exceptions based on ingredients, culture, proteins, and so on. An example is Grilled Sea Scallops with Extra Virgin Olive Oil compared to Grilled Lamb Chops with Mint Emulsion. They are cooked using the same technique, but the sea scallops are much lighter in flavor profile than grilled lamb chops, based simply on the main ingredient.

Shallow Poach

Shallow poach is a moist-heat method of cooking via steam and simmering and is intended for tender portion cuts of protein. The cooking liquid comes one-third of the way up the protein. It typically contains acid such as white wine or lemon juice and stock; the sauce is developed from the resulting cooking liquid, which is called a *cuisson*.

Using wine in the poaching liquid will create a natural bridge between the food and the wine. The resulting flavor profile is often delicate and subtle, but can vary according to the liquid and aromatics. Shallow poaching is a technique typically used to preserve the purity of delicate flavors.

Examples of Items to Shallow Poach

- Clams
- Trout
- Chicken breast
- Sole
- Flounder
- Pheasant breast

Deep Poach

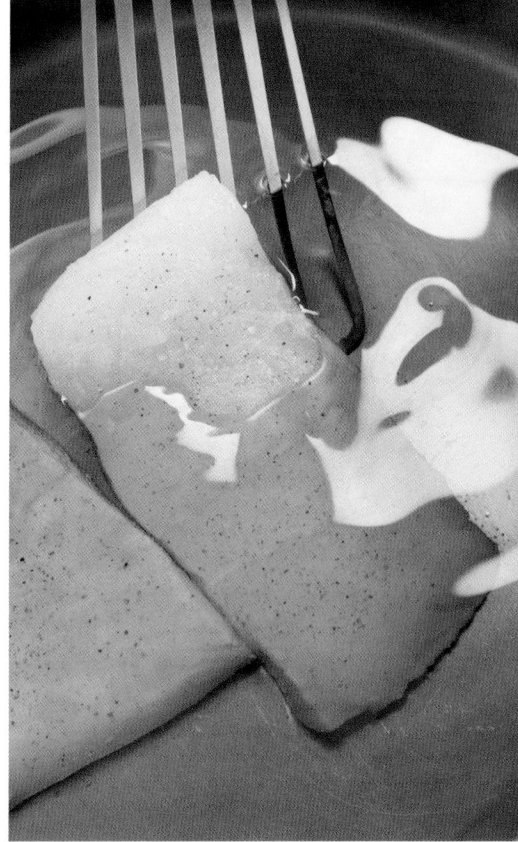

Deep poach is a moist-heat method of cooking intended for tender portion cuts and whole pieces of protein. The poaching liquid can be a stock, court bouillon, or suitable oil that completely covers the protein. The sauce is typically not derived from the poaching liquid and comes from a separate technique. Sauces would include hollandaise, beurre blanc or rouge, salsa, or compote.

Examples of Items to Deep Poach

- Salmon
- Halibut
- Lobster
- Skate
- Beef medallion
- Chicken breast

Sous Vide

Sous vide is a dry-heat method of cooking traditionally intended for tougher, more exercised whole cuts of protein. The main item is vacuum-sealed in a plastic bag and cooked in a temperature-controlled water bath using a thermal circulator at a low temperature for a prolonged period of time. The sauce is typically derived from a stock or a sauce base. Today, this technique is commonly used for both less and more exercised cuts of protein, individual portion cuts, whole pieces of protein, as well as some vegetables. Proteins may be seared before or after vacuum sealing.

It is critical to have complete knowledge of this technique prior to execution because prolonged exposure for proteins at low temperatures as well as the anaerobic environment can be potentially hazardous because these conditions can be ideal for bacterial growth. Many states require a Hazard Analysis Critical Control Points Plan (HACCP) for each item being served in a restaurant utilizing this technique.

Examples of Items to Sous Vide

- Lamb leg/shank
- Beef short ribs
- Veal osso bucco
- Beef medallion
- Pork tenderloin
- Chicken legs
- Duck breast
- Salmon
- Striped bass
- Lobster

Stir-Fry

Stir-fry is a dry-heat method of cooking intended for tender portion cuts of protein. The proteins are usually cut into bite-sized pieces and the cook time is very short. The protein, vegetables, and sauce are typically cooked in a wok over high heat. The temperature is controlled by "stirring" the ingredients with a special spatula and spoon, using the cooler sides when necessary to regulate the heat.

Stir-fry quickly cooks the protein and vegetables; the flavor can vary greatly from mild to intense based on the ingredients. Examples of sauces and ingredients include hoisin sauce, oyster sauce, dark soy sauce, garlic, ginger, scallions, Szechuan peppercorns, and dried chili peppers.

Examples of Items to Stir-Fry

- Boneless chicken thighs
- Shrimp
- Lobster
- Skirt steak
- Pork shoulder
- Scallops

Pan-Fry

This is a dry-heat method of cooking intended for tender portion cuts of protein and vegetables. The main item is typically breaded, battered, or coated with a starch and cooked in a suitable fat, lard, or another animal fat such as duck fat. The fat must come two-thirds of the way up the main item to ensure even cooking and browning. There will be a flavor transfer with certain fats (olive and peanut oil/lard). Sauces and accompaniments are not typically derived from the cooking method and vary in flavor profile; some examples include sauce remoulade and lemon wedges.

Pan-frying is where we start to develop a more complex flavor system from texture and richness. There is no *Maillard reaction* (see Chef's Note) of the protein; however, the coating (batter, breadcrumbs, potatoes, etc.) can add an element of sweetness from browning.

Examples of Items to Pan-Fry

- Flounder
- Eggplant
- Pork cutlet
- Oysters
- Veal scallopine
- Chicken breast

Certain cooking techniques result in a well-browned exterior and thus add a rich element and texture to the final flavor. This is called the Maillard reaction, often referred to as caramelization, it is a chemical reaction between amino acids and a carbohydrate unit. This occurs in meats, bread, coffee beans, nuts, beef and dark chocolate.[1] Examples of techniques that benefit from the Maillard reaction are stir-fry, sauté, roast, braise, stew, and grill.

[1] Howard McGee, *On Food and Cooking: The Science and Lore of the Kitchen* (New York: Scribner, 2004), 778.

Deep-Fry

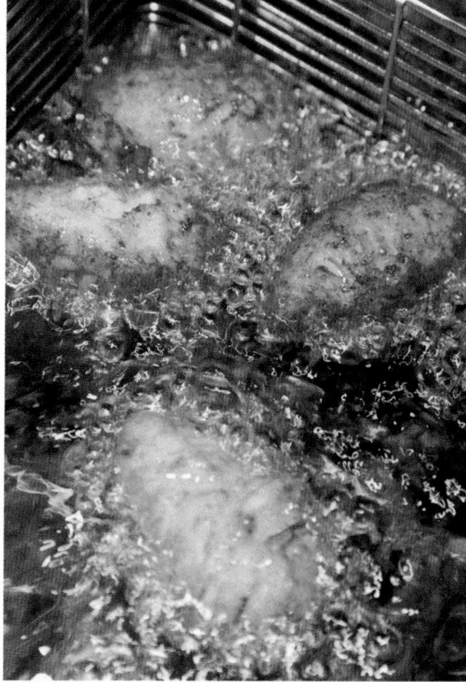

Deep-fry is a dry-heat method of cooking intended for tender portion cuts of protein and vegetables. The main item is typically breaded, battered, or coated with a starch and cooked in suitable frying oil—one with a relatively high smoking point, 400 F (204 C) degrees or above.

As stated above for pan-fry, the selection of cooking fat is important. Sauces and accompaniments are not derived from the cooking method and vary in flavor profile. Typical sauces include soy dipping sauce, tartar sauce, aioli, and vinegar or lemon sauce.

Examples of Items to Deep-Fry

- Asparagus
- Calamari
- Catfish
- Chicken legs
- Cod filets
- Fritters

Sauté

Sauté is a dry-heat method of cooking intended for tender portions of protein and vegetables. The sauce is developed in the pan from the fond formed during cooking. Deglazing the pan with wine when building the sauce creates a bridge between the food and the wine.

The sauté method can vary in flavor intensity depending on the main item and the sauce base. The Maillard reaction also plays a key role in flavor development.

Examples of Items to Sauté

- Tuna steak
- Monkfish
- Chicken breast
- Veal medallion
- Beef tournedos
- Striped bass filet

Roast

Roasting is a dry-heat method of cooking intended for whole tender pieces of protein and vegetables. The sauce is traditionally formed from the juices or drippings released during the cooking process—examples are jus lie or pan gravy.

This cooking technique moves toward the more intense end of the flavor scale. Roasting creates deep flavors and, in general, more Maillard reaction. This adds a crispy texture and a hint of sweetness.

Examples of Items to Roast

- Leg of lamb
- Fresh ham
- Prime rib
- Whole chicken/turkey/duck
- Whole red snapper
- Beets

Grill

This dry-heat method of cooking is intended for tender portion cuts, whole cuts of protein, and vegetables. Sauces and accompaniments are not derived from the cooking method and vary in flavor profile. Examples of sauces include compound butters, salsas, chutneys, relishes, and barbecue-style sauces.

When certain woods are used (apple wood, cherry wood, mesquite, or hickory), there is a transfer of flavor, which should be factored into the pairing decision. Grilling results in bold flavor. The main item can be marinated and takes on a fair amount of Maillard reaction during cooking as well as a smoky character.

Examples of Items to Grill

- Chicken
- Beef tenderloin
- Veal chop
- Pork tenderloin
- Lamb chops
- Scallops
- Pompano
- Onions

Stew

This is a combination-heat method of cooking using dry and moist heat. It is intended for tougher, more exercised cuts of protein that have been cut into bite-size pieces. The diced protein is typically seared and then is completely covered with stock during cooking. Vegetables are usually added during cooking and the sauce is the cooking liquid.

Generally, the flavor intensity for these dishes is at the upper end of the scale.

Examples of Items to Stew

- Beef shank/shoulder/neck
- Pork shank/shoulder
- Lamb shoulder
- Venison shank/shoulder

Braise

Braising is also a combination-heat method of cooking using dry and moist heat that is intended for tougher, more exercised portion and whole cuts of protein. The protein is typically seared first and then stock is added to come one-half to three-quarters of the way up the main item. Once the protein is tender, the cooking liquid is reduced and thickened to create the sauce. Braising yields the same flavor and texture attributes as stewing.

Examples of Items to Braise

- Beef shank/shoulder/short ribs
- Veal breast/neck
- Pork shank/shoulder
- Duck legs
- Lamb shanks
- Rabbit legs
- Chicken legs

Convection oven temperatures run approximately 30–50 F degrees hotter than conventional ovens based on the circulation of air, when using a conventional oven increase the temperature accordingly. The temperature may need to be adjusted based on your individual oven.

DRIVERS OF FOOD AND WINE PAIRINGS

The main drivers of food and wine pairing fall into three camps: main ingredient, techniques, and accompaniments. The starting point is to understand the main ingredient and its characteristics; this in turn drives the best-suited techniques and lastly the sauce, accompaniments, and/or sides.

Main Ingredient Tendencies

Main ingredients have a natural affinity towards certain ingredients and accompaniments that will guide the pairing. This can be as simplistic as lemon and butter with shellfish, or more complex as fruit sauces and acidity with duck. The richness of the duck naturally gravitates towards sweet fruit sauces such as cherry and orange. It also benefits from the presence of acidity, which cuts through the richness/fat and brightens the flavor. Lastly, some items are so bold on their own that they require very little or no accompaniment as in a roasted prime rib.

Weight of the Main Ingredient

The main ingredient's inherent flavor profile, weight, and texture will have a significant impact on the food and wine pairing. Halibut is a mild fish best suited for poach or sauté and accompanied by a light- to medium-bodied sauce, which will gravitate towards a light- to medium-bodied wine. On the opposite end of the spectrum is a beef shank. It is rich and higher in fat which is more suited for stewing and braising, generally accompanied by a rich sauce and will gravitate towards a complex full-bodied wine. The same holds true for desserts comparing the weight of Lemon Pound Cake to that of a Chocolate Mousse.

Cooking with Wine

Using wine as an ingredient while cooking is a technique that can be used to create a flavor bridge for food and wine pairings. This can be accomplished in several ways: a marinade, deglazing a pan, finishing a sauce with a wine reduction. We utilized this technique in several recipes included in the book (e.g., Beef Bourguignon served with Bodega Chacra Barda Pinot Noir, where the beef was marinated with a basic burgundy).

Marinades

Marinades can enhance the flavor and potentially texture of a dish and thus impact the food and wine pairing. Marinades can be classified by their components: oil, acid, and aromatics. Any aromatics, herbs and spices used will add complexity to the dish and the type of acid, vinegar, juice or wine used will also drive the pairing. For example, the lime and lemon juice in the Ceviche steered the pairing towards a delicate citrusy Vinho Verde.

Accompaniments

Many recipes have traditional accompaniments and/or sides that impact and guide pairings (e.g., tempura and soy). Our recipe for grilled flank steak sandwich has Manchego Cheese, grilled peppers, oven-dried tomatoes, and a pimenton mayonnaise. These provided additional complementary and contrasting elements to the Carménère that paired well.

Other Items That Can Dramatically Impact Pairing

The following ingredients can strongly impact and sway a food and wine pairing. They can influence a pairing's balance (acid) or their flavors have the potential to clash (capers) or cause a compounding reaction (dry spices). Care should be taken to taste the dish with the wine to determine if any adjustments are necessary.

- ***Acid*** – citrus, vinegar, etc.
- ***Artichokes***
- ***Asparagus***
- ***Avocado***
- ***Butter and cream***
- ***Capers***
- ***Olives***
- ***Chili peppers*** – jalapeño, serrano, habanero, crushed red pepper, etc.
- ***Dried fruit*** – raisins, apricots, cherries, prunes, cranberries, apples, pears, etc.
- ***Dry spices*** – cayenne, cardamom, coriander, allspice, nutmeg, clove, fennel, anise, curry, turmeric, mustard, etc.
- ***Herbs*** – basil, mint, cilantro, tarragon, sage, thyme, chives, rosemary, etc.
- ***Horseradish and wasabi***
- ***Nuts*** – walnut, pecan, macadamia, pistachio, almond, pine nut, hazelnut/filbert, etc.

SUMMARY

All of the cooking techniques discussed and various ingredients can affect the taste of the main protein and flavors of a dish. This is crucial to understand because it directly impacts the type of wine that can be paired well with that dish.

In this book, one common theme for successful food and wine pairing is balance. Balance, with regard to flavor intensity, texture, and weight, is important. The more intensely flavored the dish is, the more intensely flavored the wine needs to be in order to balance it. This is also true at the opposite end of the spectrum—milder flavored dishes require milder wines.

If there is an imbalance in either the intensity of flavor, texture, and/or weight in the pairing, there is a risk of the dish overpowering the wine or vice versa. Each change in ingredients or cooking technique can change the flavors, textures, and weight of a dish and, as a result, the wine with which it should be paired.

It is incredibly gratifying to create delicious food at home or in a restaurant. Successful cooking relies upon a complete understanding of fundamental techniques, knowledge of ingredients, and experience through repetition. These aspects of cooking allow you to be comfortable in the kitchen and execute dishes successfully with confidence. With that said, at some point your experiences should lead to culinary intuition and the making of a chef.

3
Wine Primer

This chapter provides you with a basic understanding of wine, its components and flavor characteristics. It also explains most of the terminology that you will see in the coming chapters of this book. We recommend you supplement your knowledge by taking a wine tasting course so that you can build your taste memory for wines.

Grape varieties differ in shape, size, aroma, sugar, weight, acid, and tannin, all of which leads to different basic profiles. Grapes are also grown in different areas around the world with varying climates and winemaking philosophies.

Noble versus Regional Grape Varieties

To simplify things, grape varieties roughly break down into two camps: noble and regional.

Noble White Grapes: **Chardonnay, Sauvignon Blanc, Riesling, Chenin Blanc**

Noble Red Grapes: **Cabernet Sauvignon, Merlot, Pinot Noir, Syrah, Grenache**

It is likely that you have heard of the grape varieties above. Wines are generally made with grapes from the species *Vitis vinifera*. They are grown in a variety of countries, regions, and climates around the world. While climate, vintage, region, and style all have an impact on the wine, many typical aromas, flavors, and structural components are consistent with noble grape varieties.

Regional grapes demonstrate their typical characteristics and greatness best in their country or region of origin. Generally speaking, however, you will not often see them outside of their region of origin and, if you do, they will display less consistent characteristics than they're known for. Additionally, they also have a more limited price range, whereas noble grape varieties can be found in both the value as well as in the high end of the price spectrum.

A few examples of regional grapes found in this book include:

Regional White Grapes: **Albariño, Arneis, Grüner Veltliner**

Regional Red Grapes: **Sangiovese, Tempranillo, Malbec, Zinfandel**

Grape Variety Differences

There are nearly 4,000 different types of grape varieties. Only those from the *Vitis vinifera* species (which include the above noble and regional grape varieties) are known for making quality wine. Grape varieties vary in their size, thickness of skin, potential for sugar, density of the grape cluster, and flavonoid compounds. This contributes to the immense diversity of flavors, textures, and structures found in wines.

Aromas and Flavors

As we've just mentioned, grapes have different compounds that are responsible for aroma and flavor. Each of these compounds has different molecular weights and volatilities. Some will leap from the glass while others will stay in there until you stick your nose in the glass and take a big sniff.

How to Taste for a Wine's Aromas and Flavors

To test the wine's aromatic intensity, conduct the *chest, chin, nose* test.

1. ***Chest***: First, hold the glass of wine at your chest. If you smell any wine aromas from this distance it is a very aromatic wine. That means there are aromatic compounds in the wine that are so volatile and pronounced, they hit your olfactory receptors from a distance.
2. ***Chin***: Hold the glass at your chin. If you can't smell anything at your chest and you can smell aromas at your chin, it's a moderately aromatic wine. Even when you have aromatic wines, the aromas may smell different at your chin than at your chest.
3. ***Nose***: For some wines, you won't be able to smell anything at your chin. You need to literally stick your nose in the glass and take a big sniff. For less aromatic varieties and more neutral grape varieties, this is the only way you are going to smell anything. If you have an aromatic wine, see how the aromas change again when you stick your nose in the glass.

One of the recipes in this book, Thai Beef with Massaman Curry, is paired with a Moscato d'Asti. Moscato (Muscat) is one of the most aromatic grape varieties in the world. Chances are you will smell it as soon as you open the bottle; you don't have to hold the wine glass at your chest.

At the other end of the spectrum is an Italian white, an Orvieto, which is made from a blend of white fairly neutral grape varieties in Umbria, Italy. The aromatics in this wine are quite subtle.

How Aromas and Flavors Impact Food and Wine Pairings

Intense aromas typically translate to intense flavors on the palate. There are risks at both the high end and the low end of the aromatic spectrum.

Food Pairing Risks

Food Pairing Risks with Highly Aromatic Wines	Food Pairing Risks with Low Aromatic Wines
The wine may be too intense and overpower a dish.	The subtle aromas and flavors will be overpowered by the dish.
The wine may have strong flavors that will intensely clash with flavors in the dish.	

When it comes to food and wine pairing, there is a higher risk for intensely aromatic wines to not pair well than there is for low aromatic wines. However, as with most things in life, when there is more risk, that risk can be rewarded. In this case, when highly aromatic and flavorful wines are paired with cuisines of equal intensity, they make for quite bold pairings.

Body

Grape varieties vary in body just as people do. The spectrum ranges from fashion models to body builders.

How to Taste for a Wine's Body

You identify aromas and flavors with your nose. If you hold your nose closed, you will not be able to tell what aromas or flavors a wine has. However, when you taste the wine you will be able to tell the level of body, acid, and tannin in the wine.

If you have ever tasted the difference between skim milk, whole milk, and heavy cream, this will be an easy analogy for you. Your palate can feel the weight difference between these three, and it's the same with wine. When using this analogy, we call those wines at the skim milk end of the spectrum "light-bodied." Those at the heavy cream end of the spectrum we call "full-bodied." The wines don't actually feel like milk on the palate, but the concept of how your palate determines body is similar.

In this book we recommend a dry Riesling from the Mosel region in Germany that is quite delicate and light-bodied. At the other end of the spectrum is a Cabernet Sauvignon from Chile that is rich and full-bodied. If you close your eyes (and nose) and taste these two wines blindly, your tongue will tell you which is the more full-bodied of the two.

How Body Impacts Food and Wine Pairings

In terms of body, the key to pairing wine with food is balance. If you saw an average-sized person paired in a Sumo wrestling match with a champion Sumo wrestler, chances are the Sumo wrestler would win. This is the same with food and wine pairing. Wines that are light-bodied are at risk of being pummeled by a full-bodied dish, and vice versa.

Acid

Grapes vary widely in their acid levels. Wines that are high in acidity are said to be "crisp" (sometimes "racy," synonymous for even more acidity), while wines low in acidity (and unbalanced) are said to be "flabby."

How to Taste for a Wine's Acid Level

Lemonade and milk both have acid (albeit different types of acid). The lemonade makes your mouth pucker, while the milk does not. Your palate picks up acid on the sides of your tongue, generally speaking. This is probably why it puckers there when you drink tart lemonade; very high acid can make it seem as though you are impersonating a fish. The same is true with wine.

We discuss grape varieties at both ends of the acid spectrum. A Riesling from Eden Valley is paired with poached salmon. The dry Rieslings from Eden are quite racy and they make your mouth pucker a bit. We also selected a Viognier from the Rhone Valley in France that would be an example of a wine fairly low in acid. This is evident in red grapes as well. Pinot Noirs generally have much higher acidity than, say, a Grenache or a Garnacha.

How Acid Impacts Food and Wine Pairings

Acid is the great refresher. It cleanses the palate of fats and creates a sensation that makes you think you are eating food that is lighter than perhaps you really are.

Acid is also a flavor enhancer. It makes flavors more pronounced, or makes them "pop." This is why wedges of lemon are added to certain seafood dishes to bring out some of the more subtle, delicate flavors. Fresh seafood also has an inherent sweetness, so the acid–sweetness balance here is very important as well.

Acid can also reduce the impression of saltiness in a dish. Champagne is paired with a few dishes, including a tempura shrimp that is served with a soy dipping sauce. The saltiness is softened by the high acidity of the Champagne. This explains why some high-acid wines (Chablis, Sancerre, or Muscadet) pair wonderfully with briny oysters.

With food and wine pairing, however, it is not always preferable to have more acid. When the acid of a wine is too high, it can strip the flavor of the dish, or worse, compound the acidity in the dish for an unpleasant sting.

Sweetness

There are many wines that have a perceptible level of sweetness. Professional tasters generally perceive sweetness in a still table wine when it has residual sugar above 5 grams per liter (g/l). That's not to say that wines with 6 grams of residual sugar per liter will taste sweet, but they may have a more round mouthfeel and possibly taste more "fruity."

The opposite of sweet is dry, and generally still table wines with less than 5 grams of residual sugar per liter are considered "dry."

How to Taste a Wine's Sweetness Level

Many of us don't walk around like winemakers with a device called a refractometer to measure sugar, and so we rely on our taste perception. However, if a wine has a high level of acid with some sweetness, the amount of sugar can be deceiving.

Therefore, try this test: Close your nose with one hand and take a sip of the wine with the other. Keep your nose closed while you take the sip so that you are not tempted to "smell" anything (make sure you can breathe; we don't want anyone passing out doing this test).

Your sense of smell can get in the way of your ability to perceive sweetness, and sometimes very ripe, fruity wines may make you think they are sweet when they are not.

Once you take your hand away from your nose, you will notice an influx of aromas that may change your perception of the wine. However, your tongue will not lie and will tell you if the wine is sweet or not.

Some say that the receptors for sweetness are more concentrated towards the tip of the tongue. While this is a good way to begin focusing your thoughts, the reality is you have taste buds all over your tongue. Therefore, pay attention to what all of your tongue is telling you.

How Sweetness Impacts Food and Wine Pairings

Sweetness can do quite a few things to a dish. On the positive side, it can:

- Soften the heat impression from spice
- Contrast nicely with salt and/or acid
- Complement sweetness in the dish

On the negative side, sweetness can also:

- Mute flavors of the dish
- Compound with the sweetness in the dish to overpower everything

It is important to understand a wine's residual sugar level and to taste it to see how it will work (or not work) with your dishes.

Wines in this book have a wide range of sweetness levels and they work with a variety of different dishes. For example, a Mosel Spätlese Riesling softened some of the heat from the Spicy Chipotle Pepper Sauce. Another example is the Moscato d'Asti pairing with the rich spice of the Thai Beef with Massaman Curry. In this case, sweetness offsets some of the intense spice so that it's not overpowering, but also complements some of the sweetness in the dish.

Tannin

If you have ever had a strongly brewed black tea, you know there is a drying and slight bitterness to the taste. The compound responsible for this sensation is *tannin.* In wine tannin comes from the skins, seeds, and stems of the grapes and from the oak in the winemaking process. Usually red wines have more tannin than white wines. In order to get the red color, red wines sit on their grape skins, similar in concept to steeping a tea bag, and gain tannin. Although some white wines do see skin contact, they still do not have the tannin levels that red wines have.

How to Taste for a Wine's Tannin Level

Some red wines have more tannin than others. Generally, those grape varieties with thick skins have more tannin (and color) than those with thinner skins. Cabernet Sauvignon, Syrah, and Merlot are examples of thick-skinned varieties of grapes. Pinot Noir is an example of a thin-skinned variety.

To improve your recognition of tannin, taste a Pinot Noir (New Zealand or California) side-by-side with a Cabernet Sauvignon or a Nebbiolo. Make sure they are near the same vintage because age softens tannins. Taste each wine, making sure you have enough in your mouth, and roll it around your tongue. Then wait for the drying sensation and slight bitterness towards the finish. You should find the Cabernet Sauvignon or Nebbiolo to be much higher in tannin.

You can also buy tannin powder at winemaking supply stores. Have two glasses of the same low-tannin red wine (Pinot Noir or Barbera). With the same wine in both glasses, make one the control and add some tannin powder to the second. Taste back and forth between them and you will taste the difference. If not, add more tannin powder to the second glass.

How Tannin Impacts Food and Wine Pairing

A wine's tannins can be drying, somewhat bitter, and sometimes astringent. This can be softened or exacerbated by elements in a dish:

- ***Tannin + Protein in the Dish*** – One reason why the traditional rule has been "red meat with red wine" is because the protein in the meat combines with the tannin in the wine and makes the wine seem softer on the palate. This reaction is also why people add milk to black tea.
- ***Tannin + Bitterness in the Dish*** – Sometimes the bitterness in a dish can complement some of the bitterness in the wine, or add some depth or structure to low-tannin wines. However, be careful, as bitterness can be compounded (meaning bitterness of the wine tannin + bitterness of the dish = bitterness^2). This happened when we tried a red Zinfandel with the Mezze Rigatoni with Broccoli Rabe and Sausage. The bitterness of the tannins combined with the bitterness in the broccoli rabe and compounded it.
- ***Tannin + Salt in the Dish*** – Salt in a dish intensifies the tannins of a wine. This happened when we tried Barolo (a highly tannic wine made from Nebbiolo) with the Beef and Broccoli Stir-Fry. The salty ingredients of the dish clashed with the tannins, making the wine taste more tannic despite the protein in the dish.

Alcohol

To understand alcohol in wine, it's important to understand the fermentation process:

$$\text{Sugar} + \text{Yeast} = \text{Alcohol} + CO_2$$

When grapes have higher sugar content, the resulting wine is higher in alcohol. This is one reason why different grape varieties have varying alcohol levels (also see *terroir,* discussed later in this chapter and in the Glossary).

How to Taste for a Wine's Alcohol Level

When tasting a spirit straight (such as vodka, whiskey, etc.), you will feel heat in the back of your palate and down your throat. That's the alcohol. Alcohol in wine manifests itself on the palate with a heat reaction (albeit less intense than in spirits).

A medium alcohol level is considered to be approximately 12% to 13% alcohol by volume (abv). The original purpose of "old-world" wines being chaptalized (meaning adding sugar before fermentation is complete) was to heighten the level of alcohol to increase the wine's body and give an impression of ripeness. However, when the wine is unbalanced, with too high an alcohol content, it can taste hot and sometimes bitter.

How Alcohol Impacts Food and Wine Pairings

Alcohol in wine is softened by sweetness in a dish, yet is intensified by a dish's spice and salt. For example, we pair Tandoori Chicken with a Shiraz from Hunter Valley. The alcohol is about 13.5%, and the wine worked well with this dish. However, when we tried a Shiraz from Barossa (14.5%+ alcohol), the pairing was a train wreck. It was way too hot. The level of alcohol can make or break the pairing.

Wines with more alcohol have more weight and body to them. A Chardonnay at 14% alcohol is going to have much more body than one at 12% alcohol. Because one of the key pairing elements is *matching*, be mindful of this when pairing.

Oak

Many wines are fermented or aged in oak. At wine tastings, you often hear references to a wine's "oaky" character. Winemakers think of oak similarly to how a chef might think of a spice rack.

Oak adds flavors to a wine (vanilla, toast, etc.) and adds more richness and weight. In red wines, oak also adds more tannin and structure.

The intensity of oak flavors and richness depends on a number of factors:

- ***Size of the Barrel*** – The smaller the barrel, the more of the barrel's surface comes into contact with the wine. Therefore, wines fermented and matured in barriques (or small barrels) are higher in oak flavor and richness.
- ***Percentage of New Oak*** – Barrels throw the most intense flavor when they are new. With each subsequent year's use, they lose their flavor. In winemaking notes, "100% new oak" means the wine entered a brand new oak barrel and is likely to be fairly intense in its oak flavors versus a wine that has only 15% new oak.
- ***Length of Time in the Barrel*** – The longer a wine sits in an oak barrel, the more flavor it extracts from the oak. Therefore, wines that have been aged for 24 months in oak barrels are more intense in their oak characteristics than those aged only eight months.

There is such a thing as 200% new oak, usually reserved for red wines. The winemaker will sometimes place the new wine in a 100% new-oak barrel. Then, after nine months or so, transfer the wine to a different, but entirely untouched, 100% new-oak barrel. This compounds the impact of the oak flavor and tannin. These wines can be intensely oaky.

How to Taste for a Wine's "Oakyness"

Wines that have seen some oak have some telltale flavors such as vanilla, caramel, toast, coconut, chocolate, coffee, brown spice, bacon fat, tobacco, and smoke. In some wines you may actually taste some raw wood, which is not so nice and usually indicates poor winemaking.

Taste test two Chardonnays, one oaked and one unoaked; they should be from the same vintage and region. The unoaked Chardonnay will taste of fruit while the oaked Chardonnay will taste of fruit plus other things (vanilla and spice). This is the impression oak makes on a wine.

To determine if a Chardonnay has oak, look on the back label. In an oaked Chardonnay often you will find certain words on the back label describing the wine's flavors: "vanilla," "spice," "oak," or "barrels." You can also refer to the winery's website where this information may be listed.

Origin of Oak

Factor	Types of Flavors
French Oak	Vanilla and Spice
American Oak	Vanilla, Coconut, and Dill
Slavonian Oak	Similar to French, but more Neutral

Other Oak Factors

Factor	Oak Flavor	Body	Tannin
Small Barrels/Barriques (225L)	Increases	Increases	Increases
Large Barrels/Foudres/Tonneaux	Decreases	Decreases	Decreases
The Newer the Barrel	Increases	Increases	Increases
The Older the Barrel	Decreases	Decreases	Decreases
The More Time Spent in Barrel	Increases	Increases	Increases
The Less Time Spent in Barrel	Decreases	Decreases	Decreases

How Oak Intensity Impacts Food and Wine Pairings

Wines with oak flavors can complement flavors found in food, but be careful because these flavors can be compounded and overpower a dish.

This is the reason we paired an oaked Sonoma County Chardonnay with the Mezze Rigatoni Salad with Roasted Butternut Squash, Red Onions, Sage, and Pumpkin Seeds. In addition to matching in weight, the toasty flavors of the oak in the wine complement some of the toasty and nutty flavors in the dish.

Some associate Chardonnay's "butter" note with the oak. Buttery flavors in a Chardonnay (or in other white wines) come from a reaction called malolactic fermentation. It is a microbial reaction that turns the malic acid (the tart acid also found in green apples) to lactic acid (the acid also found in milk). The reaction creates a chemical called diacetyl, which tastes buttery. Wines that have undergone malolactic fermentation (or MLF) and have buttery notes can complement a dish by creating a bridge if there is a creamy or buttery note in the dish.

Wine Components Summary for White Wines

Wine Components	Low	Medium	High
Aromatic Intensity	Chardonnay Champagne Orvieto Muscadet	Pinot Grigio Chenin Blanc*	Muscat/ Moscato Gewürtraminer Sauvignon Blanc Riesling
Body	Sauvignon Blanc* Riesling	Pinot Grigio Albariño Chenin Blanc*	Chardonnay* Viognier Gewürtraminer
Acid	Chardonnay* Viognier Gewürtraminer Fino Sherry	Pinot Grigio Soave/Arneis Grüner Veltliner	Brut Champagne Riesling Sauvignon Blanc
Sweetness	Gewurztraminer* Pinot Gris*	Riesling*	Moscato Sauternes
Alcohol	< 11% abv Riesling* Moscato	11.5%–13.5% abv Riesling* Pinot Grigio Sauvignon Blanc Chardonnay*	> 14% abv Chardonnay* Viognier Fino Sherry

*Placement varies widely depending on terroir and winemaking style.

Wine Components Summary for Red Wines

Wine Components	Low	Medium	High
Aromatic Intensity	N/A	Shiraz/Syrah Merlot Cabernet Sauvignon Sangiovese	Pinot Noir
Body	Pinot Noir* Cabernet Franc (Chinon)* Barbera	Sangiovese Tempranillo	Grenache/Garnacha Cabernet Sauvignon
Acid	Grenache/Garnacha	Merlot* Syrah/Shiraz Cabernet Sauvignon*	Sangiovese Barbera Pinot Noir Nebbiolo
Sweetness		Brachetto Lambrusco*	Port Banyuls
Alcohol	< 11% abv Lambrusco*	11.5%–13.5% abv Pinot Noir Merlot* Syrah/Shiraz* Cabernet Sauvignon*	> 14% abv Zinfandel Amarone Port
Tannin	Pinot Noir Barbera Tempranillo	Sangiovese Merlot Syrah/Shiraz*	Aglianico Tannat Nebbiolo Cabernet Sauvignon

*Placement varies widely depending on terroir and winemaking style.

WINE TEXTURES

Wines have texture just as foods have texture. Some common wine textures we reference in this book are:

- ***Effervescent*** – Refers to *bubbles*—an effervescent wine provides a different textural experience. The smaller the bead of the bubble, the finer the texture (e.g., fine bubbles of Champagne versus larger froth of Moscato d'Asti).
- ***Soft*** – Wines with a soft texture tend to be those with moderate structure, medium body, medium acid, medium alcohol, and so on. There are no rough edges or anything standing out. There are no gripping tannins, no cutting acidity, and no hot alcohol. These wines are very easygoing. For your palate, it's like falling into a pillow.
- ***Oily*** – This may sound like a negative, but it's not. Some wines have a more viscous texture, such as Gewürztraminer or Viognier, for example, which can feel more *oily* in texture than other wines.
- ***Chocolaty*** – When we say a wine has a "chocolaty" texture, we don't mean it tastes like chocolate. We are referring to how some red wines can have a density and texture to them. This is similar to how one tastes chocolates with different levels of cocoa in them. The higher the cocoa, the more dense and rich the character. Likewise, wines with a fair amount of oak influence and dense tannins may feel this way on the palate.

Complementing and *contrasting* textures are some tools you can use to enhance a pairing.

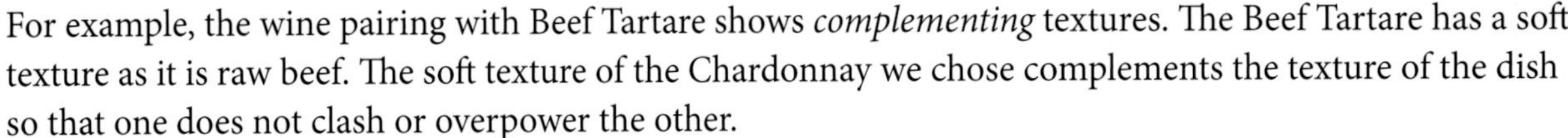

For example, the wine pairing with Beef Tartare shows *complementing* textures. The Beef Tartare has a soft texture as it is raw beef. The soft texture of the Chardonnay we chose complements the texture of the dish so that one does not clash or overpower the other.

Another example of complementing textures is the Chocolate Soufflé with Orange Crème Anglaise and the Rosé Champagne. The Rosé Champagne is effervescent, so the bubbles are airy and dynamic. The soufflé is also airy so the pairing is complementary.

Textures can also contrast for great effect. The prime example is Fried Chicken Legs with Chablis or Champagne. The light body of Chablis and Champagne is a stark contrast to the weight of buttermilk fried chicken. With Champagne specifically, its effervescence contrasts with the rich and crunchy texture of the batter coating and the oil from the frying. Both wines add refreshment to the dish and work extremely well.

WINE AROMA/FLAVOR DESCRIPTOR CHART

Some of the aromas we mention in the book may sound unpleasant in wine (e.g., gun flint, fresh cut grass, or brine); however, these are some of the typical characteristics found in wine that can help you complement flavors in dishes. Below are wine descriptors chart for whites and reds that may help you.

The following tables provide you with some basic characteristics of the grapes without the influence of climate and other aspects of terroir, winemaking style, or vintage. It may be an oversimplification, but we hope it will help you get a better understanding of some of the grapes.

Popular White Grapes

Grape	Region	Typical Aromas/Flavors
Riesling	Mosel, Germany	Citrus, Floral, Minerals (like Slate), sometimes Diesel Fuel
Pinot Grigio	Friuli	Floral, Citrus, Pear, Minerals
Pinot Gris	Alsace, France	Peach/Apricot, Honey, Spice, Minerals
Sauvignon Blanc	Pouilly-Fumé, France	Citrus, Gooseberry, Minerals (Gunflint), Fresh Cut Grass
Sauvignon Blanc	New Zealand	Passion Fruit, Citrus, Fresh Cut Grass, sometimes Asparagus
Sauvignon Blanc	Napa Valley, California	Melon, Fresh Fig, Vanilla and Spice with Fumé-Blanc Style
Chardonnay	Chablis, Burgundy	Green Apple, Chalky Minerals
Chardonnay	Napa Valley, California	Red Apple, Baked Apple, Butter (Malolactic Fermentation), Vanilla, Spice (if oaked)
Chenin Blanc	Vouvray	Tree Fruit (Pear/Quince), Minerals, sometimes Wet Wool
Chenin Blanc	South Africa	Tree Fruit (Pear/Quince), Guava, Vanilla/Spice (if oaked)
Gewürztraminer	Alsace, France	Litchi, Peach/Apricot, Spice, Honey, Minerals
Viognier	Languedoc, France	Floral (White Flowers), Peach/Apricot, Minerals, some Vanilla and Spice with Condrieu
Albariño	Rias Baixas, Spain	Floral, Citrus, Light Stone Fruit (White Peach), Minerals
Grüner Veltliner	Wachau, Austria	Citrus, White Pepper, Minerals, sometimes Lentils
Muscadet (Sur Lie)	Sèvre et Maine, Loire, Valley	Citrus, Minerals, Brine, Yeasty

Popular Red Grapes

Grape	Region	Typical Aromas/Flavors
Pinot Noir	Burgundy, France	Strawberry, Cherry, Minerals, Vanilla and Spice (if oaked)
Merlot	St. Emilion, France	Blackberry, Plum, Vanilla and Spice, Minerals
Cabernet Sauvignon	Pauillac, France	Black Currant, Blackberry, Lead Pencil Shavings, Cedar, Vanilla and Spice, sometimes Green Bell Pepper
Cabernet Sauvignon	Napa Valley, California	Black Currant Jam, Vanilla and Spice, sometimes Green Bell Pepper
Syrah	Rhône Valley, France	Raspberry, Black Pepper, Herbs, Spice, Minerals, sometimes Vanilla
Shiraz	Barossa, Shiraz	Raspberry Jam, Black Pepper, Mint/Eucalyptus, sometimes Vanilla, Coconut, Spice
Grenache	Châteauneuf-du-Pape	Cherry, Licorice, Herbs, Spice, Minerals

(continues)

Popular Red Grapes (*continued*)

Grape	Region	Typical Aromas/Flavors
Tempranillo	Rioja, Spain	Cherry, Minerals, Spice, Earth (Leather with Gran Reserva Aged Riojas)
Carmenère	Chile	Black Cherry, Grilled Meat, Spice (Vanilla if oaked)
Petite Sirah	California	Blackberry, sometimes Coconut and/or Vanilla (if oaked)
Zinfandel	Sonoma, California	Black Cherry (sometimes Dried Cherry), sometimes Tobacco, Coconut, and/or Vanilla
Sangiovese	Chianti Classico, Tuscany, Italy	Cherry (sometimes Sour Cherry), Dried Herbs, Spice, Minerals
Aglianico	Campania, Italy	Black Fruit, Earth, Spice, Minerals
Touriga Nacional	Duoro Valley, Portugal	Black Fruit, Licorice, Spice, Minerals

HYPERTASTERS, NONTASTERS, AND TASTERS

People are divided into three camps in terms of their ability to taste—*hypertasters, nontasters, and tasters.*

Hypertasters (supertasters) are those who have more taste buds on their tongues than the average person. Those increased numbers of taste buds make hypertasters more sensitive to all taste sensations, and particularly to bitter sensations. To a hypertaster, many things taste bitter or too intense. Statistics suggest hypertasters comprise between 9% and 25% of the population.

Nontasters are at the opposite end of the spectrum. Nontasters have fewer taste buds on their tongues than the average person. This makes them less sensitive to taste sensations. These are usually people who enjoy their food intense in flavor. They need that intensity to perceive any flavor at all.

Tasters are where most of us lie—between hypertasters and nontasters. This variability in people's ability to taste makes food and wine pairing somewhat difficult.

Please bear in mind that these three types of tasters may experience slightly different reactions or taste sensations when pairing food and wine based on their personal perception of taste.

Terroir

The French term *terroir* is the reason why wines from one area can taste completely different than those from a mere short distance away (all other things being equal). Terroir doesn't translate directly into English, but roughly it is the combination of natural factors that impact a wine's taste including climate, sun exposure topography, and soil.

Differences in terroir can have a dramatic effect on a wine's aromas, flavors, and structure. For instance, an unoaked Chardonnay in the region of Chablis is higher in acidity, more delicate in body and has marked chalky mineral aromas. However, an unoaked Chardonnay in California will taste much riper in its fruit, fuller in body, lower in acidity and potentially higher in alcohol (with no mineral aromas). Both are unoaked Chardonnays. These differences are primarily due to terroir.

The following table summarizes a few things to keep in mind regarding terroir.

Terroir

	Body	Acidity	Alcohol	Tannin
Warm Climate (and/or More Sun)	Increases	Decreases	Increases	Softer Texture
Cool Climate (and/or Less Sun)	Decreases	Increases	Decreases	Harder Texture
Increasing Altitude	Decreases	Increases	Decreases	Increases
Limestone/Chalky Soils	Leaner	Increases	N/A	N/A
Clay/Sandy (and Sandy) Soils	Broader	Decreases	N/A	N/A

The reason we bring up terroir is that it can explain why a grape from one area works well with a dish, yet why the same grape in another area may not. For example, while a Chardonnay from Carneros paired beautifully with the Sautéed Sea Scallops with a Truffle Goat Cheese Sauce, Chardonnays from Burgundy did not. The acidity was too cleansing and stripped the flavor of the dish.

Winemaking Style

We had an interesting tasting experience while creating Chapter 8, Pasta and Pizza. We tasted two wines from the same region, grape variety, and vintage. One was magical with the pizza the other was not. The reason wasn't terroir; it was winemaking style. The winemaker can impact the style of a wine from the vineyard through the cellar.

Winemakers in the vineyard have different techniques they can choose to impact the wine. For instance, they can leave grapes hang on the vine a bit longer than others and the result can be a riper, fuller wine. They may choose to reduce the number of grapes per vine to concentrate a wine's flavor.

In the cellar a winemaker can do all kinds of adjustments to wines (e.g., acid, alcohol, etc.) and we have discussed earlier the impact of the origin, type, size and time in oak barrels.

This is why it is important to taste wines even if they may seem to be the same. The grape variety and the region of two wines may be alike, but the winemaking style just may make one wine pair beautifully, and the other a train wreck.

Taste the Possibilities

There are many factors to keep in mind when pairing food and wine. Unfortunately, there are no rules that will work for every situation.

If there is one thing we learned from working together it is not to take anything for granted. We realized that there is absolutely no substitute for actually tasting. To create great pairings, you should taste the possibilities.

You have an incredible opportunity to take something from mediocre to marvelous. Tasting in advance and making adjustments is one of the most important things you can do to ensure success each and every time.

Image © Cengage Learning 2013

4
Shellfish

Seafood is one of the most delicate proteins that you will work with. Thus the wine pairings reflect this and they generally lean towards the lighter, more delicate end of the wine spectrum.

The subtle and sweet flavors of shellfish, which are easy to cover up, require a degree of finesse. You should also note how the variety of ingredients and techniques changes the pairing. Techniques used in this chapter are: cure, steam, sauté, roast, pan-fry, deep-fry, and grill.

We see more sparkling wines in this chapter than in any other as they add lightness and a refreshing element. Although the two red wines in this chapter show shellfish's versatility, they are far from being considered fat, big, and bold red wines.

Dish	Wine
Crab	
Jumbo Lump Crab with Cocktail Sauce and Fresh Horseradish	Domaine Carneros Sparkling Brut Rosé "Cuvée de la Pompadour," California, USA ($33)
Crab and Avocado Salad with Hazelnut Vinaigrette	Louis Jadot Beaune Clos des Ursules, Burgundy, France ($50)
Chesapeake Crab Cake with Spicy Chipotle Pepper Sauce	Selbach-Oster Zeltinger Schlossberg Spätlese Riesling, Mosel, Germany ($26)
Shrimp	
Shrimp and Scallop Ceviche	Fâmega Vinho Verde, Vinho Verde, Portugal ($7)
Shrimp Tempura with Soy Dipping Sauce	Champagne Piper-Heidsieck Brut, Champagne, France ($32)
Shrimp Scampi	Penfolds Bin 311 Chardonnay, Tumbarumba, New South Wales, Australia ($22)
Scallops	
Grilled Sea Scallops with Extra Virgin Olive Oil	Michel Redde La Moynerie Pouilly-Fumé, Loire, France ($25)
Sautéed Sea Scallops with Truffle Goat Cheese Sauce	Sequoia Grove Carneros Chardonnay, California, USA ($23)
Prosciutto-Wrapped Sea Scallops with Basil-Walnut Pesto	Benton Lane Oregon Pinot Noir, Oregon, USA ($23)
Lobster	
Steamed Lobster with Drawn Butter and Lemon	Caposaldo Pinot Grigio, Veneto, Italy ($9)
Lobster Bisque	Olivier Leflaive Puligny-Montrachet, Burgundy, France ($50)
Lobster Thermidor	Agrapart & Fils, 7 Crus, Blanc de Blancs Champagne, France ($37)

SOURCING AND STORING SEAFOOD

Many factors will impact the quality of shellfish—type of harvest, vendor, time elapsed to consumer, storage, handling, and fabrication. When sourcing seafood, use a vendor with extensive knowledge and one that you can develop a reliable relationship with. Inspect all seafood upon purchase and use quality identifiers to evaluate. When possible, buy products with the least amount of processing.

Proper storage is critical to maintaining the best possible quality. While stored under refrigeration, seafood should be kept on ice—in a perforated lined pan, covered with plastic wrap, with a layer of crushed ice on top. Alternately place sealed bags of crushed ice on top of the seafood and maintain a temperature of 32–34 F (0–1 C) degrees. Seafood should be used within two days of receiving or frozen, if applicable.

QUALITY IDENTIFIERS FOR SHELLFISH

- Bivalves (clams, mussels, oysters, cockles) should be closed or should close when squeezed.
- Inspect all bivalves for split or cracked shells; if you find any, discard them immediately.
- Lobsters and fresh crabs—including soft-shells—should be alive. Shrimp should be plump and firm with a fresh sea aroma.

CRAB

The following recipes utilize crabmeat. Below is an illustration that explains where the marketing names come from: colossal, jumbo lump, lump, special, backfin, and claw.

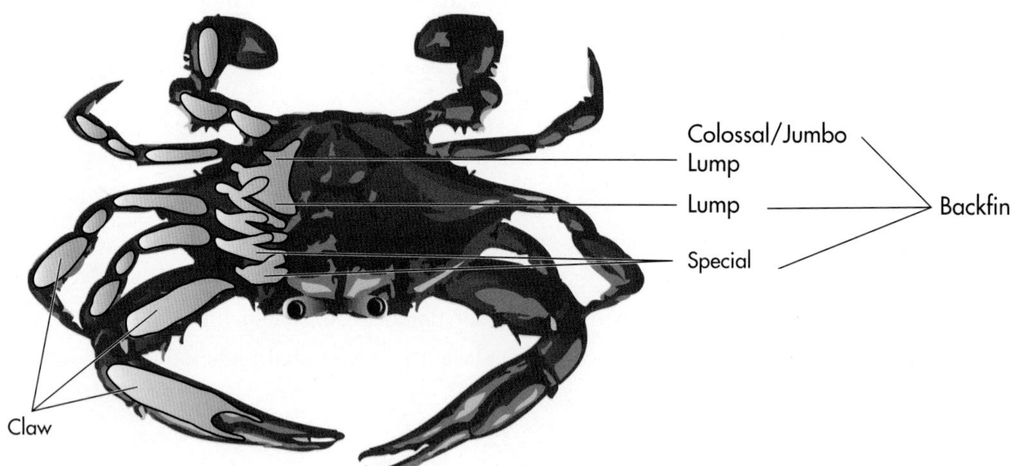

Crabmeat may contain small shell pieces and should be gently picked through to remove all shells. This can be done by hand or by placing the crab pieces in a single layer on a parchment-lined sheet and placing it under a broiler/salamander for a few seconds. The shell pieces will turn white and can easily be seen and removed.

Jumbo Lump Crab with Cocktail Sauce and Fresh Horseradish

JUMBO LUMP CRAB WITH COCKTAIL SAUCE AND FRESH HORSERADISH

Yield: 10 portions

Ingredients	Amounts - US	Volume	Metric
For the Crab with Cocktail Sauce			
Jumbo lump crab	20 oz.	5 cups	568 grams
Cocktail sauce	10 fl. oz.	1 ¼ cups	300 ml
For the Cocktail Sauce Yield: 16 oz.			
Ketchup	8 fl. oz.	1 cup	240 ml
Horseradish, prepared, drained lightly	2 oz.	3 Tbl.	56 grams
Horseradish, fresh, grated fine	⅜ oz.	1 ½ Tbl.	10 grams
Lemon juice		1 ½ tsp.	
Worcestershire sauce		½ tsp.	
Salt, kosher		¼ tsp.	
Black pepper, fresh ground		⅛ tsp.	
For the Garnish			
Horseradish, fresh, grated fine		as needed	
Lemon wedge, ends trimmed, seeds removed		20 each	
Romaine lettuce, chiffonade		2 ½ cups	
Crushed ice		as needed	

Cocktail Sauce

1. Combine all ingredients for the cocktail sauce and mix thoroughly. Refrigerate until needed.
2. Taste and adjust the seasoning.

Assembling the Crab and Cocktail Sauce

1. Place a small amount of crushed ice in the base of the serving vessel, add the romaine on top, and then add the crab.
2. Serve the cocktail sauce in a ramekin and grate fresh horseradish on top.
3. Garnish the crab with the lemon wedge.

WINE SELECTED with Jumbo Lump Crab with Cocktail Sauce and Fresh Horseradish

Wine: Domaine Carneros Sparkling Brut Rosé "Cuvée de la Pompadour" ($33)

Origin: Carneros, California, USA

Taste and Texture Comparisons

Dish: Delicate, Sweet, Spice, Sweetness (Ketchup, Crab), Spice

Wine: Fairly Delicate Structure, Fruity, Effervescent, Medium Acidity and Alcohol

This sparkling rosé is made with 58% Pinot Noir and 42% Chardonnay. Some Pinot Noir red wine is added to give it that great color. Rosé sparklers have the crispness of a sparkler with more red berry fruitiness than white sparklers.

Why This Is a Good Pairing

- ***Matching Intensity*** – The dish and the wine match in intensity of flavor. The crab has a delicate sweetness, while the wine has a delicate fruitiness that matches.
- ***Complementing*** – The sweet flavor of the crab built a bridge to the ripe red berry fruit in the wine, which makes both flavors pop even more.
- ***Contrasting*** – The effervescence and the wine's crisp acidity create a cleansing sensation that is refreshing and amplifies the dish's flavors. Additionally, the fruitiness of the rosé sparkler balances the heat of the horseradish quite well.

Wines That Didn't Work

NV Brut Champagne (blend) – The champagne's high acidity (higher than the sparkling wine from California) compounds with the acid in the dish, particularly with the lemon, making the wine too acidic. The horseradish in the sauce also clashes with the champagne and augments the dish's spice a bit too much.

Oregon Pinot Gris – The thought process was the sweetness of the crab would be augmented by the fruitiness of the wine; but without the sauce, the wine overpowers the dish. With the cocktail sauce, they both seem to wash out the other's flavor.

Beaujolais-Villages – We tested a soft, delicate red before testing any other red. The Beaujolais overpowers the dish. Additionally, the spice in the dish clashes with the tannins in the wine, making it taste bitter and diminishing the wine's fruit.

SUMMARY	Domaine Carneros Sparkling Brut Rosé	NV Brut Champagne	Oregon Pinot Gris	Beaujolais-Villages
Matching	+			
Complementing	+			
Contrasting	+			
Compounding		(–)		
Complexing				
Cleansing	+			
Covering			(–)	(–)
Clashing		(–)	(–)	(–)

Crab and Avocado Salad with Hazelnut Vinaigrette

CRAB AND AVOCADO SALAD WITH HAZELNUT VINAIGRETTE

Yield: 10 portions

Ingredients	Amounts - US	Volume	Metric
For the Crab and Avocado Salad			
Jumbo lump crab	20 oz.	5 cups	568 grams
Avocado, medium dice	1 oz.	¼ cup	28 grams
Hazelnut vinaigrette	2 fl. oz.	¼ cup	60 ml
Hazelnuts, toasted, chopped	1 oz.	¼ cup	28 grams
Chives, sliced thin	¼ oz.	2 Tbl.	8 grams
Salt, sea		as needed	
Black pepper, fresh ground		as needed	
Tomatoes, ripe, sliced ⅛-inch		30 slices	
Arugula, baby	1 ¼ oz.	2 ½ cups	36 grams
Extra virgin olive oil	½ fl. oz.	1 Tbl.	15 ml
Salt and black pepper, fresh ground		as needed	
For the Hazelnut Vinaigrette Yield: 2 ½ cups			
White balsamic vinegar	4 fl. oz.	½ cup	120 ml
Red wine vinegar	2 fl. oz.	¼ cup	60 ml
Shallots, minced	¾ oz.	2 Tbl.	22 grams
Paprika		1 tsp.	
Dijon mustard		1 tsp.	
Olive oil, pure	10 fl. oz.	1 ¼ cups	300 ml
Hazelnut oil	2 fl. oz.	¼ cup	60 ml
Salt, kosher		¾ tsp.	
Black pepper, fresh ground		¼ tsp.	
For the Garnish			
Hazelnut vinaigrette	1 fl. oz.	2 Tbl.	30 ml
Hazelnuts, roasted, chopped	½ oz.	2 Tbl.	14 grams
Chives, sliced thin, bias		1 ½ tsp.	

(Continues on next page)

Hazelnut Vinaigrette

1. Combine the white balsamic vinegar, red wine vinegar, shallots, paprika, Dijon mustard, salt, and pepper in a stainless steel bowl and whisk well to evenly combine.
2. Slowly drizzle in the oils while whisking to emulsify the dressing.
3. Taste the dressing with a small amount of lettuce and adjust the seasoning.

Toasted Hazelnuts

1. Preheat oven to 300 F (148 C) degrees convection.
2. Place the hazelnuts on a sheet pan and bake until they are light brown in the center, approximately 12–15 minutes.
3. If the nuts have the skins on, place them in a clean kitchen towel and gently rub to remove the skins.

Crab and Avocado Salad

1. Combine the crab, avocado, hazelnut vinaigrette, hazelnuts, and chives in a mixing bowl; season with salt and pepper. Mix gently to coat evenly, being careful not to break up the crab pieces. Taste the crab mixture and adjust the dressing and seasoning.
2. Place the sliced tomatoes in a circular pattern, overlapping slightly, in the center of the plate.
3. Place a 3-inch ring mold in the center of the tomatoes and place the crab mixture inside of the mold. Pack down the crab gently and remove the ring mold.
4. Place the arugula in a mixing bowl and add the olive oil, salt, and pepper; mix well to coat. Taste and adjust the seasoning.
5. Place the arugula on top of the crab.
6. Garnish the plate with the vinaigrette, hazelnuts, and chives.

Nuts are very perishable and should be purchased from a reputable source. If nuts are old or stored improperly they will have a rancid aftertaste. Purchasing small amounts and storing unused products in the freezer will help preserve the best possible quality. When checking a dressing for seasoning it is always best to taste it on lettuce to give you an accurate flavor profile.

WINE SELECTED with Crab and Avocado Salad with Hazelnut Vinaigrette

Wine: Louis Jadot Beaune Clos des Ursules, Pinot Noir ($50)

Origin: Beaune, Burgundy, France

This is a red Burgundy with lots of finesse and complexity, showing its merit of Premier Cru status. It is also a monopole of the Jadot family since 1826, meaning the vineyard is a solely owned property.

Taste and Texture Comparisons

Dish: Sweet, Rich, Light Acidity Slight Bitterness, Herbal

Wine: Aromatic, Crisp, Light Tannin, Complex, Moderate Body and Alcohol

Why This Is a Good Pairing

- ***Complementing*** – The ripe red berry fruit of the wine brings out the sweetness in the crab and the sweetness of the tomatoes.
- ***Cleansing*** – The hazelnut oil and avocado are cut by the crisp acidity of the wine, creating a refreshing sensation.
- ***Complexing*** – There is considerable complexity to this wine in the flavors of fruit, and with touches of spice, earth, and minerals. When paired with this dish you taste all of these with the layers of the flavors of the dish (sweet flavor of the crab, hazelnuts, avocado, and tomatoes).
- ***Dance*** – The fats from the avocado and nuts hold the flavor and extend the dance longer, elongating the finish.

Wines That Didn't Work

New Zealand Sauvignon Blanc – The intensity of the tropical passion fruit flavors of this wine is too overpowering for this dish.

Rias Baixas Albariño – The mild white peach flavor of the wine disappears when paired with this dish. The acidity comes forward in an unpleasant way (due to the compounding with the acidity in the dressing and/or the contrast to the fat in the dish).

Meursault – Meursault is known for its hazelnut-like aroma. In this case, it compounds with the hazelnuts in the dish (hazelnut + hazelnut = hazelnut^3). Additionally, the weight of the wine compounds with the fat in the dish, creating an unpleasant oily texture on the palate.

SUMMARY	Louis Jadot Beaune Clos des Ursules, Pinot Noir	New Zealand Sauvignon Blanc	Rias Baixas Albariño	Meursault
Matching				
Complementing	+			
Contrasting			(–)	
Compounding			(–)	(–)
Complexing	+			
Cleansing	+			
Covering		(–)	(–)	
Clashing				

Chesapeake Crab Cake with Spicy Chipotle Pepper Sauce

CHESAPEAKE CRAB CAKE WITH SPICY CHIPOTLE PEPPER SAUCE

Yield: 10 portions (10 4-oz. cakes)
Cooking Method: Pan-Fry

Ingredients	Amounts - US	Volume	Metric
For the Crab Cakes			
Jumbo lump crab	2 lbs.	8 cups	908 grams
Crabmeat, special	4 oz.	1 cup	114 grams
Eggs, large, whisked	3 ½ oz.	2 each	100 grams
Mayonnaise	3 oz.	½ cup	85 grams
Dijon mustard		1 tsp.	
Worcestershire sauce		1 tsp.	
Old Bay seasoning		½ tsp.	
Tabasco sauce		¼ tsp.	
Salt, kosher		½ tsp.	
Black pepper, fresh ground		¼ tsp.	
Panko breadcrumbs, ground fine		2 Tbl.	
Panko breadcrumbs		as needed	
Extra virgin olive oil		as needed	
For the Chipotle Pepper Sauce Yield: 1 ½ cups			
Mayonnaise	8 ¼ oz.	1 cup	232 grams
Roasted red peppers, cleaned	5 ½ oz.	¾ cup	142 grams
Chipotle peppers, canned, chopped	½ oz.	1 Tbl.	14 grams
Lemon juice	½ fl. oz.	1 Tbl.	15 ml
Honey	½ fl. oz.	1 Tbl.	15 ml
Salt, kosher		½ tsp.	
Black pepper, fresh ground		¼ tsp.	
For the Garnish			
Cilantro, chopped	¼ oz.	2 Tbl.	8 grams

Chipotle Pepper Sauce

1. Combine all ingredients and process in a blender until smooth.
2. Taste and adjust the seasoning.
3. Reserve under refrigeration until needed.

(Continues on next page)

Crab Cakes

1. Combine the eggs, mayonnaise, Dijon mustard, Worcestershire sauce, Old Bay, Tabasco, salt, and pepper; whisk well to evenly incorporate.
2. Add both types of crab and the 2 Tbl. of Panko breadcrumbs; mix gently with your hands to combine evenly. *It is important not to break up the large pieces of Jumbo lump when mixing.*
3. The crab cake mixture should be able to hold together when loosely formed into a cake. If the mixture is not holding, add a small amount of mayonnaise to lightly bind the mixture.
4. Form a small cake and cook a test cake; taste and adjust the seasoning.
5. Form the cakes into 4 oz. portions, approximately a ½-cup volume, and form in a 3-inch ring mold.
6. Preheat oven to 375 F (190 C) degrees convection.
7. Preheat a sautoir with enough oil to be roughly ½ the height of the crab cakes over medium heat.
8. Gently coat the top and bottom of the crab cakes in Panko breadcrumbs.
9. When the oil is hot enough it will have a slight shimmer; test by sprinkling a small pinch of Panko in the oil. If it begins to sizzle and turns light brown, it is ready.
10. Carefully add the crab cakes, laying them gently in the oil away from you so that the oil doesn't splatter in your direction. There should be space between each crab cake; do not overcrowd the pan or the temperature will drop and the cakes will steam and absorb oil.
11. Once the crab cakes are golden brown on the bottom, using a slotted spatula or small offset spatula, turn the cakes gently away from you. Once the bottom is golden brown, remove the cakes to a sheet pan.
12. Bake until they are hot in the center, approximately 6 minutes.
13. Sauce each plate with 1 oz. of chipotle pepper sauce, garnish with cilantro, and serve immediately.

Roasted Red Peppers

1. Wash the peppers and coat them lightly with oil.
2. Place on a sheet pan and roast at 425 F (218 C) degrees until the skin is blistered and turning black on all sides. Alternately, grill the peppers until the skin is blistered and turning black on all sides. Note the flesh should be soft but not mushy.
3. Remove from the oven and place in a paper bag or a stainless steel bowl covered with plastic wrap until they have cooled. This step will make it easy to peel the skin off.
4. Peel the skin off the peppers and remove the seeds.

WINE SELECTED with Chesapeake Crab Cake with Spicy Chipotle Pepper Sauce

Wine: Selbach-Oster Zeltinger Schlossberg Spätlese Riesling ($26)

Origin: Zeltinger Schlossberg, Mosel, Germany

Taste and Texture Comparisons

Dish: Slight Sweetness (Pepper Sauce and Crab), Spice, Rich, Crispy

Wine: Sweet, Aromatic, Mineral, Fruity, Crisp, Low Alcohol

Mosel Spätlese Rieslings like this one tend to have sweetness and relatively low alcohol (9% abv).

Why This Is a Good Pairing

- ***Complementing*** – The sweetness of the pepper sauce creates a bridge to the sweetness in the wine and brings out the flavor of the wine's fruit and the sweetness of the crab.
- ***Contrasting*** – The sweetness in the wine balances the spice of the chipotle sauce.
- ***Cleansing*** – The light body of the wine and its high acidity slightly cleanse the richness of the dish, making the pairing seem light and refreshing.

Wines That Didn't Work

Austrian Grüner Veltliner – The white pepper spice for which Grüner Veltliner is known and the spice in the dish are compounded (spice + spice = spice^2). The fruit disappears and the wine tastes too acidic.

Alsatian Gewürztraminer – "Gewürz" means "spice" in German and indeed this wine has a spice to it. However, when combined with the dish, the spice is amplified, although slightly less so than with the Grüner Veltliner. The slight sweetness is slightly balancing, but the wine's alcohol (14% abv) intensifies the spice and makes the wine taste too "hot."

Argentinean Torrontés – Although *matching* in weight, the wine's floral and fruit intensity overpowers this dish. There is also a clash between the spices in the dish, which makes the wine's floral notes taste like soap when paired with this dish.

SUMMARY	Selbach-Oster Zeltinger Schlossberg Spätlese Riesling	Austrian Grüner Veltliner	Alsatian Gewürztraminer	Argentinean Torrontés
Matching				+
Complementing	+		+	
Contrasting	+			
Compounding		(–)	(–)	
Complexing				
Cleansing	+			
Covering				(–)
Clashing				(–)

Shrimp and Scallop Ceviche

SHRIMP

There are several species of shrimp available on the market today, for example, black tiger, white, brown, and pink. It is important to note that there are taste and quality differences among these products. When available, fresh wild-caught shrimp are preferred.

SHRIMP AND SCALLOP CEVICHE

Yield: 10 portions

Cooking Method: Cure

Ingredients	Amounts - US	Volume	Metric
For the Ceviche			
Shrimp, 16/20, peeled, deveined	20 oz.	32 each	566 grams
Sea scallops, 10/20, heel removed, medium dice	12 oz.	10 each	340 grams
Extra virgin olive oil	2 fl. oz.	¼ cup	60 ml
Lime juice, fresh	6 fl. oz.	¾ cup	180 ml
Lemon juice, fresh	6 fl. oz.	¾ cup	180 ml
Tomato, small dice	8 oz.	1 ½ cup	255 grams
European cucumber, small dice	4 ½ oz.	1 cup	128 grams
Red onion, brunoise	2 oz.	½ cup	56 grams
Scallions, sliced thin, bias cut	1 oz.	½ cup	28 grams
Jalapeño pepper, seeded, minced	¾ oz.	2 Tbl.	20 grams
Cilantro, chopped		1 ½ Tbl.	
Salt, kosher		½ tsp.	
Black pepper, fresh ground		¼ tsp.	
For the Dressing Yield: 12 oz.			
Lime juice, fresh	3 fl. oz.	⅓ cup	90 ml
Lemon juice, fresh	3 fl. oz.	⅓ cup	90 ml
Honey	1 fl. oz.	2 Tbl.	30 ml
Lime zest, finely grated		½ tsp.	
Tabasco		2 dashes	
Extra virgin olive oil	6 fl. oz.	¾ cup	180 ml
Salt, kosher		½ tsp.	
Black pepper, fresh ground		¼ tsp.	

Ceviche can be found in most South American countries and is the national dish of Peru. This dish varies tremendously from town to town, using fish or shellfish that can be raw, seared, or fully cooked. The seafood is typically diced and is "cooked/cured" in an acidic marinade, such as lemon and/or lime juice, and is mixed with a variety of local ingredients such as onions, tomatoes, cucumbers, avocado, corn, spicy peppers, and herbs.

(Continues on next page)

Dressing

1. Combine the lime juice, lemon juice, honey, lime zest, Tabasco, salt, and pepper; whisk well.
2. Slowly drizzle in the olive oil while whisking to incorporate.
3. Taste and adjust the seasoning.

Ceviche

1. Preheat a sauté pan over medium heat. Add the oil and then the shrimp. Sauté for 20 seconds on each side, remove from the pan, cool, and then cut into medium dice.
2. Place the shrimp and scallops in a non-reactive pan (e.g., glass), add the lemon and lime juice, cover with plastic wrap, and refrigerate.
3. Mix the shrimp and scallops gently every hour. It will take approximately 3–4 hours to cure the shrimp and scallops; they will turn white in the center. The amount of cure time will vary based on the acidity in the lemons and limes.
4. Once the shrimp and scallops are fully cured, drain the mixture and discard the liquid.
5. Combine the cured mixture with the tomatoes, cucumber, red onions, jalapeño, cilantro, salt, pepper, and approximately 6 oz. of the dressing; mix well to combine. *Re-whisk the dressing just prior to using.*
6. Taste and adjust the dressing and seasonings as needed.
7. Mix well before serving.

WINE SELECTED with Shrimp and Scallop Ceviche

Wine: Fâmega Vinho Verde ($7)
Origin: Vinho Verde, Portugal

Taste and Texture Comparisons

Dish: Fresh, Light, Acidic, Herbal
Wine: Fresh, Light, Acidic, and Modest Alcohol

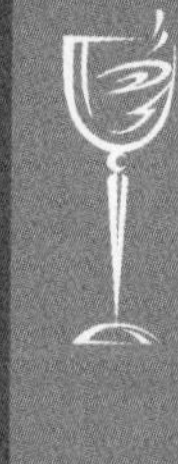

Vinho Verde literally translates to "green wine" in Portuguese. Fâmega's is a blend of indigenous white grapes—Avesso, Azal, and Pedernã—and is fresh, delicate, and only about 9.5% abv, which adds to its lightness.

Why This Is a Good Pairing

- ***Matching Body and Intensity*** – The dish and the wine are delicately structured and have crisp acidity. This does not allow one to overpower the other. The dish is a bit bolder in its flavors, but does not overpower the wine.
- ***Complementing*** – The wine's crisp acidity and light citrus notes link to the citrus notes in the dish, creating a connection. However, it does not compound the citrus notes or the high acid.
- ***Contrasting*** – The herbal notes and the slight briny nature of the shrimp contrast with the delicate fruit in the wine, and the dish's strong acidity makes the fruit flavors of the wine pop. This reaction makes the wine taste luxurious.

Wines That Didn't Work

Muscadet – While the acid in the Vinho Verde and Eden Riesling do not compound with the dish, the acid in the Muscadet compounded with the dish because it doesn't have enough fruit to balance it out. The finish was drying and fairly unpleasant.

NV Brut Champagne (blend) – The bubbles augment the black pepper and spice in the dish a bit too much, and the dish's high acidity strips the flavor of the champagne.

Argentinean Torrontés – The wine's full body overpowers the dish. Also, the contrast between the dish's high acidity and the wine's low acidity augments the wine's already intense flavor and masks the delicate flavors of the fish.

Alternatives: This was one of the dishes we found a few alternatives that paired well. Eden Valley Riesling went very well with this dish for similar reasons as the Vinho Verde (light-bodied, crisp acidity), and shared a similar reaction. The Beaujolais-Villages (a red alternative) is a bit softer in its acidity, especially in comparison to the dish, but the dish's acid makes the raspberry fruit flavors of the wine pop.

SUMMARY	Fâmega Vinho Verde	Muscadet	NV Brut Champagne	Argentinean Torrontés
Matching	+	+	+	(–)
Complementing	+			
Contrasting	+			
Compounding		(–)		
Complexing				
Cleansing	+			
Covering			(–)	(–)
Clashing		(–)	(–)	

Shrimp Tempura with Soy Dipping Sauce

SHRIMP TEMPURA WITH SOY DIPPING SAUCE

Yield: 10 portions

Cooking Method: Deep-Fry

Ingredients	Amounts - US	Volume	Metric
For the Shrimp Tempura			
Shrimp, 16/20, peeled, deveined, stretched	1 ½ lbs.	30 each	680 grams
Flour, all-purpose	5 ¾ oz.	1 ¼ cups	164 grams
Cornstarch	¾ oz.	3 Tbl.	20 grams
Baking powder		1 tsp.	
Salt, kosher		½ tsp.	
Seltzer water, well chilled	10 fl. oz.	1 ¼ cups	300 ml
Sesame oil		¾ tsp.	
For the Soy Dipping Sauce Yield: 16 oz.			
Dashi	8 fl. oz.	1 cup	240 ml
Soy sauce	2 ½ fl. oz.	¼ cup, plus 1 Tbl.	75 ml
Mirin	1 fl. oz.	2 Tbl.	30 ml
Daikon, grated finely	1 ½ oz.	¼ cup	42 grams
Scallions, thin sliced, bias cut	⅝ oz.	⅓ cup	18 grams
For the Dashi Broth Yield: 32 oz.			
Water	32 fl. oz.	1 qt.	1 L
Kombu, (dried kelp)		6 in. square	
Bonito flakes		½ cup	

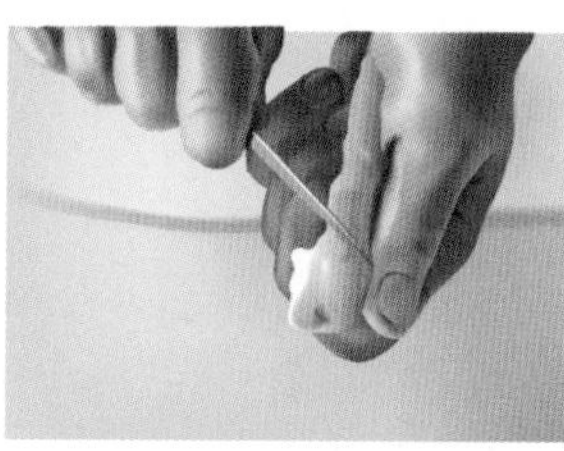

Lightly score the underside of the shrimp with a knife.

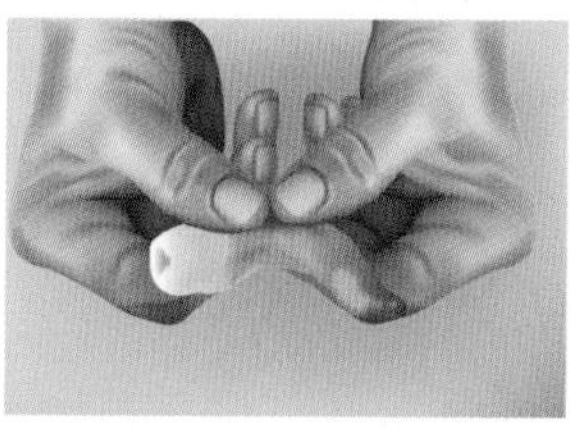

Shrimp are naturally arched in the center and the objective is to straighten them out. Using your fingers apply gentle pressure to shrimp while moving to opposite ends so it begins to straighten.

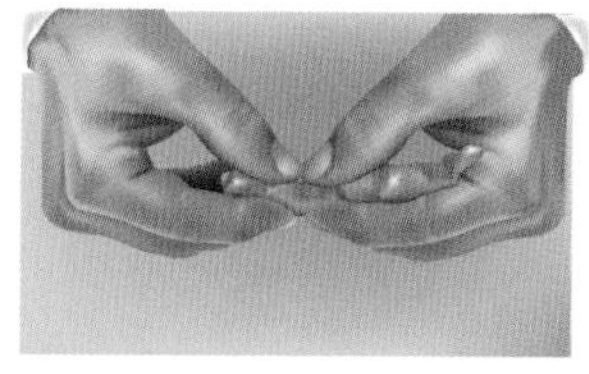

Continue to apply pressure from head to tail so that the shrimp is now completely straight. This is often referred to as 'massaging' the shrimp.

(Continues on next page)

For the Dashi Broth

1. Place the water and Kombu in a saucepan and bring to a gentle simmer.
2. Remove the Kombu, add the Bonito flakes and return to a simmer.
3. Remove from the heat and allow to steep for 5 minutes.
4. Strain through a cheesecloth-lined chinois.
5. Reserve for use.

Soy Dipping Sauce

1. Combine all ingredients and mix well.
2. Reserve under refrigeration.

Shrimp Tempura

1. Combine the dry ingredients.
2. Add the wet ingredients to the dry and mix gently with a whisk to combine evenly. Store the batter under refrigeration or on ice until needed.
3. Preheat a fryer to 365 F (185 C) degrees. Ensure that the oil is clean and clear.
4. Working in batches, holding the tail shell of the shrimp, dip each piece in the batter to coat evenly. Gently draw the shrimp on the side of the bowl to remove excess batter and then gently float, with a back and forth motion, in the oil until the batter begins to set. Do not overcrowd the fryer or the temperature will drop and the batter will absorb oil.
5. Once the shrimp are light golden and cooked, drain well. Cook time will be approximately 2 ½ minutes.
6. Serve immediately with the Soy Dipping Sauce.

If a deep fryer is not available, a heavy-bottomed saucepan or stockpot can be used. Please note the following key points: select a pot that is large enough to cook the main item and still allow plenty of space to the top of the pot, approximately 8 inches from the top of the oil; preheat the oil and adjust the heat using a thermometer to maintain the proper temperature; and use a spider or appropriate strainer to carefully remove the cooked food from the pot.

WINE SELECTED with Shrimp Tempura with Soy Dipping Sauce

Wine: Champagne Piper-Heidsieck Brut ($32)
Origin: Champagne, France

This Grande Marque champagne is made mostly from Pinot Noir with some Pinot Meunier and 15% Chardonnay. It is aged for more than two years on lees, which adds complexity. Although champagne is a delicate wine generally, this is a more aromatic and medium-bodied champagne.

Taste and Texture Comparisons

Dish: Crunchy, Rich, Umami/Saltiness, Sweetness
Wine: Effervescent, Crisp, Complex Flavors

Why This Is a Good Pairing

- ***Matching*** – The wine and the dish match in intensity of flavor. The shrimp tempura has a soft, mild flavor as does the champagne.
- ***Complementing*** – The toastiness of the fried batter connects with the champagne's autolytic character (biscuit, yeasty, toastiness), which augments the flavor of both in a good way.
- ***Contrasting*** – The richness from the batter and frying is a contrast to the high acidity and structure of the champagne. This creates a cleansing sensation, refreshing the palate.
- ***Complexing*** – The contrasting also allows the palate to focus on the layers of flavors in the wine (green apples, floral note, biscuits, minerals) and the dish (shrimp, batter, mirin, scallions).
- ***Dance*** – The richness of the batter elongates the finish, carrying the flavors for quite some time.

Wines That Didn't Work

New Zealand Sauvignon Blanc – The dish overpowers the wine and the flavors clash a bit. The wine is more than 14% alcohol and tasted warm, making the dish taste a bit bitter.

Beaujolais-Villages – The acidity in the sauce amplifies the fruit in the wine, but a bit too much, making it taste candied. However, the scallions in the dish help to create some complexity.

Barbera d'Asti – The high acidity of Barbera is refreshing; however, there is a clash between the toasty character of the sesame oil and the wine's fruit. Additionally, the earthiness of the wine and the tannins are amplified, especially with the sauce.

This pairing works well with and without the dipping sauce. Keep in mind, many wines may or may not work with or without an accompanying sauce.

SUMMARY	Champagne Piper-Heidsieck Brut	New Zealand Sauvignon Blanc	Beaujolais-Villages	Barbera d'Asti
Matching	+			
Complementing	+			
Contrasting	+		(–)	
Compounding				
Complexing	+		+	
Cleansing	+			+
Covering		(–)		
Clashing				(–)

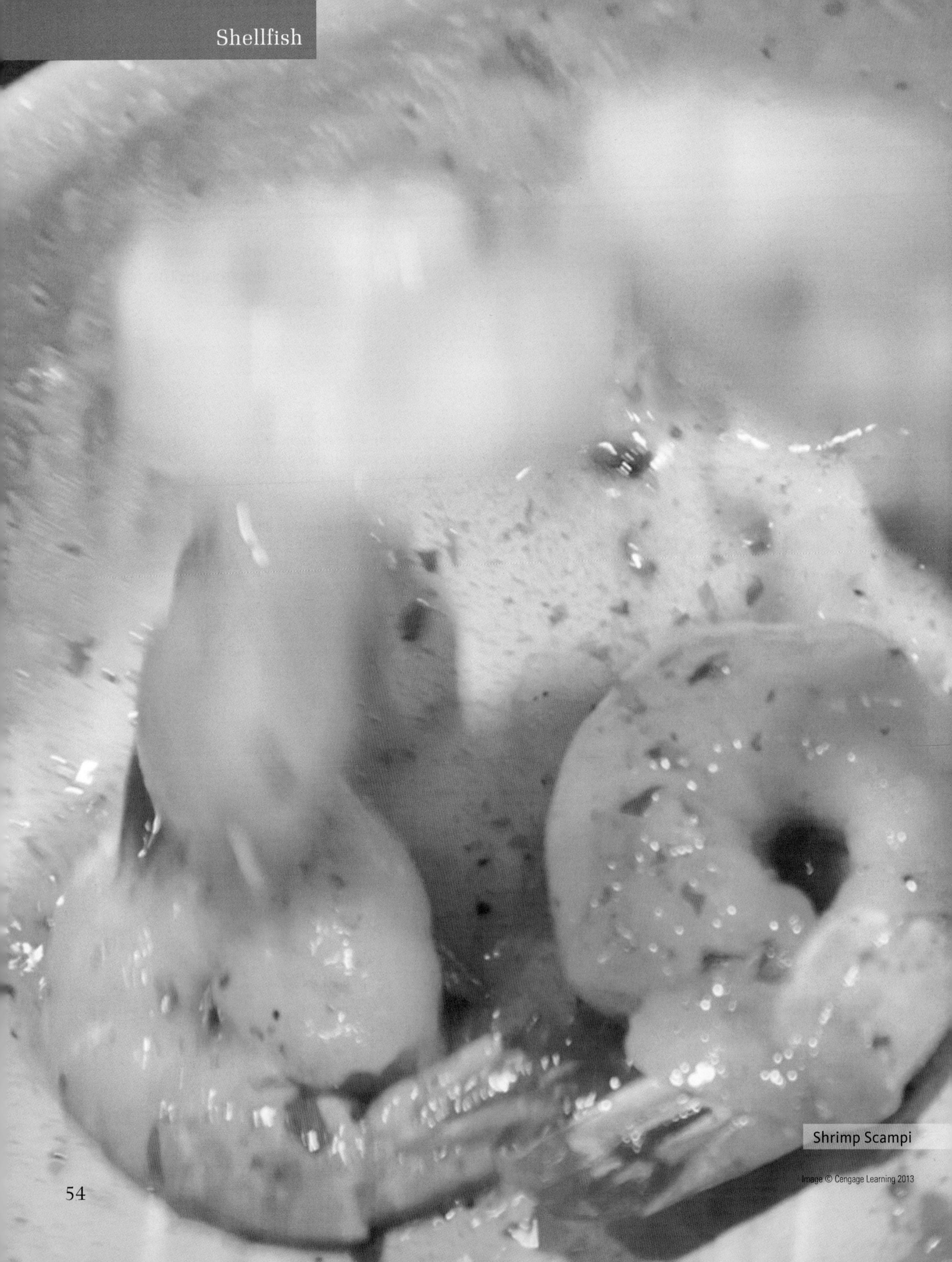

Shrimp Scampi

SHRIMP SCAMPI

Yield: 10 portions

Cooking Method: Sauté

Ingredients	Amounts - US	Volume	Metric
Shrimp, 16/20, peeled and deveined	1 ½ lb.	30 each	680 grams
Extra virgin olive oil	3 fl. oz.	6 Tbl.	90 ml
Butter, unsalted, cubed	3 oz.	6 Tbl.	85 grams
Garlic, sliced	¾ oz.	2 ½ Tbl.	20 grams
White wine, Chardonnay	4 fl. oz.	½ cup	120 ml
Lemon juice, fresh	1 ½ fl. oz.	3 Tbl.	45 ml
Italian parsley, chopped	¼ oz.	2 Tbl.	8 grams
Crushed red pepper		¼ tsp.	
Lemon zest, fine		½ tsp.	
Salt, sea		½ tsp.	
Black pepper, fresh ground		¼ tsp.	
Baguette, bias cut ¼-inch thick		10 each	
Extra virgin olive oil	1 ½ fl. oz.	3 Tbl.	45 ml

Scampi

1. Brush the baguette slices on both sides with extra virgin olive oil.
2. Grill on both sides until lightly toasted; reserve the crostini for plating.
3. Preheat a large sauté pan over medium heat. Work in batches so that you do not overcrowd the pan and drop the heat. The amount of shrimp you cook in each batch is determined by the size of the pan. *Adjust the amount of oil and butter for each batch.*
4. Add the oil and half the butter to the pan and then a single layer of shrimp.
5. Once the shrimp has sautéed for approximately 1 minute, add the garlic and mix well, ensuring that the shrimp are turned to cook evenly.
6. When the shrimp are cooked three-quarters of the way and the garlic is light brown, add the wine and reduce by half. Add the lemon juice, parsley, crushed red pepper, lemon zest, salt, and pepper; mix well to combine. At this point the shrimp will be cooked and slightly opaque in the center.
7. Turn off the heat and add the remaining butter; swirl the pan to emulsify into the sauce.
8. Place the shrimp scampi on top of the grilled crostini and top with the remaining garlic butter sauce.

The term *scampi* actually refers to *a prawn* in Italian and has become known as the method of preparation listed above.

WINE SELECTED with Shrimp Scampi

Wine: Penfolds Bin 311 Chardonnay ($22)
Origin: Tumbarumba, New South Wales, Australia

Taste and Texture Comparisons

Dish: Bold, Garlic, Slightly Spicy, Light Acidity, Herbal
Wine: Fruity (Apple), Moderate Acidity, Alcohol and Body, Slightly Round Texture

Tumbarumba is at the foothills of the snowy mountains in New South Wales, Australia. The climate is cool, resulting in a more delicate Chardonnay. It is mildly oaked, showing only hints of vanilla and spice.

Why This Is a Good Pairing

- ***Matching Intensity*** – Both the dish and the wine are about the same intensity in flavor and body. This even matching reduces the risk of one overpowering the other.
- ***Complementing*** – Although a different Chardonnay was added in the cooking, the Chardonnay in the sauce connects with the wine, creating better harmony between them. Additionally, the crostini's toastiness connects with the light touch of oak in the wine.
- ***Complexing*** – Given the layers of flavors in this pairing, there is a lovely complexing reaction. You taste all of the nuances of the dish (shrimp, garlic, slight buttery note, spice) with the layers of flavors in the wine (apple, spice, and slight hazelnut note).
- ***Cleansing*** – The acidity in the wine cuts through the richness in the sauce. The acidity in the dish also makes the apple fruit pop in the Chardonnay.

Wines That Didn't Work

Heavily Oaked California Chardonnay – We tested the recipe with a heavily oaked California Chardonnay and the wine's oak character is augmented and tastes strongly of clove when paired with this dish. Additionally, the wine's alcohol is also a bit high and mutes the flavors in the dish.

Gavi – While you may assume an Italian white would go with an Italian seafood dish, the dish is a bit overpowering for the wine and the dish's acidity from the lemon makes the fruit in the wine disappear, rather than augment it.

Alternative: Muscadet Sèvre et Maine Sur Lie—There is a complementing between the flavor of the shrimp and the slight briny flavor typically found in Muscadet. There is also a complementing of the lemon juice in the dish and the soft citrus notes in the wine. Given this Muscadet is Sur Lie, the crostini also complements the yeasty, bread-like flavor found in the wine. Additionally, the crisp acidity of the Muscadet creates a refreshing cleansing sensation with the dish.

SUMMARY	Penfolds Bin 311 Chardonnay	Muscadet Sèvre et Maine Sur Lie	Oaked California Chardonnay	Gavi
Matching	+			
Complementing	+	+		
Contrasting				
Compounding			(–)	
Complexing	+			
Cleansing		+		(–)
Covering				(–)
Clashing			(–)	

Grilled Sea Scallops with Extra Virgin Olive Oil

SCALLOPS

Scallops are typically marketed in two types: bay scallops and sea scallops. Bay scallops are smaller in size. Sea scallops are typically larger and marketed as 10/20—10 to 20 per pound, or U10—under 10 per pound. Many scallops are soaked in a phosphate solution before reaching the market to keep them white and to retain moisture. These scallops are typically not the best quality and can be more difficult to brown during cooking because of their moisture content. Dry pack scallops have not been treated are preferable.

GRILLED SEA SCALLOPS WITH EXTRA VIRGIN OLIVE OIL

Yield: 10 portions

Cooking Method: Grill

Ingredients	Amounts - US	Volume	Metric
Sea scallops, 10/20, side muscle removed	22 oz.	30 each	638 grams
Extra virgin olive oil	2 fl. oz.	¼ cup	60 ml
Salt, sea		as needed	
Black pepper, fresh ground		as needed	
Italian parsley, chopped	⅛ oz.	1 Tbl.	4 grams
Sicilian extra virgin olive oil	1 fl. oz.	2 Tbl.	30 ml

Grilled Scallops

1. Preheat a grill to medium high heat.
2. Coat the scallops with the extra virgin olive oil and season them with the salt and black pepper.
3. Place the scallops on the grill, allowing space between each scallop.
4. Cook for approximately 45 seconds and turn the scallops 45 degrees to achieve a crosshatch mark. Continue cooking until the scallops are cooked halfway and turn over.
5. Repeat the above procedure to crosshatch the other side of the scallops. Total cook time is approximately 3 minutes and the scallops should be slightly opaque in the center. The cook time will vary according to the size of the scallops and the heat of the grill.
6. Place the scallops on a plate and garnish with parsley and the Sicilian olive oil.

WINE SELECTED with Grilled Sea Scallops with Extra Virgin Olive Oil

Wine: Michel Redde La Moynerie Pouilly-Fumé ($25)
Origin: Pouilly-Fumé, Loire Valley, France

Taste and Texture Comparisons

Dish: Slight Sweetness, Herbal, Rich, Smoky/Grilled Flavor
Wine: Intense Aroma/Flavor, Dry, Fruity, Slight Herbal, High Acidity, Delicate Body, Mineral Notes

This is an unoaked Sauvignon Blanc that has strong mineral notes that remind some people of "gunflint." The wine is also known for its high acidity.

Why This Is a Good Pairing

- ***Contrasting Textures and Sweetness*** – Scallops have a rich, sweet texture, while the wine is delicate and dry. This works well as the scallops are rich enough to not be neutralized by the high acid of the wine. In fact, the acidity of the wine allows more flavors in the dish to pop.
- ***Complementing*** – There is a bridge between the smokiness from the grilling of the scallop and the minerality ("gunflint") of the wine. Additionally, the slight sweetness of the scallop is also augmented by the sweetness of the fruit in the wine.
- ***Contrasting Flavors*** – The citrus fruit in the wine contrasts with the grilling notes, making the fruit taste more ripe.
- ***Complexing*** – The complementing and contrasting create a *complexing* effect where you taste all the layers of flavor in both the dish and the wine.

Wines That Didn't Work

Dry White Sparkling – We tried many types of dry white sparkling wines from many regions and none of them worked well. Even though sparkling wines generally lighten and add freshness (and the champagne's minerality complemented the grilling notes), the acidity is a bit too high and, combined with the bubbles, is a bit too cleansing, neutralizing the flavors of the dish.

Oaked California Chardonnay – The weight of the dish and the wine match, but the flavors of the Chardonnay (particularly oaked Chardonnay with notes of vanilla, spice, and butter) overpower the freshness of the dish. You might pair this dish with an unoaked Chablis, but the flavors may not pop as much as with the Loire Sauvignon Blanc.

Oregon Pinot Noir – The acidity cleanses the palate in a similar way to the Pouilly-Fumé and the grilling notes bring out some of the toasty and earthy notes in the wine. However, the intensity of the flavors and the weight of the Pinot Noir overpower the scallop and cover the flavors of the dish.

SUMMARY	Pouilly-Fumé	Dry White Sparkling	Oaked California Chardonnay	Oregon Pinot Noir
Matching			+	
Complementing	+	+		+
Contrasting	+	+		
Compounding				
Complexing	+			
Cleansing	+	(–)		+
Covering			(–)	(–)
Clashing				

SAUTÉED SEA SCALLOPS WITH TRUFFLE GOAT CHEESE SAUCE

Yield: 10 portions

Cooking Method: Sauté

Ingredients	Amounts - US	Volume	Metric
Sea scallops, 10/20, side muscle removed	22 oz.	30 each	638 grams
Salt, sea		as needed	
Black pepper, fresh ground		as needed	
Extra virgin olive oil	3 fl. oz.	⅓ cup	90 ml
White wine, Chardonnay California, medium oak	2 fl. oz.	¼ cup	60 ml
For the Sauce Base			
Extra virgin olive oil	1 fl. oz.	2 Tbl.	30 ml
Shallots, minced	½ oz.	2 Tbl.	14 grams
Heavy cream	16 fl. oz.	2 cups	500 ml
Dijon mustard		½ tsp.	2 grams
Sophie goat cheese, diced	2 oz.	⅓ cup	56 grams
For the Black Truffles			
Black truffles, sliced thin	⅜ oz.	1 ½ Tbl.	10 grams
Butter, unsalted	½ oz.	1 Tbl.	14 grams
Thyme, leaves		1 tsp.	

Sophie is a bloomy, rind-ripened pasteurized goat's milk cheese from Sprout Creek Creamery that has been aged for three to four weeks.

Truffles

1. Preheat a saucepan over low heat; add the butter, truffles and thyme; sauté until the truffles are aromatic and slightly softened.
2. Reserve until needed.

Sauce Base

1. Preheat a saucepan over medium heat; add the extra virgin olive oil and the shallots; sweat until tender and translucent; do not color.
2. Add the cream and the mustard, whisk well to combine, and bring to a gentle simmer.
3. Reduce until the sauce is a light nape consistency; it will lightly coat the back of a spoon.
4. Whisk in the cheese slowly until fully melted and incorporated. Strain the sauce through a fine mesh strainer. Reserve the sauce until needed.

Sautéed Scallops

1. Season the scallops with salt and pepper.
2. Preheat a large sauté pan over medium heat; add the olive oil and the scallops to the pan. Work in batches so that you do not overcrowd the pan and drop the heat.
3. Once the scallops are cooked halfway and light brown, approximately 1½ minutes, turn over and finish cooking until they are slightly opaque in the center.
4. Remove the scallops from the pan and deglaze with the white wine; reduce by one-half and then add to the sauce base.
5. Add the truffles to the sauce, return the sauce to a gentle simmer, taste, and adjust the seasoning.
6. Plate and serve immediately.

WINE SELECTED with Sautéed Sea Scallops with Truffle Goat Cheese Sauce

Wine: Sequoia Grove Carneros Chardonnay ($23)
Origin: Carneros, California, USA

Taste and Texture Comparisons

Dish: Rich, Creamy Texture, Earthy, Slightly Sweet

Wine: Rich, Creamy Texture, Spice, Vanilla, Apple Fruit

A full-bodied California Chardonnay with over 14% alcohol. Creamy texture from lees stirring and rich French oak notes (vanilla, spice). This wine also does not go through malolactic fermentation so its acidity is well balanced for this dish.

Why This Is a Good Pairing

- ***Matching*** – Both are bold, rich, and have a creamy texture so neither overpowers the other; they are evenly matched.
- ***Complementing*** – The cream in the dish connects and builds a bridge with the cream notes in the wine.
- ***Contrasting*** – The earthiness of the truffles contrasts with and augments the apple fruit in the wine.
- ***Long Dance*** – The acidity is not too high (which is good for this dish!) and doesn't cleanse too much, which allows the richness in the dish to carry the flavor on your palate for a long time, elongating the dance back and forth.

Wines That Didn't Work

Light-Bodied or Unoaked Chardonnay – Be careful with Chardonnays that are unoaked or those that are not full-bodied enough for this dish; they will disappear on the palate. Additionally, we tried this dish with a few white Burgundies and while there were many complementing flavors and good matching weights and textures, their acidities are a bit too cleansing and they have a tendency to neutralize the dish.

Sauvignon Blanc – Whether from New Zealand or from France, their acidities, in general, are too high and strip the fat from your palate, thereby cutting the length and neutralizing the flavors. Even oaked versions (Fumé Blanc and Pessac-Léognans) are too high in acidity and strip the flavor of this dish.

New World Pinot Noir – We tried several New World Pinot Noirs including some from New Zealand and the United States. Truffle notes complement some of the earthy notes in the Pinot Noir, but the Pinot Noir covers up the flavors of the scallops and the cream.

The wine made the dish pop, and the dish made the wine sing. This was a magical two-way pairing for us.

SUMMARY	Sequoia Grove Carneros Chardonnay	Light-Bodied/ Unoaked Chardonnay	Sauvignon Blanc	New World Pinot Noir
Matching	+	+		
Complementing	+	+		
Contrasting	+			
Compounding				
Complexing				
Cleansing	+	(–)	(–)	(–)
Covering				(–)
Clashing				

Prosciutto-Wrapped Sea Scallops with Basil-Walnut Pesto

PROSCIUTTO-WRAPPED SEA SCALLOPS WITH BASIL-WALNUT PESTO

Yield: 10 portions

Cooking Method: Sauté

Ingredients	Amounts - US	Volume	Metric
For the Scallops			
Sea scallops, 10/20, side muscle removed	22 oz.	30 each	638 grams
Prosciutto di Parma, sliced thin		10–15 each	
Black pepper, fresh ground			
Olive oil, pure	3 fl. oz.	⅓cup	90 ml
For the Basil-Walnut Pesto			
Extra virgin olive oil	4–5 fl. oz.	½ cup plus	120–150 ml
Garlic, crushed	⅜ oz.	2 each, medium	10 grams
Walnuts, toasted	1 ½ oz.	½ cup	44 grams
Pine nuts, toasted	1 oz.	¼ cup	28 grams
Basil, leaves	1 ¼ oz.	2 cups	36 grams
Italian parsley, leaves		2 Tbl.	
Parmigiano-Reggiano, grated	1 ⅛ oz.	½ cup	34 grams
Black pepper, fresh ground		½ tsp.	

Basil-Walnut Pesto

1. Combine the olive oil, garlic, walnuts, and pine nuts in a blender and puree until smooth. Do not over puree this mixture as the oil will heat quickly and this will negatively impact the flavor and the color of the basil.
2. Add the basil, parsley, Parmigiano-Reggiano, and the black pepper; puree until the pesto is smooth. The amount of oil may need to be adjusted in order to achieve a smooth puree. Again, take care not to over puree and heat the pesto.
3. Taste and adjust the seasoning; drizzle a thin layer of extra virgin olive oil on top of the pesto to delay oxidation.
4. Reserve under refrigeration until needed.

Scallops

1. Season the scallops with black pepper on both sides.
2. Cut the prosciutto into strips wide enough to cover three-quarters of the surface and long enough to overlap. Wrap each scallop with a piece of prosciutto, positioning the seam in the center of one of the flat sides of the scallops.
3. Preheat a large sauté pan over medium heat; add the olive oil and the scallops. Work in batches so that you do not overcrowd the pan and drop the heat.
4. Once the scallops have cooked halfway and the prosciutto is golden brown (approximately 1 ½ minutes), turn the scallops over and finish cooking until they are slightly opaque in the center.
5. Plate and garnish each scallop with the pesto.

WINE SELECTED with Prosciutto-Wrapped Sea Scallops with Basil-Walnut Pesto

Wine: Benton Lane Oregon Pinot Noir ($23)

Origin: Willamette Valley, Oregon, USA

Taste and Texture Comparisons

Dish: Herbal/Aromatic, Umami/Salt, Slightly Sweet

Wine: Fruity, Aromatic, Slight Earthy Soft Texture, Crisp

Oregon Pinot Noir is a little darker in its fruit character than its California cousin in general, and at this price point, it can be a good value.

Why This Is a Good Pairing

- ***Match Intensity, Texture, and Weight*** – There is a variety of textures and intensity here, but each seems to find its match (aromatic pesto: aromatic wine; slightly sweet scallop: sweet impression of fruit in wine; soft texture in wine: soft texture in scallop; slight bitterness with walnuts in pesto: slight tannins in Pinot Noir).
- ***Complementing*** – The slightly bitter notes from the walnuts in the pesto creates a bridge to the texture of the tannins in the Pinot Noir. Your palate focuses on it (without the tannin compounding), adding another dimension.
- ***Contrasting*** – The cherry fruit in the Pinot Noir and the sweetness of the scallop are augmented by the savory flavors of the prosciutto.
- ***Complexing*** – The richness in the dish makes the flavors dance on your palate so that you taste all the layers: pesto, fruit, earthiness, herbal notes, meat, and sweetness of the scallop.

Wines That Didn't Work

New Zealand Sauvignon Blanc – Sauvignon Blancs are known for an herbaceous aroma. This herbaceousness compounds with the pesto (green + green = green^2) and is unpleasant.

Alsatian Gewürztraminer – Although matching the dish's intensity, Gewürztraminer's litchi and spice flavors make it too much for the pairing. There is too much going on and the flavors all clash.

Dry White Sparkling – We tried a variety of dry sparkling wines. All are a bit cleansing at first, but then the dish overpowers the wine.

When Pinot Noirs are being made, sometimes winemakers include the stems from the clusters to beef up the structure, and sometimes not. We have found that those with "stems in" or that use whole-cluster fermentation taste astringent with this dish. This is a compounding reaction with the herbal notes and slight tannins with the pesto. Make sure you test before you pair!

SUMMARY	Benton Lane Oregon Pinot Noir	New Zealand Sauvignon Blanc	Alsatian Gewürztraminer	Dry White Sparkling
Matching	+		+	
Complementing	+			
Contrasting	+		(–)	
Compounding	+	(–)		
Complexing	+			
Cleansing				(–)
Covering				(–)
Clashing			(–)	

LOBSTER

The first commercial lobster fishery was founded in the mid 1800s in Maine. As a prized delicacy, lobsters are known for their tenderness and sweet flavor. Lobsters are very perishable; they should be purchased and consumed as close to harvest as possible.

STEAMED LOBSTER WITH DRAWN BUTTER AND LEMON

Yield: 10 portions

Cooking Method: Steam

Ingredients	Amounts - US	Volume	Metric
Lobster, Maine, 1½ pounds		10 each	
Butter, drawn	20 fl. oz.	2 ½ cups	620 ml
Lemon, wedge		20 each	

Steamed Lobster

1. Steam the lobsters in a covered pot over gently simmering salted water for approximately 11–12 minutes until just cooked; the flesh will be slightly opaque in the center.
2. Split the lobsters in half lengthwise. Clean the tomalley out of the cavity.
3. Crack the claws and knuckles to allow easy removal.
4. Serve immediately with drawn butter and lemon wedges.

WINE SELECTED with Steamed Lobster with Drawn Butter and Lemon

Wine: Caposaldo Pinot Grigio ($9)
Origin: Veneto, Italy

This wine comes from the Veneto in northeast Italy, west of Venice. Pinot Grigio is known for soft floral notes and moderate structure, which makes it a crowd pleaser and a great pairing for this dish.

Taste and Texture Comparisons

Dish: Sweet Flavor, Soft Texture, Rich, Light Acid
Wine: Fruity, Soft Texture, Lightly Floral, Citrus and White Peach Notes, Moderate Acid, Body, and Alcohol

Why This Is a Good Pairing

- ***Matching Intensity*** – The flavors in both are pure, clean, and on the medium side in flavor intensity. Additionally, both the wine and the dish have a soft texture. This makes for a balanced pairing where one does not overpower the other.
- ***Complementing*** – The lobster has a distinct sweet flavor that connects with the fruit in the Pinot Grigio. This makes the fruit in the wine pop. It augments the wine without losing the flavor of the dish.
- ***Contrasting*** – The acidity in the wine contrasts with the richness from the drawn butter, which creates a slight cleansing sensation that is refreshing, but the acid doesn't cut the flavor of the dish. Additionally, the richness from the drawn butter elongates the flavors on the palate, making the dance of flavors last just a bit longer.

Wines That Didn't Work

Puligny-Montrachet – The wine's intensity overpowers the dish. Additionally, the wine has buttery notes from malolactic fermentation that compound with the drawn butter in the dish and yield a buttery texture on your palette. This is a bit overwhelming.

NV Brut Champagne (blend) – There is a bit of a contrast and dance between the toasty notes in the wine and the sweet impression of the lobster, but the wine's high acidity is too cleansing, stripping the dish's flavor.

Roero Arneis – The soft lemony character of Arneis compounds with the lemon in the dish, making the pairing taste too lemony, ultimately washing away the flavor of the dish.

Alternative: Muscadet Sèvre et Maine Sur Lie also pairs well with this dish for similar structural reasons as the Pinot Grigio. Muscadet is also known for a slightly briny flavor that augments the lobster's flavor.

SUMMARY	Caposaldo Pinot Grigio	Puligny-Montrachet	NV Brut Champagne	Roero Arneis
Matching	+			
Complementing	+			
Contrasting	+		+	
Compounding		(–)		(–)
Complexing			+	
Cleansing	+		(–)	
Covering		(–)		
Clashing				

Lobster Bisque

LOBSTER BISQUE

Yield: 10 portions

Cooking Method: Simmer

Ingredients	Amounts - US	Volume	Metric
Lobster, Maine, 1½ pounds		4 each	
Extra virgin olive oil	2 fl. oz.	¼ cup	60 ml
Butter, unsalted	1 oz.	2 Tbl.	28 grams
Onions, large dice	8 oz.	2 cups	226 grams
Leeks, large dice	4 oz.	1 cup	114 grams
Celeriac, large dice	4 oz.	1 cup	114 grams
Carrots, large dice	4 oz.	1 cup	114 grams
Garlic, crushed	¼ oz.	2 each, medium	6 grams
Tomato paste	2 oz.	¼ cup	56 grams
Cognac	4 fl. oz.	½ cup	120 ml
Lobster stock	64 fl. oz.	8 cups	2 L
Chicken stock	64 fl. oz.	8 cups	2 L
Sachet		1 each	
Rice, Carolina	3 oz.	½ cup	84 grams
Lobster stock		as needed	
Heavy cream, hot	8–12 fl. oz.	1–1 ½ cups	240–360 ml
Butter, unsalted	4 oz.	½ cup	114 grams
Salt, sea		to taste	
Black pepper, fresh ground		to taste	
Cognac	½ fl.oz.	1 Tbl.	15 ml
Lemon juice	½ fl. oz.	1 Tbl.	15 ml
For the Garnish			
Lobster, steamed, small dice		2 each	
Tarragon, chopped	½ oz.	2 Tbl.	14 grams

(Continues on next page)

Lobster Bisque

1. Steam the lobsters until slightly undercooked (approximately 7 minutes), shock in ice water, and drain well.
2. Preheat oven to 375 F (190 C) degrees convection.
3. Remove the lobster meat from the shells, medium dice the garnish, and reserve under refrigeration. The remaining lobster meat can be used for an alternative dish/use.
4. Place the shells on a sheet pan and roast in the oven until completely dry and brittle.
5. Place the shells in a stockpot or cheesecloth and crush with a meat mallet until the pieces are no larger than 1 inch.
6. Preheat a stockpot over medium heat; add butter and oil, then the onions, leeks, celeriac, and carrots. Sauté until vegetables are lightly caramelized and begin to soften.
7. Add the garlic and sweat until aromatic.
8. Reduce the heat to low. Add the tomato paste and stir well to coat. Cook until the tomato paste is caramelized and brick red.
9. Add the first cognac and reduce by three-quarters.
10. Add the stocks, crushed lobster shells, sachet, and the rice; bring to a simmer and cook for 45 minutes to 1 hour.
11. Once the flavor has fully developed, remove from the heat. Remove the sachet from the soup and use an immersion blender to puree the base and thicken the soup. Ensure that the blender base is flat against the bottom of the pot as this will allow the rice to be pureed and will draw more flavor from the shells.
12. Strain the soup through a China cap and then a chinois.
13. Refresh the strained shells with enough water to just cover, bring to a simmer, and cook for 20 minutes. Strain and add to the soup base. This maximizes the flavor drawn out of the shells.
14. Return the soup base to a gentle simmer and add the hot cream; season with salt and pepper; taste and adjust the seasoning.
15. Reduce the heat, mount with butter, and add the lemon juice and cognac.
16. Add the diced lobster and the tarragon.
17. Serve immediately.

Lobster Bisque is a classic soup that is derived from a stew-like dish that originated in the Bay of Bisque. Traditionally, it is thickened with rice but can also be thickened with a roux. Replace the rice with 12 oz. of blond roux. This is a great option if you do not have an immersion blender.

WINE SELECTED with Lobster Bisque

Wine: Olivier Leflaive Puligny-Montrachet ($50)
Origin: Côte de Beaune, Burgundy, France

Taste and Texture Comparisons

Dish: Rich, Creamy Texture, Sweet, Bold Flavor
Wine: Medium Body and Alcohol, Slight Creamy Texture, Apple, Vanilla, Toast, Spice, Minerals, Crisp Acidity

Puligny-Montrachet is one of the top appellations in Burgundy for white wine made from Chardonnay. They are wines of great depth and finesse.

Why This Is a Good Pairing

- ***Matching Intensity*** – The bold flavors of the soup match in intensity with the depth and rich, complex flavor of the Puligny-Montrachet.
- ***Complementing*** – The light toasty and spice flavors in the wine create a bridge to the roasted flavor of the lobster shells used for the bisque. Additionally, the wine's hint of butter connects with the soup's touch of cream.
- ***Contrasting*** – The moderately high acidity of the wine cuts through some of the creamy texture and richness of the dish, but not too much. It didn't strip any of the flavors. On the contrary, it allows for the flavors of the dish and the wine to come through. This creates a *complexing* reaction. The fat from the dish carries the flavors, allowing the dance to last for a longer time.

Wines That Didn't Work

Italian Pinot Grigio – The richness and boldness of the dish overpower the delicate floral and light fruity aromas of the Pinot Grigio. The dish wins the struggle and you lose the flavor of the wine.

California Fumé Blanc – This wine clashes with the dish. The acidity strips the flavor of the bisque and the alcohol (14.5% abv) is amplified by the dish, making the wine taste hot on the palate. From a flavor perspective, something clashes that makes the wine taste like lavender perfume. Yeah, weird.

California Pinot Noir – Given that lobster is a rich, sweet shellfish and bisque is a bold dish, we thought Pinot Noir would work. We tried several. The weights match and the slight spicy nature of the oak connects with the flavor of the roasted lobster shells. However, the bisque diminishes the fruit completely, augmenting the wine's earthy character. Additionally, there is a slightly astringent note to the tannins.

SUMMARY	Olivier Leflaive Puligny-Montrachet	Italian Pinot Grigio	California Fumé Blanc	California Pinot Noir
Matching	+	(–)		+
Complementing	+			+
Contrasting	+			
Compounding			(–)	(–)
Complexing	+			
Cleansing			(–)	
Covering		(–)		(–)
Clashing			(–)	

Lobster Thermidor

LOBSTER THERMIDOR

Yield: 10 portions

Cooking Method: Roast

Ingredients	Amounts - US	Volume	Metric
Lobster, Maine, 1 ½ pounds, steamed*		5 each	
Butter, unsalted	1 oz.	2 Tbl.	28 grams
Shallots, minced	2 oz.	½ cup	56 grams
White wine, Chardonnay California, medium oak	2 fl. oz.	¼ cup	60 ml
Heavy cream	10 fl. oz.	1 ¼ cups	300 ml
English mustard, dry		¾ tsp.	
Lemon juice	½ fl. oz.	1 Tbl.	15 ml
Parsley, chopped		1 Tbl.	
Salt, sea		to taste	
White pepper, fresh ground		to taste	
Egg yolks, large	2 ¼ oz.	4 each	64 grams
Parmigiano-Reggiano, grated fine	⅜ oz.	3 Tbl.	2 grams

*The lobsters should be slightly undercooked when initially steamed.

Lobster Thermidor

1. Preheat oven to 400 F (205 C) degrees convection.
2. Remove the lobster meat from the tail, body, and claws—keeping the body and tail intact. Slice the tail on a slight bias into pieces ¼-inch thick. Reserve the remaining shells for another use (lobster stock, butter, etc.).
3. Preheat a saucepan over medium-low heat, add the butter, and cook until melted.
4. Add the shallots and sweat until tender.
5. Add the wine and cook until almost dry.
6. Add the heavy cream and simmer gently to reduce by half.
7. Mix the English mustard and the lemon juice to combine evenly; add to the sauce base while whisking to evenly incorporate.
8. Add parsley, salt, and pepper; taste and adjust the seasoning as needed. Remove from the heat.
9. Cool the mixture slightly, add the yolks and whisk well to combine. Refrigerate this mixture until it is well chilled before using.
10. Place the lobster bodies on a sheet pan; spoon 1 oz. of sauce into the shell cavity. Shingle the lobster slices evenly back into the opposite shells. Place the claw and knuckle meat on top of the head portion.
11. Top the lobster with an additional 1 oz. of sauce; sprinkle the cheese over the top of the sauce.
12. Bake the lobsters for approximately 10 minutes or until light brown and hot in the center.

WINE SELECTED with Lobster Thermidor

Wine: Agrapart & Fils, 7 Crus ($37)
Origin: Blanc de Blancs Champagne, France

Taste and Texture Comparisons

Dish: Bold, Rich, Creamy, Piquant

Wine: Delicate, High Acidity, Slightly Toasty, Biscuity

This champagne is made up of only Chardonnay grapes from seven villages in the Côte des Blancs region in Champagne. In general, Blanc de Blancs are lighter in body and higher in acidity than those blended with Pinot Noir and Pinot Meunier. Aging on lees for three years gives this champagne toasty, biscuity flavors on the palate.

Why This Is a Good Pairing

- ***Complementing*** – The slightly nutty notes of the parmesan and the creaminess of the sauce connect with the autolytic flavors of the champagne. Additionally, the richness from the sauce allows the flavors to linger on your palate for a longer period of time. Quite a magical experience.
- ***Contrasting*** – This traditionally rich dish contrasts exceptionally well with the more delicate acidic champagne.
- ***Cleansing*** – This dish is very rich. The high acidity of the Blanc de Blancs cuts through the richness without stripping the flavor. Additionally, the high acid also makes the flavors of the dish pop even more.

Wines That Didn't Work

Puligny-Montrahet – The acidity of the wine brings out the complexities of the dish, but the pairing feels like a struggle as opposed to a dance.

New World Dry Riesling – We tried a few dry Rieslings from the New World (Australia, New Zealand, etc.). The high acidity cleanses the palate, but so much that it strips the flavors of the dish. The richness of the dish also clashes with the wine, making the wine taste too much like bitter grapefruit.

California Pinot Noir – Again, we tried a red wine, given the boldness of the dish. The touch of oak in the Pinot Noir is augmented by the dish and it tastes like tobacco. The dish also strips the fruit from the wine.

SUMMARY	Agrapart Blanc de Blancs Champagne	Puligny-Montrachet	New World Dry Riesling	California Pinot Noir
Matching			(–)	
Complementing	+			
Contrasting	+			
Compounding				(–)
Complexing		+		
Cleansing	+	+	(–)	(–)
Covering				
Clashing		(–)	(–)	

SHELLFISH PAIRING SUMMARY AND CONCLUSIONS

Crab

Dish	Method	Wine
Jumbo Lump Crab	—	Sparkling Brut Rosé, Domaine Carneros
Crab and Avocado Salad	—	Pinot Noir, Jadot Beaune Clos des Ursules
Chesapeake Crab Cake	Pan-Fry	Spätlese Riesling, Selbach-Oster

- ***Main ingredient tendencies:*** Crab's light weight and texture are suitable for light-to medium-bodied wines. Its purity of flavor pops with high acid wines and its slight sweet flavor can complement a wine's fruit flavor.
- ***Specific techniques that changed the pairing:*** The jumbo lump crab on its own is already cooked, so with these recipes it is more the ingredients that impact the pairing than the technique.
- ***Specific ingredients that changed the pairing:*** Horseradish contrasted nicely with fruit in the rosé sparkler and spicy chipotle contrasted with the sweetness of Mosel Riesling, yet both spices clashed with the tannin in red wine.

Shrimp

Dish	Method	Wine
Shrimp and Scallop Ceviche	Cure	Vinho Verde, Fâmega Vinho Verde
Shrimp Tempura	Deep-Fry	Champagne Piper-Heidsieck Brut
Shrimp Scampi	Sauté	Chardonnay, Penfolds Bin 311

- ***Main ingredient tendencies:*** Shrimp is quite aromatic and the best wine pairings revolve around delicate whites with subtle aromatics. These recipes were overpowered by fuller-bodied whites and light-to medium-bodied red wines.
- ***Specific techniques that changed the pairing:*** The champagne slightly cleanses the oil present from the deep-frying of the Tempura, but it strips the flavor in the Ceviche and Scampi.
- ***Specific ingredients that changed the pairing:*** The tempura batter added a richness with which the champagne's acidity was able to contrast, but also complemented the champagne's autolytic character. The ceviche's acidic marinade and fruit were complemented by a light, fruity wine.

Scallops

Dish	Method	Wine
Grilled Sea Scallops	Grill	Sauvignon Blanc, Pouilly-Fumé, Michel Redde
Sautéed Sea Scallops	Sauté	Chardonnay, Sequoia Grove
Prosciutto-Wrapped Sea Scallops	Sauté	Pinot Noir, Benton Lane

- ***Main ingredient tendencies:*** Scallops have a soft texture and are sweet. These recipes allow a range of wines to be paired from delicate, crisp whites to low tannin, fruity reds.
- ***Specific techniques that changed the pairing:*** Grilling the sea scallops complements the mineral notes in the Pouilly-Fumé.
- ***Specific ingredients that changed the pairing:*** Truffle goat cheese sauce and prosciutto add weight to the second two dishes, allowing for a richer wine. The cheese sauce complemented the buttery notes and creamy texture in the Chardonnay, while the prosciutto wrapping contrasts with the Pinot Noir, making its fruit pop and tannins even softer.

Lobster

Dish	Method	Wine
Steamed Lobster	Steam	Pinot Grigio, Caposaldo
Lobster Bisque	Simmer	Chardonnay, Puligny-Montrachet, Olivier Leflaive
Lobster Thermidor	Roast	Blanc de Blancs Champagne, Agrapart & Fils

- ***Main ingredient tendencies:*** Lobster is rich in weight and texture and has a sweet flavor which pairs well with crisp white wines, yet is overpowered by low-tannin, fruity reds.
- ***Specific techniques that changed the pairing:*** Steaming preserves the pure lobster flavor and lighter weight, allowing for a delicate moderate white. Roasting intensifies the flavors and the Pinot Grigio was overpowered by the lobster bisque.
- ***Specific ingredients that changed the pairing:*** The richness from the roasted lobster shells, stock, and the cream in the Lobster Bisque called for a richer wine, and the Puligny-Montrachet's high acidity created the right amount of cleansing. The Thermidor required more of a cleansing reaction to cut through the richness of the cheese and to accent the lobster's flavor.

5
Fish

Fish is a very versatile protein that can vary greatly in flavor, body, and texture. This versatility lends well to a variety of cooking techniques in this chapter including: cure, poach, sauté, roast, and grill.

An herb-crusted salmon and a Sancerre sparked my first interest in wine more than 10 years ago. The pairing took place at a client lunch while I was working for Citibank in London. It was so delicious that I lost concentration in the meeting. It was at that moment I realized that wines and dishes were intentionally paired with one another for delightful sensory experiences! From then on, I was smitten with wine (and food and wine pairing). We have a very similar pairing in this chapter, Grilled Salmon with a Sancerre. Perhaps it will inspire you.

Dish	Wine
Halibut	
Poached Halibut with Fennel and Orange Slaw	Valdinera Roero Arneis, Piedmont, Italy ($16)
Sautéed Halibut with Tomatoes, Capers, and Mint	Trimbach Muscat, Alsace, France ($22)
Halibut Wrapped in Phyllo with Marjoram and Chive Beurre Blanc	Ruffino Orvieto Classico, Umbria, Italy ($8)
Tuna	
Tuna Poke	Guigal Côtes du Rhône Blanc Viognier, Rhone, France ($12)
Seared Tuna with Sesame and Coriander	Willm Gewürztraminer Vin d'Alsace, Alsace, France ($15)
Grilled Tuna Skewers with Yellow Peppers and Cherry Tomatoes	Yerring Station Yarra Valley Pinot Noir, Victoria, Australia ($16)
Salmon	
Gravlax	Veuve Clicquot Yellow Label Brut Champagne, Champagne, France ($45)
Poached Salmon with Sauce Hollandaise	Pewsey Vale Eden Valley Dry Riesling, South Australia, Australia ($15)
Grilled Salmon with Dill Butter	Vincent Gaudry Sancerre "Melodie de Vieilles Vignes," Loire, France ($24)

QUALITY IDENTIFIERS FOR FISH

When purchasing whole fish, look for the following:

- Eyes should be bulging and clear.
- Flesh should be firm to the touch and bounce back slightly.
- Gills should be bright pink.
- The cavity should have a fresh sea aroma.
- Scales should hold tight to the skin.

When purchasing fish filets or portions, look for the following:

- The fish should have a fresh sea aroma.
- Flesh should be firm to the touch and bounce back slightly.
- There should be little or no separation in the flesh.

HALIBUT

Halibut are noted as the largest of the flat fish, and they thrive in deep, cold water. Their flesh is firm, flaky, and has a mild sweet flavor.

POACHED HALIBUT WITH FENNEL AND ORANGE SLAW

Yield: 10 portions

Cooking Method: Poach

Ingredients	Amounts - US	Volume	Metric
For the Halibut			
Halibut filet, 5 oz., skin off		10 each	142 grams
Salt, sea		as needed	
White pepper, fresh ground		as needed	
Extra virgin olive oil		as needed	
For the Fennel and Orange Slaw			
Fennel, shaved thin, core removed	8 oz.	3 cups	224 grams
Red onion, sliced thin	4 oz.	1 cup	112 grams
Orange segments	6 oz.	1 ¼ cup	168 grams
Orange juice, fresh	1 ½ fl. oz.	3 Tbl.	45 ml
Fennel fronds, chopped	¼ oz.	1 ½ Tbl.	6 grams
Extra virgin olive oil	1 ½ fl. oz.	3 Tbl.	45 ml
Fennel pollen		to taste	
Salt, kosher		to taste	
Black pepper, fresh ground		to taste	

(Continues on next page)

Poached Halibut with Fennel and Orange Slaw

Halibut

1. Place enough oil in a rondeau to cover the halibut pieces by 1 inch, preheat the oil to 150 F (65 C).
2. Combine the ingredients for the Fennel and Orange Slaw, taste, and adjust the seasoning.
3. Season the halibut with salt and pepper on both sides.
4. Place the halibut carefully in the oil. Cook for approximately 8–10 minutes until the fish is just cooked throughout; it should be slightly opaque in the center.
5. Remove the fish carefully with a fish spatula and drain well.
6. Plate with the Fennel and Orange Slaw and serve immediately.

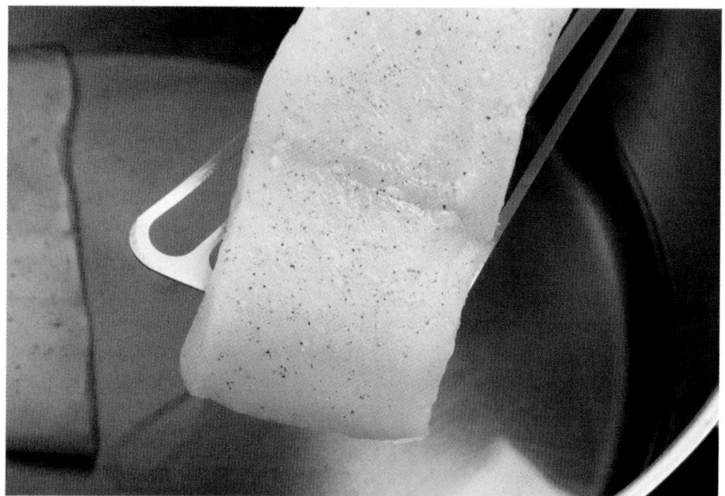

If fennel pollen is unavailable, you can substitute lightly toasted fennel seeds that have been finely ground.

WINE SELECTED with Poached Halibut with Fennel and Orange Slaw

Wine: Valdinera Roero Arneis ($16)

Origin: Roero, Piedmont, Italy

Taste and Texture Comparisons

Dish: Mild Flavor, Herbal, Sweet, Slight Spice

Wine: Mild Flavor, Medium Body, Acidity, and Alcohol with Citrus, Floral, and Slight Almond Flavors

Arneis is a white grape from Piedmont that in the past was blended with the red grape Nebbiolo to soften its tannins. However, on its own it can be a lightly fragrant, delicately floral white.

Why This Is a Good Pairing

- ***Matching Body and Flavor*** – The Arneis matches the dish in both body and intensity of flavor.
- ***Complementing*** – The wine's citrus character provides a nice complement to the fresh orange in the dish, creating a bridge of flavor. Given it is not an overly crisp or acidic wine, it doesn't cleanse/strip the flavor of the dish from your palate. Likewise, the amount of orange is just enough so that the wine is balanced and still remains fruity.
- ***Contrasting*** – The floral and slightly almond notes provide a great contrast to the herbal nature of the Fennel and Orange Slaw and the flavor of the Halibut. This extends the finish of the dish.

Wines That Didn't Work

Muscadet – Muscadet Sur Lie is not an obviously fruity wine. In fact, many times the fruit plays second fiddle to a slight brininess, reminiscent of oyster shells, that some refer to as a minerality. While this can complement some fish dishes (e.g., Shrimp Scampi), it sometimes can compound with the briny character of the fish, as it does in this case.

Dry Alsatian Muscat – The wine's floral nature clashes with the fish and the fennel, augmenting its floral notes (making it too floral). Additionally, the orange flavor in the dish compounds with a citrus/orange flavor in the wine. Muscat is also traditionally low in acid. Acid can bring freshness to a dish, but this wine doesn't have any to bring.

Orvieto – This wine is a bit too delicate for this dish. Additionally, the crisp acidity cleanses the palate too much stripping the flavor of the dish.

SUMMARY	Arneis	Muscadet	Dry Alsatian Muscat	Orvieto
Matching	+		+	(–)
Complementing	+			
Contrasting	+		(–)	
Compounding		(–)		
Complexing				
Cleansing				(–)
Covering				
Clashing				

Sautéed Halibut with Tomatoes, Capers, and Mint

SAUTÉED HALIBUT WITH TOMATOES, CAPERS, AND MINT

Yield: 10 portions
Cooking Method: Sauté

Ingredients	Amounts - US	Volume	Metric
Halibut filet, 5 oz., skin off		10 each	
Salt, sea		as needed	
White pepper, fresh ground		as needed	
Flour, all-purpose		as needed	
Extra virgin olive oil	3 fl. oz.	⅓ cup	90 ml
Shallots, minced	1 oz.	¼ cup	28 grams
Garlic, chopped	½ oz.	1 Tbl.	14 grams
Extra virgin olive oil		as needed	
Tomato, peeled, seeded, small dice	16 oz.	3 cups	448 grams
Capers, salt-packed, rinsed	¾ oz.	2 Tbl.	24 grams
Mint, chopped	¼ oz.	4 tsp.	4 grams
Parsley, chopped		2 ½ tsp.	
Salt, kosher		to taste	
Black pepper, fresh ground		to taste	

Halibut

1. Preheat a sauté pan over medium heat.
2. Season the fish with salt and pepper; dredge in flour.
3. Add the oil to the pan and then the fish. Do not overcrowd the pan; work in batches as necessary.
4. Sauté the fish until it is cooked almost halfway and the bottom surface is light golden brown; control the heat as needed.
5. Turn and repeat until the fish is cooked, it should be opaque in the center; remove to a rack and hold warm.
6. Reduce the heat to low, add the shallots to the pan and sauté until they begin to soften; add the garlic and sauté until aromatic and the garlic begins to brown. Add additional oil as needed to cook the shallots and garlic.
7. Add the tomatoes and the capers and sauté until heated throughout.
8. Add the mint and parsley, season to taste with salt and pepper.
9. Plate the fish and top with the tomato, caper, and mint sauce.

WINE SELECTED with Sautéed Halibut with Tomatoes, Capers, and Mint

Wine: Trimbach Muscat ($22)

Origin: Alsace, France

Taste and Texture Comparisons

Dish: Sweet, Herbal, Crisp Acidity Salt, and Maillard Reaction Flavors

Wine: Dry, Floral (Rose), Mineral, Honey, Medium Body and Alcohol with Low Acidity

One of the most aromatic varieties in the world, Muscat can make very sweet wines, sparkling, and still wines. In Alsace it is typically dry, yet still showcases its powerful aromas.

Why This Is a Good Pairing

- ***Matching*** – The wine and the dish match in intensity, flavor, and body. The dish has some bold flavors, as does the wine.
- ***Contrasting*** – Muscat is low in acid, so it does not strip the flavors of the dish from the palate and balances nicely with the tomatoes which do add fresh acidity.
- ***Complexing*** – A lovely dance plays between the flavor of the fish, the floral character of the wine and the freshness of the tomatoes, and the slight bite of the capers. You taste all of the layers.

Wines That Didn't Work

Orvieto – This delicate white wine's minerality and slight herbal nature make the herbs in the dish stick out like a sore thumb. The sweetness of the tomatoes and the capers also clash with the wine for an unpleasant finish.

Alsace Gewürztraminer – It is said that Gewürztraminer goes well with tomatoes; however, we found this wine to overpower the dish. When paired, the flavors in the dish are lost. There is also a compounding between the sweetness of the tomatoes and the slight sweetness of the wine. The wine's alcohol is also brought to the forefront by the mint.

Savennières – The wine is a bit overpowering for the dish. The freshness of the dish makes the wine taste more evolved (older) than it is, creating a strong unpleasant nutty character on the palate.

SUMMARY	Muscat	Orvieto	Alsace Gewürztraminer	Savennières
Matching	+	(–)	(–)	
Complementing				
Contrasting	+	(–)		(–)
Compounding				
Complexing	+			
Cleansing				
Covering			(–)	(–)
Clashing		(–)		

HALIBUT WRAPPED IN PHYLLO WITH MARJORAM AND CHIVE BEURRE BLANC

Yield: 10 portions

Cooking Method: Roast

Ingredients	Amounts - US	Volume	Metric
For the Halibut			
Halibut filet, 5 oz., skin off		10 each	
Phyllo dough		8 sheets	
Extra virgin olive oil		as needed	
Marjoram, chopped		1 Tbl.	
Bread crumbs, finely ground, lightly toasted		1 Tbl.	
Black pepper, fresh ground		as needed	
Salt, sea		as needed	
Chives, short cut		1 Tbl.	

For the Chive Beurre Blanc Yield: 16 oz.			
Shallots, sliced	2 oz.	½ cup	56 grams
Black peppercorns, cracked		2 tsp.	
Thyme, sprigs		2 each	
White wine, Chardonnay California, medium oak	6 fl. oz.	¾ cup	180 ml
White wine vinegar	2 fl. oz.	¼ cup	60 ml
Lemon juice, fresh	2 fl. oz.	¼ cup	60 ml
Heavy cream	6 fl. oz.	¾ cup	90 ml
Butter, unsalted, cubed	16 oz.	32 Tbl.	448 grams
Chives, blanched, drained well	1 oz.	1 bunch	28 grams
Salt, kosher		to taste	
Black pepper, fresh ground		to taste	

Chive Beurre Blanc

1. Combine the shallots, peppercorns, thyme, wine, vinegar, and lemon juice in a saucepan and reduce until almost dry (approximately 2 oz. remaining); strain through cheesecloth.
2. Add the heavy cream and reduce by one-third.
3. In a blender puree the cream reduction and the chives until smooth.
4. Return to a saucepan over low heat and begin slowly adding the butter while whisking constantly to emulsify and incorporate. Remove from the heat as necessary to not break the emulsion; the sauce should not simmer.
5. Strain through a chinois.
6. Taste and adjust the seasoning; hold over low heat, or in a water bath, until needed.

Halibut

1. Preheat oven to 425 F (218 C) degrees convection.
2. Lay the phyllo dough on a flat surface on a piece of plastic film; cover with an additional piece of plastic film and a slightly damp towel.
3. Place one sheet of phyllo on a cutting board; always keep the remaining phyllo covered while working.
4. Brush the sheet of phyllo with olive oil and lightly sprinkle the marjoram, bread crumbs, and black pepper across the sheet of phyllo dough. Repeat with 3 more sheets of phyllo; do not place any marjoram or bread crumbs on the last sheet.
5. Cut the phyllo into strips that are approximately 6–7 inches long and 2 inches wide (the size will vary according to the shape of the halibut). They should be long enough to wrap around the center of the fish and overlap by 1 inch, covering approximately half the surface of the fish, leaving the ends exposed.
6. Season the fish with salt and pepper; sprinkle bread crumbs on both sides of the fish where the phyllo dough will cover. Wrap the phyllo around the fish and brush the outside of the phyllo with oil.
7. Place the fish on a sheet pan and bake until the phyllo is golden brown and the fish is just cooked throughout, approximately 8 minutes.
8. Place the fish in the center of the plate and add ¾ oz. of the sauce on each side of the filet; garnish with chives.

WINE SELECTED with Halibut Wrapped in Phyllo with Marjoram and Chive Beurre Blanc

Wine: Ruffino Orvieto Classico ($8)

Origin: Orvieto Classico, Umbria, Italy

Taste and Texture Comparisons

Dish: Rich, Crisp Acidity, Mild Flavor, Herbal

Wine: Delicate, Crisp, Mild Citrus Flavor, Minerality, and Moderate Alcohol

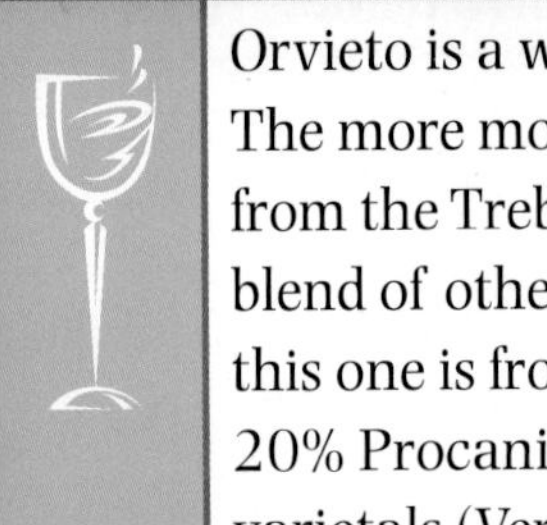

Orvieto is a white wine from Umbria. The more modern ones are made from the Trebbiano grape with a blend of other white grapes. However, this one is from 40% Grechetto, 20% Procanico, and 40% other white varietals (Verdello, Canaiolo Bianco).

Why This Is a Good Pairing

- ***Contrasting Flavor*** – The Chive Beurre Blanc focuses the palate on the fruit of the wine, making the wine taste fruitier.
- ***Complexing*** – The contrast in body, intensity, and flavor creates a *complexing* reaction that allows you to taste all of the layers of flavors in the dish and the wine.
- ***Cleansing*** – The wine's crisp acidity cuts through the Chive Beurre Blanc, which brightens the flavors.
- ***Dance*** – The richness of the butter elongates the flavors of both the wine and the dish.

Wines That Didn't Work

Roero Arneis – The dish and the wine match in intensity, but the floral nature of the Arneis compounds with the herbal character of the Chive Beurre Blanc making it overbearing.

Hunter Valley Semillon – The acid is a bit too high in the wine and is too cleansing (similar reaction with Champagne). It strips the flavor of the dish. The herbal nature of the dish also clashes with the lemon/lime fruit, making the wine taste somewhat sour.

California Fumé Blanc – The wine overpowers the dish and the acidity of the wine strips your palate of the dish's flavor.

SUMMARY	Orvieto	Roero Arneis	Hunter Valley Semillon	California Fumé Blanc
Matching		+		
Complementing				
Contrasting	+			
Compounding		(–)		
Complexing	+			
Cleansing	+		(–)	(–)
Covering				(–)
Clashing			(–)	

TUNA

There are several varieties of tuna available on the market: bluefin, blackfin, yellowfin, skipjack, albacore, and bigeye. They are very fast swimmers and can cruise at over 50 miles per hour, and the largest of the species can grow to over 1,000 pounds. Tuna flesh is rich, firm, and can be fatty. Its texture and flavor lend themselves to a wide variety of cooking techniques.

TUNA POKE

Yield: 10 portions

Cooking Method: Raw

Ingredients	Amounts - US	Volume	Metric
Ahi tuna, sushi grade 1, small dice	1 ½ lbs.	3 cups	672 grams
Scallions, sliced thin	1 oz.	⅓ cup	28 grams
Macadamia nuts, roasted, chopped	4 oz.	⅓ cup	112 grams
Soy sauce	2 fl. oz.	¼ cup	60 ml
Sesame oil	⅜ fl. oz.	2 tsp.	10 ml
Ginger, chopped fine		1 tsp.	
Crushed red pepper		½ tsp.	
Salt, sea		to taste	

Tuna

1. Combine all ingredients in a bowl and mix gently to evenly incorporate.
2. Serve immediately.

WINE SELECTED with Tuna Poke

Wine: Guigal Côtes du Rhône Blanc ($12)
Origin: Côtes du Rhône, Rhone Valley, France

Taste and Texture Comparisons

Dish: Fresh, Salty, Mild Spice, Rich, Aromatic
Wine: Aromatic, Floral, Low Acidity, Oily Texture, Full Body, Moderate Alcohol

This wine is predominantly Viognier. Viognier is a very floral and fragrant, low-acid white grape variety on the medium plus- to full-bodied side. In Côtes du Rhône, it is unoaked, as opposed to the higher quality appellation of Condrieu.

Why This Is a Good Pairing

- ***Matching*** – The wine is fairly full-bodied and the texture of the fish is rich. This makes them fairly well balanced.
- ***Complementing*** – The rich texture of the fish with the sesame oil creates a bridge to the oily texture of the wine with no compounding.
- ***Contrasting*** – Contrast between the floral nature of the wine (jasmine/acacia) and the mild spiciness of the dish makes the floral notes come out in the wine and the flavors of the dish dance through to the finish. However, because the acid in the wine is low, the dance is more elegant (like a waltz as opposed to a tango).
- ***Complexing*** – The contrast in flavors makes the wine taste more complex. You can taste more layers of flavors, which makes the wine taste more luxurious than it is.

Wines That Didn't Work

Dry White Sparkling – We tried several dry white sparkling wines from around the world, and in all cases, the high acidity and bubbles strip the flavor and overpower the dish.

Oaked Napa Chardonnay – The full body and rich flavor (apples, vanilla, spice) of the wine overpower the dish and focus your palate on the macadamia nuts too much.

Provence Rosé – The weight of the dish and the wine work well and the fruitiness of the wine pops, but the flavors in the dish are lost in this pairing.

SUMMARY	Guigal Côtes du Rhône Blanc Viognier	Dry White Sparkling	Oaked Napa Chardonnay	Provence Rosé
Matching	+			
Complementing	+			
Contrasting	+	+		
Compounding			(–)	
Complexing	+			
Cleansing				
Covering		(–)	(–)	(–)
Clashing				

SEARED TUNA WITH SESAME AND CORIANDER

Yield: 10 portions

Cooking Method: Sauté

Ingredients	Amounts - US	Volume	Metric
Ahi tuna, sushi grade 1, 3 oz. steak, 1 inch thick		10 each	
Salt, sea		as needed	
Black pepper, fresh ground		as needed	
Coriander, ground		as needed	
Sesame seeds	1 ½ oz.	⅓ cup	42 grams
Sesame seeds, black	¾ oz.	3 Tbl.	22 grams
Extra virgin olive oil	2 fl. oz.	¼ cup	60 ml

Tuna

1. Combine the sesame seeds and mix well.
2. Preheat a sauté pan over medium heat.
3. Season the tuna with salt, pepper, and coriander. Press the top and bottom of the tuna into the sesame seed mixture.
4. Add the oil and then the tuna to the sauté pan.
5. Sauté the tuna until it has cooked approximately ⅛ inch on the bottom and the sesame seeds are light golden brown.
6. Turn and repeat until the sesame seeds are light golden brown.
7. Slice the tuna into ¼-inch slices and serve immediately.

WINE SELECTED with Seared Tuna with Sesame and Coriander

Wine: Willm Gewürztraminer Vin d'Alsace ($15)

Origin: Alsace, France

Taste and Texture Comparisons

Dish: Spice, Light Earthiness, Rich Texture, Crunchy

Wine: Spice, Floral, Full Body, Low Acidity, Dry, Moderate Alcohol

Some Alsatian Gewürztraminers are dry while some are sweet. This one is on the lighter side for an Alsatian Gewürztraminer and dry.

Why This Is a Good Pairing

- ***Matching*** – The weight of the dish and the wine are evenly matched.
- ***Complementing*** – The spice in the dish (coriander) connects and creates a bridge with the spiciness of the Gewürztraminer.
- ***Contrasting*** – The intense flavors of the wine (litchi, spice, floral notes, light mineral) contrast with the flavors of the dish (light earthiness, Maillard reaction, tuna, sesame seeds), making all the flavors come out, creating a *complexing* reaction.
- ***Dance*** – The wine's low acid allows all the flavors to linger and dance on the palate for a long time.

Wines That Didn't Work

Sweet Riesling – There's a nice contrast between the fruit in the wine and the spice in the dish. However the sweetness is somewhat overpowering and the high acid of the wine strips the flavors of the dish, cutting the finish of the dish short, making the sweetness of the wine linger by itself.

New World Pinot Noir – The weight of the wine matches the dish; however, the intense red berry fruit covers up the flavor of the dish, particularly the tuna. The tannins from the wine clash with the sesame seeds.

Cru of Beaujolais – The earthiness and spice of the dish clash with the fruit in the wine, making the wine taste candied. Similar to the Pinot Noir, the tannins become astringent.

SUMMARY	Willm Vin d'Alsace Gewürztraminer	Sweet Riesling	New World Pinot Noir	Cru of Beaujolais
Matching	+			
Complementing	+			
Contrasting	+	+		
Compounding				
Complexing	+			
Cleansing	+			
Covering		(–)	(–)	(–)
Clashing			(–)	(–)

Grilled Tuna Skewers with Yellow Peppers and Cherry Tomatoes

GRILLED TUNA SKEWERS WITH YELLOW PEPPERS AND CHERRY TOMATOES

Yield: 10 portions

Cooking Method: Grill

Ingredients	Amounts - US	Volume	Metric
For the Tuna Skewers			
Ahi tuna, sushi grade 1, large dice	1 ½ lbs.	40 each	0.7 kilogram
Yellow peppers, large dice		40 each	
Red onions, large dice		40 each	
Tomatoes, cherry		40 each	
Extra virgin olive oil		as needed	
Salt, sea		as needed	
Black pepper, fresh ground		as needed	
Skewers		20 each	
For the Salsa Crudo Yield: 1 ½ cups			
Extra virgin olive oil	10 fl. oz.	1 ¼ cups	300 ml
Picholine olives, chopped	1 ¾ oz.	⅓ cup	50 grams
Celery hearts, minced	1 oz.	¼ cup	28 grams
Parsley, Italian, chopped	½ oz.	¼ cup	14 grams
Mint, chopped	¼ oz.	2 Tbl.	8 grams
Celery leaves, chopped	¼ oz.	2 Tbl.	8 grams
Sea salt		to taste	
Black pepper, fresh ground		to taste	

Tuna Skewers

1. Combine all of the ingredients for the Salsa Crudo and mix well, taste and adjust the seasoning. Allow the flavors to marry for 2 hours before using.
2. Assemble the skewers as follows: tuna, yellow pepper, red onion, tomato, tuna, yellow pepper, red onion, tomato.
3. Preheat a charbroiler or grill.
4. Season the skewers with salt and pepper, lightly drizzle with olive oil.
5. Place the skewers on the grill and cook for approximately 45 seconds on each side or until the tuna is rare and the vegetables have started to soften.
6. Plate and spoon the Salsa Crudo over the skewers.

If using bamboo skewers, presoak them in water for 30 minutes to help prevent burning.

WINE SELECTED with Grilled Tuna Skewers with Yellow Peppers and Cherry Tomatoes

Wine: Yerring Station Pinot Noir ($16)

Origin: Yarra Valley, Victoria, Australia

Taste and Texture Comparisons

Dish: Soft Texture, Fresh, Herbal, Earthy, Sweet

Wine: Soft Texture, Aromatic, Fruity, Crisp, Medium Body and Alcohol

Yarra Valley is a cool grape-growing region in Australia that yields very fresh, crisp Pinot Noirs with lots of ripe strawberry and cherry flavors.

Why This Is a Good Pairing

- ***Matching*** – Both the dish and the wine have a soft texture and they match in terms of intensity of flavor.
- ***Complementing*** – Although dry, the ripeness and sweet impression of the fruit in the Pinot Noir bring out the sweetness in the tomatoes and the peppers. There is also a bridge between the flavors from the grilled tuna and the light vanilla/spice flavors of the oak in the wine.
- ***Complexing*** – The mint and olives in the dish bring out some of the herbal and earthy complexities in the wine. You taste more flavors in both the dish and the wine; this *complexing* reaction makes the wine taste more luxurious.
- ***Cleansing*** – Pinot Noir, in general, has high acidity for a red grape and that adds freshness to the dish.

Wines That Didn't Work

New Zealand Sauvignon Blanc – The wine is cleansing and brings out the freshness of the sauce and the sweetness of the peppers. However, the herbaceousness of the wine brings out a vegetal character in the dish (celery, pepper, and tomato) and you lose the flavor of the tuna.

Unoaked French Viognier – The floral character clashes with the herbal/earthy nature of the dish, making it taste like perfume.

Dry Rosé – The fruit of the wine comes out too much, making the flavors of the dish disappear.

SUMMARY	Yerring Station Yarra Valley Pinot Noir	New Zealand Sauvignon Blanc	Unoaked French Viognier	Dry Rosé
Matching	+			
Complementing	+	+		
Contrasting				
Compounding		(–)		(–)
Complexing	+			
Cleansing	+			(–)
Covering		(–)	(–)	
Clashing			(–)	

Gravlax

SALMON

Salmon is one of the most widely eaten fish in the world. There are numerous species that include: Coho, Sockeye, Chinook, Chum, and Pink. Salmon is a very versatile fish and can be cooked with a wide variety of techniques; the flesh is firm, flaky, rich, and can be fatty. It is available farm raised as well as wild caught, the later being the best choice for nutrition and flavor.

GRAVLAX

Yield: 10 portions

Cooking Method: Cure

Ingredients	Amounts - US	Volume	Metric
Salmon filet, skin on, pin bones removed	2 lbs.	1 each	0.9 kilograms
For the Cure			
Salt, kosher	4 oz.	½ cup	112 grams
Sugar, granulated	3 oz.	⅓ cup	86 grams
Dill, rough chopped	1 oz.	1 bunch (about 1 ½ cups)	28 grams
Black peppercorns, cracked		1 ½ tsp.	
Vodka	½ fl. oz.	1 Tbl.	15 ml

Gravlax

1. Wipe down both sides of the salmon filet carefully to ensure that there are no scales or pin bones on the flesh.
2. Combine the salt and sugar; mix well to incorporate evenly.
3. Brush the flesh with the vodka to coat evenly.
4. Spread the cracked peppercorns evenly over the surface of the salmon.
5. Spread the salt and sugar mixture onto the surface; the mixture should be slightly thinner towards the tail where the filet is thinner. Depending on the size of the filet, all of the cure may not be necessary.*
6. Place the dill on top of the salt and sugar mixture.
7. Wrap the filet in cheesecloth and place in a large perforated pan (hotel pan) inside another large pan. The pans should be large enough for the fish to lay flat.
8. Place another hotel pan on top of the salmon and weigh down the pan with 2 lbs of weight, ensuring that the weight is distributed evenly (small 1-lb. cans work well).
9. Allow the salmon to cure for 48 to 72 hours under refrigeration (the amount of cure time will vary according to the thickness of the salmon). When fully cured, the flesh will be slightly firm to the touch.
10. Remove the cheesecloth from the salmon and gently remove the dill and any excess cure.
11. Slice the salmon as thin as possible while still maintaining a uniform slice.

* A large side of salmon will require more salt/sugar cure; increase the amount accordingly.

WINE SELECTED with Gravlax

Wine: Veuve Clicquot Yellow Label Brut Champagne ($45)
Origin: Champagne, France

Taste and Texture Comparisons

Dish: Bold, Briny, Herbaceous
Wine: Effervescent, Dry, High Acidity, Autolytic (Toasty, Biscuity), Moderate Alcohol

Veuve Clicquot is one of the most popular champagnes on the market. Some champagnes are on the light and fruity end of the spectrum, but this one is aged for nearly three years for a fuller body and autolytic notes.

Why This Is a Good Pairing

- ***Complementing*** – The autolytic character and mineral notes of the champagne bring out some of the briny notes of the salmon.
- ***Contrasting*** – The flavor of the salmon contrasts with some of the subtle green apple flavors of the champagne. This makes the flavor of both stand out more.
- ***Cleansing*** – The high acidity from the champagne cleanses the palate, making the dish more refreshing and light. The high acidity also makes the flavors of the salmon pop.

Wines That Didn't Work

New Zealand Sauvignon Blanc – We tried the dish with a Sauvignon Blanc that has bold passion-fruit flavors and strong herbaceous notes. The wine overpowers the dish and the dill flavors compound with the wine's herbal notes in a negative way. However, the wine's high acidity is refreshing.

Vouvray – With this pairing, we experienced a weird clash of flavors. The contrast between the salmon and the floral notes in this Loire white makes the wine taste like floral air freshener. A similar reaction occurs with a Pinot Grigio that is also floral.

Australian Pinot Noir – The oak in the wine makes the salmon taste like it is smoked. While some of the flavors seem to dance, it is a bit like dancing partners stepping on each other's feet.

SUMMARY	Veuve Clicquot Brut Yellow Label	New Zealand Sauvignon Blanc	Vouvray	Australian Pinot Noir
Matching				
Complementing	+			
Contrasting	+			+
Compounding		(–)		
Complexing				
Cleansing	+	+		
Covering		(–)		(–)
Clashing			(–)	(–)

Poached Salmon with Sauce Hollandaise

POACHED SALMON WITH SAUCE HOLLANDAISE

Yield: 10 portions

Cooking Method: Poach

Ingredients	Amounts - US	Volume	Metric
For the Salmon			
Salmon, darne, 8 oz.		10 each	
Salt, sea		as needed	
White pepper, fresh ground		as needed	
For the Court Bouillon			
Water	1 gallon	16 cups	4 liters
White wine vinegar	8 fl. oz.	1 cup	240 ml
Onions, sweet, sliced ¼"	1 lb.	4 cups	452 grams
Carrots, sliced ¼"	1 lb.	4 cups	452 grams
Celery, sliced ¼"	8 oz.	2 cups	226 grams
Parsley, stems		12 each	
Thyme, sprigs		4 each	
Bay leaf		1 each	
Salt, kosher	1 ½ oz.	3 Tbl.	40 grams
Black peppercorns, crushed	⅜ oz.	1 ½ Tbl.	10 grams
For the Sauce Hollandaise			
Reduction			
White wine vinegar	2 fl. oz.	½ cup	60 ml
Peppercorns, cracked		¾ tsp.	
Water	1 ½ fl. oz.	3 Tbl.	45 ml
Sauce Ingredients			
Water	¾ fl. oz.	1 ½ Tbl.	25 ml
Egg yolks, large	2 ⅝ oz.	5 each	72 grams
Butter, unsalted, melted	14 oz.	1 ¾ cups	392 grams
Lemon juice, fresh	1 fl. oz.	2 Tbl.	30 ml
Tabasco		dash	
Salt, kosher		to taste	
White pepper, fresh ground		to taste	

Court Bouillon

1. Combine all of the ingredients for the court bouillon in a stockpot and bring to a simmer. Simmer gently for 30 minutes.
2. Strain the court bouillon through a fine mesh strainer.
3. Reserve until needed.

Hollandaise

1. Combine the ingredients for the reduction in a small saucepan and reduce until it is almost dry (approximately 1 Tbl. of liquid remaining). Refresh with the second amount of water and strain through cheesecloth.
2. Melt the butter and keep warm.
3. Combine the yolks and the reduction in a stainless steel bowl over a gently simmering water bath (ensure that water doesn't touch the bottom of the bowl). Whisk the yolks until they thicken and the whisk leaves a noticeable track.
4. Remove the saucepan from the heat; place a side towel over the top of the saucepan and replace the bowl.
5. Begin slowly adding the warm melted butter into the yolks while whisking constantly to emulsify the butter into the yolks; continue until all of the butter has been added.
6. Add the lemon juice, Tabasco, salt, and pepper; taste and adjust the seasonings.

To set up a double boiler, ensure that the stainless steel bowl will fit inside of the pot without the gently simmering water touching the bottom of the bowl, and that the outsides of the bowl do not scorch from the flame.

Hollandaise is a very delicate sauce that can break or scramble easily. Carefully control the heat when whisking the yolks, add the butter slowly and hold warm in a water bath. Some classical recipes call for clarified butter with the addition of water to adjust the consistency. I prefer to use melted whole butter which adds additional flavor from milk solids and contains a small amount of water.

Salmon

1. Place the court bouillon in a rondeau that is large and deep enough to accommodate the salmon, as it will be completely covered by the liquid.
2. Bring the court bouillon to 155–160 F (68–71 C) degrees.
3. Secure the thin belly flaps with a skewer, piercing both sides to hold them together.
4. Place the salmon portions in the court bouillon, ensuring that the pieces are not touching and that they are completely submerged.
5. Cook until the center spine bone comes out easily (test by pressing a paring knife in the center and slowly pulling upward), approximately 8–10 minutes.
6. Remove the salmon with a fish spatula to a parchment-lined sheet pan. Gently remove the skin, bones, and any cartilage. Keep the salmon warm while working.
7. Serve the salmon immediately with Hollandaise.

Care should be taken to remove the "blood line" from salmon after removing the skin. This flesh is oily and can have a very strong flavor; however, in many Asian countries this is considered a delicacy.

WINE SELECTED with Poached Salmon with Sauce Hollandaise

Wine: Pewsey Vale Dry Riesling ($15)
Origin: Eden Valley, South Australia, Australia

Taste and Texture Comparisons

Dish: Rich, Bold Flavor, Slight Acidity
Wine: Light-Bodied, Strong Lime Aromas, High Acidity, Floral Notes

Rieslings from Eden Valley, Australia, are more akin to those of Austria than of Germany. They are generally dry, light-bodied, racy in their acidity, with strong notes of lime.

Why This Is a Good Pairing

- ***Matching*** – Salmon has a bold flavor, as does the wine. Despite the contrasting textures and weights of the dish and the wine, their flavor intensities match and so one does not overpower the other.
- ***Complementing*** – There is a bridge between the lemon in the sauce and the citrus lime notes in the wine.
- ***Contrasting*** – The flavor of the salmon contrasts with the wine, making the flavors of both stand out.
- ***Cleansing*** – Eden Valley Rieslings are known for intense acidity. The acid cuts through the richness of the salmon and the Hollandaise sauce. Additionally, the acid makes the flavors of the salmon and the sauce pop.

Wines That Didn't Work

NV Brut Champagne (blend) – The acidity is high enough for a cleansing reaction, but the flavor of the champagne is not intense enough to balance the wine with the dish. In the end, the dish covers the wine.

California Chardonnay – We tried a moderately oaked Sonoma Chardonnay, thinking the butter in the Hollandaise would complement the wine's soft buttery notes, but it makes the dish taste heavy and oily.

Alternative: Nuits-St.-Georges Burgundy—Pinot Noir is known to pair well with salmon. Pinot Noir in Burgundy has soft, red berry fruit aromas that are augmented by the salmon. Similar to the Riesling, its high acidity cuts through the richness in the Poached Salmon with Sauce Hollandaise, making the dish more refreshing.

We also tried a few New World Pinot Noirs that did not work as well as the Burgundy. The fruit of the wine is heightened, and although the dish works with the Riesling, the intense fruitiness of the New World Pinot Noirs covers the flavor of the salmon.

SUMMARY	Pewsey Vale Eden Valley Dry Riesling	Nuits-St.-Georges, Burgundy, Pinot Noir	NV Brut Champagne	Oaked California Chardonnay
Matching	+	+		
Complementing	+			
Contrasting	+	+		
Compounding				(–)
Complexing				
Cleansing	+	+	+	
Covering			(–)	
Clashing				

GRILLED SALMON WITH DILL BUTTER

Yield: 10 portions

Cooking Method: Grill

Ingredients	Amounts - US	Volume	Metric
For the Salmon			
Salmon, steak, skin off, 6 oz.		10 each	
Salt, sea		as needed	
Black pepper, fresh ground		as needed	
Olive oil, pure		as needed	
For the Dill Butter			
Butter, unsalted, room temperature	8 oz.	1 cup	226 grams
Dill, chopped	½ oz.	¼ cup	14 grams
Parsley, chopped	⅜ oz.	¼ cup	12 grams
Lemon juice, fresh	½ fl. oz.	1 Tbl.	15 ml
Salt, kosher		1 tsp.	
Black pepper, fresh ground		¼ tsp.	

Dill Butter

1. Using a stand mixer, combine all of the ingredients for the dill butter and mix until well blended. Taste and adjust the seasoning.
2. Pipe the butter in parchment paper and roll into a cylinder, approximately 1 ½ inches in diameter.
3. Refrigerate until firm, slice in ⅜-inch rounds, and remove the parchment paper. Reserve under refrigeration until needed.

Salmon

1. Preheat a charbroiler/grill.
2. Season the salmon steaks with salt and pepper on both sides.
3. Lightly oil the surface of the grill with an appropriate towel that has been coated with oil, and then place the salmon on the grill.
4. Cook for 2 minutes and then turn the salmon 90 degrees to achieve crosshatch marks and continue cooking for another 2 minutes; adjust the cook time according to thickness and desired doneness.
5. Turn the salmon and repeat the above process until the salmon is cooked.
6. Remove from the grill and top with the Dill Butter.

WINE SELECTED with Grilled Salmon with Dill Butter

Wine: Vincent Gaudry Sancerre "Melodie de Vieilles Vignes" ($24)

Origin: Sancerre, Loire Valley, France

Taste and Texture Comparisons

Dish: Bold, Maillard Reaction, Grilled/Smoky, Herbaceous, Rich

Wine: Light-Bodied, High Acidity, Finesse, Citrus, Mineral, Slight Herbal Notes

This is a typical Sancerre—unoaked Sauvignon Blanc from the region of Sancerre. Some have very grassy notes, but this one is quite delicate in its herbal tones.

Why This Is a Good Pairing

- ***Complementing*** – The wine's soft herbaceous notes build a bridge to the dill butter. The grilled notes of the salmon also complement some of the wine's mineral notes.
- ***Contrasting*** – The flavor of the salmon contrasts with the fruit in the wine, making the fruit more dynamic.
- ***Cleansing*** – Sancerre has crisp acidity and this cuts through the richness of the salmon. However, the wine does not strip the dish of its flavor. On the contrary, the acid of the wine makes the flavors of the dish pop in a refreshing way.

Wines That Didn't Work

South African Sauvignon Blanc – The Sauvignon Blanc we tried is more obvious in its herbaceous notes than the Sancerre. These herbal notes compounded with the dill. Green + Green = Green^2, which was quite unpleasant.

NV Brut Champagne (blend) – Cleansing happens, but the champagne's autolytic character clashes with the dill.

Pouilly-Fuissé – This unoaked white Burgundy made from Chardonnay seemed to overpower the dish. The grilling notes make the mineral notes in the wine stand out too much and the butter notes in the wine compound with the dill butter, making the fish and the wine taste more oily.

SUMMARY	Sancerre	South African Sauvignon Blanc	NV Brut Champagne	Pouilly-Fuissé
Matching				
Complementing	+			
Contrasting	+			
Compounding		(–)		(–)
Complexing				
Cleansing	+	+	+	
Covering				(–)
Clashing			(–)	

FISH PAIRING SUMMARY AND CONCLUSIONS

Halibut

Dish	Method	Wine
Poached Halibut with Fennel and Orange Slaw	Poach	Arneis, Valdinera Roero
Sautéed Halibut with Tomatoes, Capers, and Mint	Sauté	Muscat, Trimbach
Halibut Wrapped in Phyllo and Chive Beurre Blanc	Roast	Orvieto Classico, Ruffino

- ***Main ingredient tendencies:*** Halibut has a delicate structure and a mild flavor. This is why the range for these recipes remains in the white category while reds (and rosés) are overpowering.

- ***Specific techniques that changed the pairing:*** Despite the varied techniques, the ingredients had the largest impact on the wine pairing change.

- ***Specific ingredients that changed the pairing:*** The slaw's fennel and orange flavors complements some floral and citrus notes in the Arneis. The tomatoes in the second recipe raises the acidity of the dish, which calls for a lower-acid wine (Muscat). The Chive Beurre Blanc adds richness, which is cut by the crisp acidity of the Orvieto. The Beurre Blanc also has acidity, which complements the wine, and the chives contrast with the Orvieto's mild fruit, making the fruit pop more.

Tuna

Dish	Method	Wine
Tuna Poke	Raw	Viognier, Guigal Côtes du Rhône Blanc
Seared Tuna with Sesame and Coriander	Sauté	Gewürztraminer, Willm
Grilled Tuna Skewers	Grill	Pinot Noir, Yerring Station

- ***Main ingredient tendencies:*** Tuna has a rich structure and texture and with these recipes can pair with medium-bodied whites and low-tannin, medium-bodied reds.

- ***Specific techniques that changed the pairing:*** The Poke is raw, which keeps the purity of the flavor of the tuna and provides a soft texture that balances in weight with the Viognier. Grilling intensifies tuna's flavors and richness, which allows for a red wine to pair well, and the toasty caramelized flavors from the grilling complements the wine's hint of oak.

- ***Specific ingredients that changed the pairing:*** The coriander with the seared tuna complements the spice in the Gewürtztraminer and sweetness from the yellow peppers and cherry tomatoes complements the ripe fruit in the New World Pinot Noir.

Salmon

Dish	Method	Wine
Gravlax	Cure	Champagne Veuve Clicquot
Poached Salmon with Sauce Hollandaise	Poach	Dry Riesling, Pewsey Vale
Grilled Salmon with Dill Butter	Grill	Sauvignon Blanc, Sancerre Vincent Gaudry

- ***Main ingredient tendencies:*** Salmon's richness and intensity of flavor yield a wide wine pairing range, from sparkling to light- and medium-bodied red wines. Note that all the wines that paired are high-acid wines. Salmon has an inherent richness/fat, which high-acid wines cleanse while allowing the salmon flavor to shine.

- ***Specific techniques that changed the pairing:*** Curing focuses the palate on the brininess in the salmon, which complements the champagne's autolytic character. Grilled salmon has the most intense flavor, which pairs well with this highly aromatic Sauvignon Blanc. Additionally, the grilling notes helps the palate focus on the flinty, mineral notes in the Sancerre.

- ***Specific ingredients that changed the pairing:*** Herbs are a common ingredient with salmon recipes. So be aware when pairing with wines with an herbaceous note that they may complement the recipe or they may compound in a negative way.

6
Chicken, Duck, and Pork

Chicken, duck, and pork are generally mild to rich in flavor and thus lend themselves to a variety of cooking techniques. Those highlighted in this chapter include: poach, sauté, pan-fry, deep-fry, grill, braise, roast, sous vide, and smoke.

You will also notice their versatility with respect to wine pairings. There is a wide selection of wines that pair well with these proteins—whites, rosés, delicate reds, and rich reds. This is partly because they belong in the medium weight category. However, it is the ingredients and the techniques applied that can make them lighter or richer dishes, so their range is vast.

Dish	Wine
Chicken Breast	
Chicken Salad with Apples, Cranberries, and Pecans	Domaine Pélaquié Tavel Rosé, Rhône, France ($15)
Hot Smoked Chicken Breast with Creole Mustard Sauce	Yabby Lake Pinot Noir, Victoria, Australia ($40)
Chicken Breast Stuffed with Spinach and Gruyère Cheese	Gloria Ferrer Chardonnay, California, USA ($21)
Chicken Legs	
Buttermilk Fried Chicken	Christian Moreau Chablis, Burgundy, France ($22)
Chicken Cacciatore	Willm Gewürztraminer Vin d'Alsace, Alsace, France ($13)
Tandoori Chicken	Brokenwood Shiraz, New South Wales, Australia ($35)
Duck	
Sous Vide Duck Breast with Cardamom, Thyme, and Duck Jus	Guigal Côtes du Rhône Rouge, Rhône, France ($14)
Smoked Duck Salad with Baby Beets, Arugula, and Orange Vinaigrette	Dr. Loosen Erdener Treppchen Riesling Kabinett, Mosel, Germany ($23)
Sautéed Duck Breast with Sun-Dried Cherry Sauce	Wildekrans Pinotage, Walker Bay, South Africa ($15)
Pork	
Sous Vide Pork Tenderloin with Spicy Pineapple Salsa	Ken Forrester "Petit" Chenin Blanc, South Africa ($10)
Pork Schnitzel with Lemon	Craggy Range Pinot Noir, Martinborough, New Zealand ($35)
Grilled Pork Tenderloin with Caramelized Apple Compote	Domaine Wachau Terressen Federspiel Grüner Veltliner, Wachau, Austria ($15)

CHICKEN BREAST

Chicken breasts are an excellent source of lean protein. They are a less exercised cut, quite versatile, and lend themselves well to a variety of accompanying ingredients as well as cooking techniques.

CHICKEN SALAD WITH APPLES, CRANBERRIES, AND PECANS

Yield: 10 portions
Cooking Method: Poach

Ingredients	Amounts - US	Volume	Metric
Chicken breast, split, bone-in	2 lbs.	4 each	908 grams
Chicken stock	48–64 oz.	6–8 cups	1 ½–2 liters
Parsley stems		5 each	
Tarragon stems		5 each	
Bay leaf		1 each	
Garlic, clove, medium, crushed		1 each	
Salt, kosher		to taste	
Black pepper, fresh ground		to taste	
Mayonnaise	13 oz.	1 cup	364 grams
Lemon juice, fresh	½ fl. oz.	1 Tbl. plus 1 tsp.	15 ml
Dried cranberries	2 ⅛ oz.	½ cup	56 grams
Pecans, toasted, rough chopped	2 ¼ oz.	⅔ cup	64 grams

(Continues on next page)

Ingredients	Amounts - US	Volume	Metric
Granny Smith apples, medium diced	10 oz.	2 cups	280 grams
Celery, peeled, medium dice	4 ½ oz.	1 cup	128 grams
Red onion, small dice	2 oz.	½ cup	56 grams
Salt, kosher		½ tsp.	
Black pepper, fresh ground		½ tsp.	
Tabasco sauce		⅛–¼ tsp.	
For the Garnish			
Chives, short cut		2 Tbl.	
Pecans, chopped	½ oz.	2 Tbl.	14 grams

Chicken Salad

1. Preheat the oven to 250 F (120 C) degrees convection.
2. Place the chicken stock in a stockpot with the parsley stems, tarragon stems, bay leaf, and garlic and bring to a gentle simmer; taste and adjust the seasoning.
3. Place the chicken skin-side-up in a 4-inch hotel pan or other suitable pan. Pour the stock over the chicken, ensuring that the stock is covering the chicken. Weigh down the chicken with a rack so that it stays submerged; cook until the chicken is 165 F (74 C) degrees in the thickest part of the breast. Ensure that the tip of the thermometer doesn't touch the bone when checking the temperature or you will get a false reading.
4. Remove from the oven, and allow to cool to room temperature. Chill the chicken in the stock under refrigeration.
5. Once the chicken is cold, remove from the stock; debone and cut the chicken into medium dice. Strain and reserve the stock for another use.
6. Combine the mayonnaise, lemon juice, Tabasco, salt, and pepper. Whisk well to evenly incorporate, taste and adjust the seasoning.
7. Add the chicken, cranberries, pecans, apples, celery, and red onion; mix gently with a rubber spatula to combine evenly.
8. Taste and adjust the seasoning.
9. Plate the chicken using a 3" ring mold, garnish with chives and pecans.

WINE SELECTED with Chicken Salad with Apples, Cranberries, and Pecans

Wine: Domaine Pélaquié Tavel Rosé ($15)
Origin: Tavel, Rhône Valley, France

Taste and Texture Comparisons

Dish: Medium Body, Sweet, Nutty/Crunchy, Creamy
Wine: Medium Body, Fruity, Slightly Herbal, Mineral, Crisp/Bright

Rosés from Tavel and Provence have red berry fruit with hints of minerals and herbs (rosemary, thyme). However, Tavel rosés are a bit deeper in color, richer in flavor and body, and higher in alcohol than Provence rosés.

Why This Is a Good Pairing

- ***Matching Weight*** – The elements of the dish and the Tavel are medium-bodied and evenly matched.
- ***Complementing*** – The cranberries in the dish create a bridge to the red berry notes in the wine. The wine's fruitiness gives an impression of sweetness (though the wine itself is totally dry), but connects with the fruitiness and sweetness in the dish.
- ***Cleansing*** – The wine's crisp acidity cuts through some of the richness of the mayonnaise, creating a refreshing cleansing sensation without covering up the flavor of the chicken or other elements in the dish.
- ***Dance*** – The richness from the mayonnaise elongates all the flavors on the palate for a long finish.

Wines That Didn't Work

Chablis – The wine's crisp acidity cleanses and refreshes, but the sweetness of the apples and cranberries makes the wine taste sour.

Alsatian Gewürztraminer – Although the style of the Alsatian Gewürztraminer we tested is on the lighter, drier side, it is still too intense in flavor/richness and covers up the flavors of the dish.

Cru of Beaujolais – The raspberry flavors in the wine overpower the dish. Additionally, there is a reaction between the tannin in the wine and the dish that makes the tannins astringent and unpleasant.

SUMMARY	Domaine Pélaquié Tavel Rosé	Chablis	Dry Alsatian Gewürztraminer	Cru of Beaujolais
Matching	+			
Complementing	+			
Contrasting	+	(–)		
Compounding				
Complexing				
Cleansing	+	+		
Covering			(–)	(–)
Clashing				(–)

Hot Smoked Chicken Breast with Creole Mustard Sauce

HOT SMOKED CHICKEN BREAST WITH CREOLE MUSTARD SAUCE

Yield: 10 portions
Cooking Method: Brine–Smoke/Roast

Ingredients	Amounts - US	Volume	Metric
For the Chicken			
Chicken breast, split, bone-in		10 each	
Wood chips, apple		⅔ cup	
For the Brine			
Water	128 oz.	1 gallon	4 liters
Salt, kosher	6 oz.	1 cup	170 grams
Honey	3 fl. oz.	⅓ cup	90 ml
Garlic clove, medium, crushed	½ oz.	4 each	14 grams
Bay leaves		2 each	
Fennel seeds	½ oz.	2 Tbl.	12 grams
Mustard seeds	¼ oz.	1 Tbl.	6 grams
For the Creole Sauce Yield: 3 cups			
Olive oil, pure	1 ½ fl. oz.	3 Tbl.	45 ml
Onions, small dice	2 oz.	½ cup	56 grams
Celery, small dice	1 oz.	¼ cup	28 grams
Garlic clove, medium, chopped	½ oz.	1 ½ Tbl.	14 grams
White wine, Chardonnay	2 fl. oz.	¼ cup	60 ml
Velouté, light nappe	24 fl. oz.	3 cups	740 ml
Heavy cream	4 fl. oz.	½ cup	120 ml
Creole mustard	2 ¼ oz.	3 Tbl.	62 grams
Tabasco		to taste	
Salt, kosher		to taste	
Black pepper, fresh ground		to taste	
Thyme, chopped		2 tsp.	
Scallion, sliced thin	¾ oz.	3 Tbl.	22 grams
Butter, unsalted	½ oz.	1 Tbl.	14 grams
Lemon juice, fresh		½ tsp.	

Brining and Smoking

1. Combine all ingredients for the brine and bring to a simmer; remove from the heat and chill under refrigeration until cold.
2. Pour the brine over the chicken breasts and ensure that they are completely covered. Brine under refrigeration for 24 hours.

(Continues on next page)

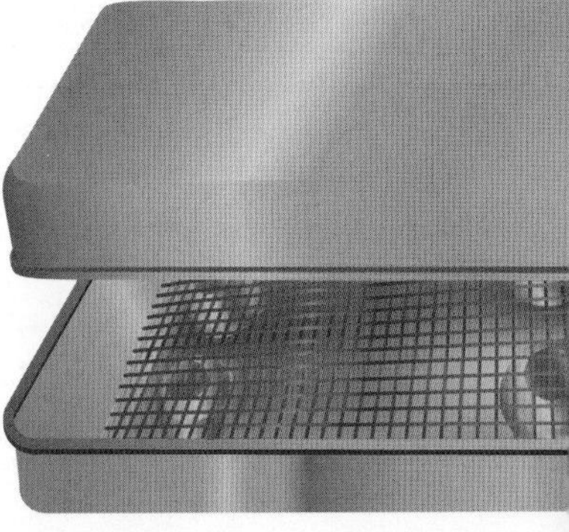

3. Remove the chicken from the brine and place on a rack. Refrigerate uncovered for 12–24 hours until the skin is dry and tacky before smoking. This step will allow a pellicle to form on the skin, which helps the skin to brown as well as aids in the absorption of smoke.
4. Set up a pan smoker with a 4-inch hotel pan, four 4 oz. aluminum cups, a rack, and a 2-inch hotel pan as a lid.
5. Preheat oven to 375 F (190 C) degrees convection.
6. Place the wood chips in the center of the base pan and heat on a burner until they begin to smoke; place the chicken on an elevated rack in the smoker and cover with another pan. Monitor and control the heat and amount of smoke (the smoke should be silver-gray and relatively heavy). Look for the skin to pick up the smoke; it will begin to turn a yellowish gray (after approximately 5–8 minutes, depending on the smoke). This step will determine how much smoke flavor the chicken will pick up.
7. Place the chicken in the oven on a racked sheet pan; cook until 165 F (74 C) degrees internal temperature in the thickest part of the breast. Ensure that the tip of the thermometer doesn't touch the bone when checking the temperature or you will get a false reading.
8. Allow the chicken to rest for 10 minutes before carving off the bone.

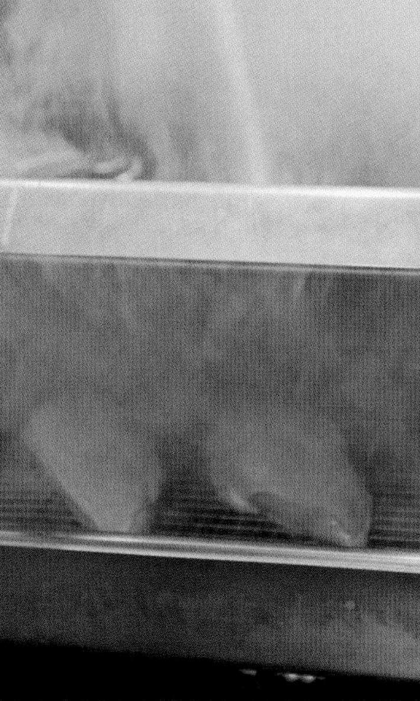

Creole Sauce

1. Preheat a saucepan over medium heat; add the oil and then the onions and celery.
2. Sauté until the onions begin to lightly caramelize; reduce the heat as needed.
3. Add the garlic and sauté until very aromatic and light brown.
4. Deglaze with the wine and reduce by two-thirds.
5. Add the velouté and bring to a simmer. Cook gently for 15 minutes; skim as needed.
6. Add the heavy cream and continue to simmer for 10 minutes.
7. Strain the sauce and return to a simmer; add the Creole mustard and whisk to evenly incorporate.
8. Add the Tabasco; taste and adjust the seasoning.
9. Add the thyme, scallions, lemon juice, and butter and whisk well to fully incorporate.

The velouté should be a light nappe, approximately 2 ½ oz. of roux per quart. This sauce should have a sharp, piquant bite and be slightly spicy. Alternately, the chicken can be cooked in a smoker or smoked in the oven.

WINE SELECTED with Hot Smoked Chicken Breast with Creole Mustard Sauce

Wine: Yabby Lake Pinot Noir ($40)

Origin: Mornington Peninsula, Victoria, Australia

Taste and Texture Comparisons

Dish: Medium/Full Body, Smoky, Earthy, Savory, Rich/Cream, Spice

Wine: Medium Body, Aromatic, Fruity, Slight Earthy, Bright Acidity, Medium Alcohol, Soft Texture

In the cooler areas of Victoria (Mornington Peninsula and Yarra Valley) Pinot Noir reigns supreme in Australia with ripe fruit yet crisp acidity and finesse.

Why This Is a Good Pairing

- ***Matching Weight and Intensity*** – The dish and the wine are evenly matched in terms of weight and intensity of flavor. This allows harmony between them and reduces the risk of one overpowering the other.
- ***Complementing*** – The earthiness in the dish (smoke and thyme) creates a bridge to some of the savory complexities in the wine (earthy, slightly herbal).
- ***Contrasting*** – The smoke and the spice in the dish contrast with the ripe red berry fruit in the wine, making the flavors of the wine pop without losing the flavors of the dish.
- ***Cleansing*** – Pinot Noir is known for crisp acidity, and this wine does not disappoint. The acidity is fresh and bright, creating a cleansing sensation on the palate that is pleasant.

Wines That Didn't Work

Dry White Sparkling – We tried a few dry white sparkling wines from around the world. The high acidity and bubbles are too cleansing and strip some of the flavor from the dish. In general, they lack the fruit and weight to balance with this dish.

California Fumé Blanc – The spice from the garlic and mustard covers the fruit and puts the focus onto the alcohol in the wine (14%+ abv), creating a thermal/heat reaction on the palate. Additionally, the spice clashes with the oak rather than complementing it.

Gigondas/Côtes du Rhône – Although it matches in weight, the wine clashes with the dish. The tannins became more astringent and the herbal notes in the wine clash with the dish.

SUMMARY	Yabby Lake Mornington Peninsula Pinot Noir	Dry White Sparkling	California Fumé Blanc	Gigondas/Côtes du Rhône
Matching	+			+
Complementing	+			
Contrasting	+		(–)	
Compounding				
Complexing				
Cleansing	+	(–)		
Covering			(–)	
Clashing			(–)	(–)

Chicken Breast Stuffed with Spinach and Gruyère Cheese

CHICKEN BREAST STUFFED WITH SPINACH AND GRUYÈRE CHEESE

Yield: 10 portions
Cooking Method: Stuff-Roast

Ingredients	Amounts - US	Volume	Metric
For the Chicken			
Chicken breast, split, boneless, skin on		10 each	
Salt, kosher		as needed	
Black pepper, fresh ground		as needed	
Olive oil, pure	2 fl. oz.	¼ cup	60 ml
For the Filling			
Spinach, baby	2 lbs.		852 grams
Extra virgin olive oil		as needed	
Extra virgin olive oil	2 fl. oz.	¼ cup	60 ml
Onion, sweet, brunoise	3 oz.	¾ cup	84 grams
Leeks, brunoise	3 oz.	1 cup	84 grams
Garlic, roasted	½ oz.	4 tsp.	14 grams
Rosemary, chopped		1 tsp.	
Parmesan cheese, grated	2 oz.	¾ cup	56 grams
Goat cheese, soft	4 oz.	⅓ cup	112 grams
Gruyère cheese, shredded	4 oz.	2 cups	112 grams
Parsley, Italian, chopped		2 Tbl.	
Nutmeg, ground		⅜ tsp.	
Salt, kosher		to taste	
Black pepper, fresh ground		to taste	

Roasting Garlic

1. Cut the top off of a head of garlic, drizzle with extra virgin olive oil, and season with salt and pepper.
2. Wrap in aluminum foil and roast at 300 F (150 C) degrees convection until the cloves are soft and light golden, approximately 1 hour. Once cool, squeeze the garlic cloves out of their skins and mash into a paste.

Filling

1. Preheat a large sauté pan over medium heat and add the oil and the spinach. Sauté the spinach quickly until just wilted; drain and cool in the refrigerator immediately to set the color. Gently squeeze the excess moisture from the spinach in a perforated pan or strainer and then rough chop.
2. Preheat a sauté pan over medium heat; add the oil and then the onions and the leeks.
3. Sweat until tender; add the rosemary and mix well. Remove from the heat and cool.

(Continues on next page)

4. Combine all of the ingredients for the filling; mix well to evenly incorporate.
5. Taste and adjust the seasoning, and chill the filling under refrigeration until it is cold and firm.

Chicken

1. Preheat a convection oven to 325 F (164 C) degrees convection.
2. Using a boning or paring knife, make an incision along the side of the thickest portion of the breast, 1 inch wide, and then carefully slide the knife gently along the inside of the breast in order to create a pocket (the pocket should be as large as possible without coming through the side or base of the breast or the filling will leak out during cooking).
3. Fill each pocket with approximately 1 ½ oz. of filling and gently spread evenly in the pocket, allowing a little room for the filling to expand during cooking. Seal the opening with a small skewer or toothpick.

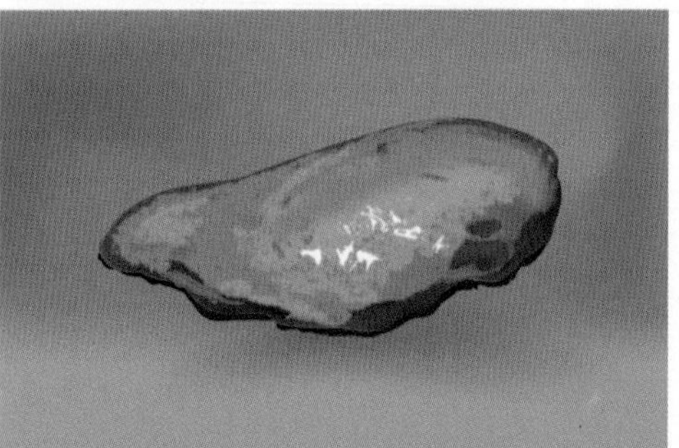

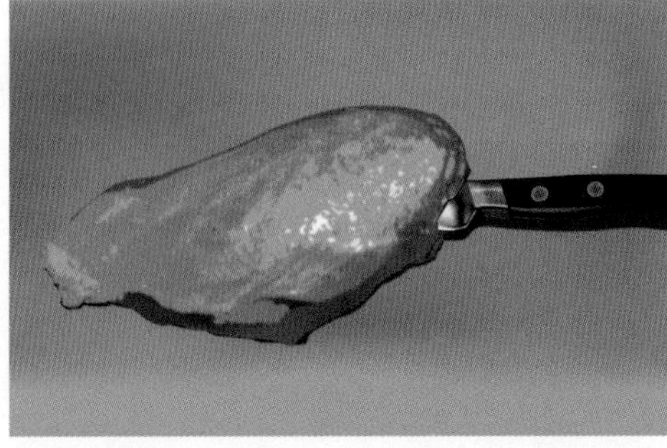

4. Season the chicken breasts on both sides with salt and pepper.
5. Preheat a sauté pan over medium heat, and add the oil and the chicken breasts skin-side-down.
6. Sauté until the skin is golden brown; turn the breasts over and cook until the bottom is light brown.
7. Place in the oven until at an internal temperature of 165 F (74 C) degrees. *Take care to insert the thermometer in the thickest part of the chicken flesh when checking the temperature.*

WINE SELECTED with Chicken Breast Stuffed with Spinach and Gruyère Cheese

Wine: Gloria Ferrer Chardonnay ($21)
Origin: Carneros, California, USA

Taste and Texture Comparisons

Dish: Herbal/Earthiness, Rich/Sharp Flavor, Nutty
Wine: Fruity, Spice, Butter, Creamy Texture, Medium Acidity, Moderate Alcohol

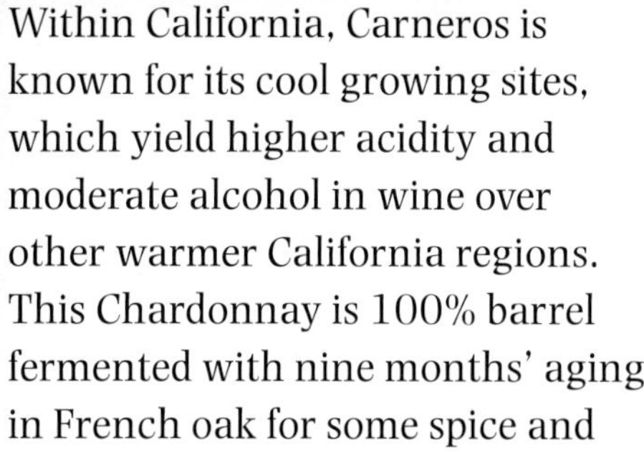

Within California, Carneros is known for its cool growing sites, which yield higher acidity and moderate alcohol in wine over other warmer California regions. This Chardonnay is 100% barrel fermented with nine months' aging in French oak for some spice and creamy texture.

Why This Is a Good Pairing

- ***Matching Weight and Intensity*** – Chardonnays such as this that have gone through some malolactic fermentation, seen oak, and bâtonnage has more richness and weight than most other whites. This wine matches the weight and intensity of the dish.
- ***Complementing*** – The flavor of the cheese creates a bridge and complements the creamy flavors and texture in the wine.
- ***Contrasting*** – The savory nature of the dish contrasts with the fruit in the wine and makes both flavors pop.
- ***Cleansing*** – The wine's acidity cuts through some of the richness from the cheese, creating a cleansing sensation. This lightens and refreshes the palate without cutting any flavor.

Wines That Didn't Work

Unoaked Australian Viognier – Initially quite floral and pretty, but the weight and alcohol of the wine overpower the dish.

Loire Cabernet Franc – The green herbal flavors of the wine with the spinach in the dish make the dish taste more green and vegetal. Green + green = $green^2$. Additionally, the tannins clash with the dish, turning astringent and drying.

Chianti Classico – The rich weight of the Chianti Classico we tested overpowers the dish, and the wine's tannins become overwhelming.

Alternative: Chablis—The spinach creates a refreshing sensation with the wine and the acid cuts through the cheese for a very nice dance. There is also a little nuttiness from parmesan cheese that comes in at the end. Although the Chablis is from the same grape as the Carneros Chardonnay, the reaction is different, but they both work well.

SUMMARY	Gloria Ferrer Chardonnay	Unoaked Australian Viognier	Loire Cabernet Franc	Chianti Classico
Matching	+			
Complementing	+			
Contrasting	+			
Compounding			(–)	
Complexing				
Cleansing	+			
Covering		(–)		(–)
Clashing			(–)	

CHICKEN LEGS

Chicken legs are more exercised than breasts, thus have a richer flavor and more fat. They are suited for both dry and moist methods of cooking.

BUTTERMILK FRIED CHICKEN

Yield: 10 portions

Cooking Method: Pan-Fry

Ingredients	Amounts - US	Volume	Metric
Chicken legs, split (thigh and drumstick)		10 each (20 pieces)	
Buttermilk	16 fl. oz.	2 cups	500 ml
Dijon mustard	1 ⅛ oz.	2 Tbl.	32 grams
Grain mustard	1 ⅛ oz.	2 Tbl.	32 grams
Salt, kosher		1 Tbl.	
Black pepper, fresh ground		1 ½ tsp.	
Tabasco sauce		½ tsp.	
Salt, kosher		as needed	
Black pepper, fresh ground		as needed	
Flour, all-purpose	8 oz.	2 cups	226 grams
Garlic, granulated		2 tsp.	
Paprika, Spanish		1 tsp.	
Cayenne		¼ tsp.	
Olive oil, pure		as needed	

Fried Chicken

1. Combine the buttermilk, mustards, Tabasco, salt, and pepper and whisk well until evenly incorporated. Place the chicken in a non-reactive pan (or a Zip-lock bag), cover with the buttermilk marinade, and mix well to coat. Marinate under refrigeration for 8–12 hours.
2. Combine the flour, garlic, paprika, and cayenne and mix well.
3. Fill a cast iron skillet with enough oil to come two-thirds of the way up the side of the chicken (approximately ½ to 1 inch of oil), and heat to 340 F (170 C) degrees. The amount of oil needed will be determined by the size of the pan and the amount of chicken. *Alternately, the chicken can be cooked in a deep-fat fryer.*
4. Remove the chicken from the marinade; season with salt and pepper. Dredge the chicken in the seasoned flour.
5. Gently place the chicken pieces in the oil, laying them away from you. Adjust the oil level as needed. Take care when adding the chicken as the oil level will rise and can possibly over flow causing a flare up.
6. Monitor the oil temperature to ensure that it remains at 340 F (170 C) degrees during cooking.
7. Turn the chicken after the bottom is golden brown and cooked halfway, approximately 8–10 minutes. Continue cooking until the chicken is 165 F (74 C) degrees and golden brown. Ensure that the tip of the thermometer doesn't touch the bone when checking the temperature or you will get a false reading.
8. Remove the chicken and drain well on absorbent towels.

It is my preference to directly season proteins with salt and pepper as opposed to seasoning the flour with salt and pepper. The reason for this is they have different weights and do not mix evenly. The salt is heavy and sinks to the bottom while the light pepper sits on top, so the first item dipped in the flour will have a lot of pepper and little salt, while the last pieces will have little pepper and a lot of salt. However, dried spices in general have a similar weight to flour and will mix relatively evenly.

WINE SELECTED with Buttermilk Fried Chicken

Wine: Christian Moreau Chablis, Chardonnay ($22)
Origin: Chablis AC, Burgundy, France

Taste and Texture Comparisons

Dish: Rich, Piquant, Crunchy, Spice
Wine: Delicate, Crisp Acidity, Mild Green Apple Flavor with Mineral Tones

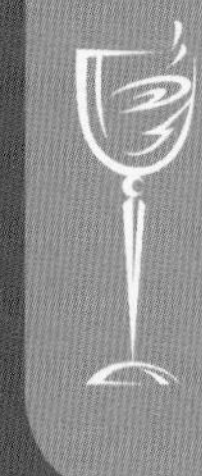

This is a village-level Chablis, from the Chablis region in Burgundy in France. These Chardonnays are generally unoaked and this producer is known for very clean, pure, and mineral flavors.

Why This Is a Good Pairing

- ***Contrasting Textures*** – This dish has some weight to it, along with richness and a crunchy texture. At the opposite end of the spectrum, the wine is delicate and has bright, crisp acidity. This structure lightens the dish.
- ***Cleansing*** – Chablis has high acidity for Chardonnay and cuts through the oil from the frying, creating a cleansing sensation while allowing the flavors of the chicken to come through.
- ***Complementing*** – Many Chablis Chardonnays go through malolactic fermentation and lees stirring, which creates creamy and yeasty flavors that bridge and connect with the flavor of the buttermilk.
- ***Dance*** – Fat is flavor and the crispy chicken skin carries the flavor of the dish on the palate for a long time. The acidity of the wine cuts through the fat in the dish without cutting the length of flavor. It's a nice, long waltz.

Alternative: NV Brut Champagne—Dry champagne pairs well with this dish for similar reasons to the Chablis, and the bubbles add another dimension that helps cut through the rich and crunchy texture of the dish, adding refreshment to the dish.

Wines That Didn't Work

Alsatian Gewürztraminer – The style of this Alsatian Gewürztraminer has a touch of sweetness. The wine matches the dish in weight, and the spice provides a nice *complexing* feature, but the low acid and its slightly oily texture compound with the richness of the dish in an unpleasant way.

Beaujolais Nouveau – The texture is okay; the mustard flavors contrast with the fruit, making them pop, but the wine's raspberry fruit is too overpowering for this dish.

New World Pinot Noir – We tested a few New World Pinot Noirs. The texture matches and the mustard flavors make the ripe berry fruit pop. Additionally, Pinot Noir's crisp acidity cleanses the palate, and does a dance with the fat, elongating the finish. However, it's a one-way pairing, meaning it is only augmenting the wine.

SUMMARY	Christian Moreau Chablis, Chardonnay	Alsatian Gewürztraminer	Beaujolais Nouveau	New World Pinot Noir
Matching		+	+	
Complementing	+			
Contrasting	+		+	+
Compounding		(–)		
Complexing		+		
Cleansing	+			+
Covering			(–)	(–)
Clashing				

CHICKEN CACCIATORE "HUNTER'S STYLE"

Yield: 10 portions

Cooking Method: Braise

Ingredients	Amounts - US	Volume	Metric
For the Chicken			
Chicken legs, split (thigh and drumstick)		10 each (20 pieces)	
Salt, kosher		as needed	
Black pepper, fresh ground		as needed	
Flour, all-purpose		as needed	
Extra virgin olive oil	3 fl. oz.	⅓ cup	90 ml
Button mushrooms, ½" pieces	12 oz.	4 cups	336 grams
Onions, red, sliced ¼"	12 oz.	4 cups	336 grams
Garlic clove, sliced thin	½ oz.	2 Tbl.	14 grams
White wine, Pinot Grigio	4 fl. oz.	½ cup	120 ml
Chicken stock	16 fl. oz.	2 cups	500 ml
Tomatoes, plum, canned, rough chopped	25 oz.	3 cups	736 grams
Roasted red peppers, batonnet	10 oz.	1 ½ cup	284 grams
Bay leaf		1 each	
Thyme sprig		6 each	
For the Garnish			
Parsley, Italian, chopped		1 Tbl.	

(Continues on next page)

Roasted Red Peppers

1. Coat the peppers lightly with olive oil; place on a sheet pan in a 425 F (215 C) degree oven.
2. Turn the peppers as the skin begins to blister and turn black.
3. Remove when all sides are slightly blackened; place in a paper bag or a bowl covered with plastic wrap.
4. Allow the peppers to steam for 15–20 minutes.
5. Peel the skin off and remove the seeds.

Chicken

1. Preheat a convection oven to 275 F (135 C) degrees.
2. Season the chicken legs with salt and pepper. Dredge the chicken in flour and shake off the excess.
3. Preheat a sautoir over medium heat.
4. Add the olive oil and then the chicken, skin side down. Work in batches as not to overcrowd the pan. Once the skin is golden brown, turn and repeat. Remove the chicken to a roasting pan. Continue until all chicken has been browned.
5. Add the mushrooms and sauté until they begin to brown; add additional oil if necessary.
6. Add the red onions and sauté until they begin to color lightly; add the garlic and sauté until very aromatic.
7. Deglaze with white wine and reduce by three-quarters, ensuring that you loosen the fond on the bottom of the pan.
8. Add the chicken stock, tomatoes, red peppers, bay leaf, and thyme; return to a simmer.
9. Pour this over the chicken. The liquid should come halfway up the chicken pieces; adjust with stock as necessary.
10. Cover the pan with plastic wrap and then aluminum foil and place in the oven.
11. Turn the chicken every 30 minutes and rotate the pan until the chicken is fork tender, approximately 1 ½ –2 hours.
12. Garnish with parsley.

Button mushrooms are grown in sterilized manure and should be washed prior to use; however, they are sensitive to moisture, absorb water, and oxidize easily. Just prior to use: wash, drain, and dry mushrooms well before cutting and cooking.

This is a traditional Italian dish; cacciatore means "in the style of the hunter."

WINE SELECTED with Chicken Cacciatore

Wine: Willm Gewürztraminer Vin d'Alsace ($13)
Origin: Alsace, France

Taste and Texture Comparisons

Dish: Soft Texture, Rich, Slightly Sweet, Earthy
Wine: Soft Texture, Medium-Bodied, Dry, Fruity, Spice, Earthy (Floral)

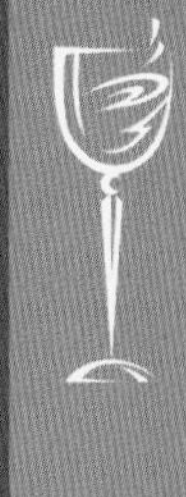

This is a fairly inexpensive Alsatian Gewürztraminer. Bear in mind that at this price point (and this producer) this Gewürztraminer is a bit lighter and drier in style (and lower in alcohol at about 13% abv) than others from Alsace.

Why This Is a Good Pairing

- ***Matching Weight, Texture, and Intensity*** – The dish and the wine were evenly matched.
- ***Complementing*** – The earthy notes in the dish bridge the spice and floral notes in the wine.
- ***Contrasting*** – "Gewürz" in German means "spice" and Gewürztraminer has a spiciness to it. This contrasts with the flavor of the chicken and the sweetness of the tomatoes and peppers, making them stand out. This also causes a *complexing* effect wherein you taste all the layers of flavors.
- ***Cleansing*** – This is one of the rare instances where the dish's acidity lifts the wine. Gewürztraminer is generally low in acid. In this instance, the slight acidity of the tomatoes refreshes the wine, making the wine's flavors pop and its overall balance more harmonious.
- ***Complexing*** – All of these varying reactions make for a complex and luxurious pairing.

Wines That Didn't Work

Chablis – The wine's crisp acidity compounds with the tomato's acidity for a sour note. Additionally, the citrus fruit in the wine clashes with the dish, making the wine taste like candy (and not in a good way).

Tavel Rosé – We tried this dish with a Tavel (a dry rosé from the Tavel region in the Rhône Valley of France). The sweet impression of the red berry fruit connects to the sweetness in the tomatoes and peppers but the alcohol at 14% stands out, creating a heat that cuts the finish short.

Hunter Valley Shiraz – The reaction is similar to that of the rosé. Additionally, the weight and the intensity of the fruit overpower and cover the flavors of the dish.

SUMMARY	Willm Gewürztraminer Vin d'Alsace	Chablis	Tavel Rosé	Hunter Valley Shiraz
Matching	+			
Complementing	+		+	+
Contrasting	+		(–)	(–)
Compounding		(–)		
Complexing	+			
Cleansing	+			
Covering				(–)
Clashing		(–)		

Tandoori Chicken

TANDOORI CHICKEN

Yield: 10 portions

Cooking Method: Roast

Ingredients	Amounts - US	Volume	Metric
For the Chicken			
Chicken legs, skinless, split (thigh and drumstick)		10 each (20 pieces)	
Ghee	3 fl. oz.	⅓ cup	90 ml
For the Marinade			
Yogurt, plain	12 oz.	1 ½ cups	348 grams
Salt, kosher	⅞ oz.	2 ½ Tbl.	26 grams
Lime juice, fresh	¾ fl. oz.	1 ½ Tbl.	22 ml
Ginger, chopped	⅝ oz.	1 ½ Tbl.	18 grams
Garlic clove, chopped	½ oz.	1 ½ Tbl.	14 grams
Cardamom, ground	¼ oz.	1 Tbl.	6 grams
Tumeric		2 tsp.	
Coriander, ground		1 ½ tsp.	
Cumin		1 ½ tsp.	
Black pepper, fresh ground		¾ tsp.	
Cayenne		¾ tsp.	
Paprika		¾ tsp.	
Cloves, ground		½ tsp.	
For the Onions			
Red onions, sliced ¼"	6 oz.	2 cups	170 grams
Extra virgin olive oil	1 fl. oz.	2 Tbl.	30 ml
Salt, kosher		as needed	
Black pepper, fresh ground		as needed	
For the Garnish			
Tomatoes, sliced ⅛", cut in half		15 each	
Cilantro, rough chopped		1 Tbl.	
Lime wedges		20 each	

(Continues on next page)

Chicken

1. Using a paring knife, make several long slits ¼ inch deep into the thickest areas of thighs and drumsticks (they should be about 1 ½ to 2 inches long).
2. Combine the ingredients for the marinade and whisk well. Place the chicken in a non-reactive container, (or a Zip-lock bag), and pour the marinade over the chicken. Gently rub the marinade into the chicken slits. Marinate for 24 hours.
3. Preheat the oven to 425 F (218 C) degrees convection.
4. Remove the chicken from the marinade, place in a roasting pan lined with a rack, and brush with the ghee. Roast until the chicken is 165 F (74 C) degrees internally and browned evenly; baste with ghee occasionally during roasting. Ensure that the tip of the thermometer doesn't touch the bone when checking the temperature or you will get a false reading.
5. Mix the onions with the olive oil, salt, and pepper; grill until they are caramelized and they begin to soften slightly. Cut the onions into quarters.
6. Place the onions and tomato slices on the plate, arrange the chicken, and garnish with cilantro and lime.

This dish is traditionally cooked in a clay oven called a Tandoor.

WINE SELECTED with Tandoori Chicken

Wine: Brokenwood Hunter Valley Shiraz ($35)
Origin: Hunter Valley, New South Wales, Australia

TASTE AND TEXTURE COMPARISONS

Dish: Medium/Full Body, Rich Flavor, Spice, Sweet, Acidic

Wine: Medium Body, Spice, Raspberry Fruit

This Hunter Valley Shiraz has a milder alcohol level (13.5% abv) than some of its Barossa brethren (which can easily reach above 14.5% abv). Wines at a milder alcohol level are more suitable for spicy cuisines.

Why This Is a Good Pairing

- ***Matching Weight and Flavor Intensity*** – The wine and the dish are evenly matched and are rich in flavor. The dish is rich in spice, although not necessarily in heat, and the wine has a dense concentration of raspberry fruit and spice.
- ***Complementing*** – The spice in the dish augments the spice in the wine. Shiraz (also known as Syrah) is known for an aroma and flavor that is reminiscent of black pepper spice that comes through in the wine.
- ***Contrasting*** – The rich, concentrated raspberry fruit in the wine contrasts with the spice in the chicken, augmenting all of the flavors. In this respect, it is a two-way pairing, as both the dish and the wine are enhanced.

Wines That Didn't Work

Chablis – This delicate wine is overpowered by the intensity of this dish.

Moscato d'Asti – The wine matches the weight of the dish and its sweetness balances the spice. In addition, the low alcohol (5%) does not exacerbate the spice in the dish, but the wine's intense flavors are somewhat overpowering and you lose the flavors of the dish.

Zinfandel – The intensely concentrated fruit contrasts nicely with the chicken and spices, but the high alcohol (above 14.5%) cuts the finish very short and makes it unpleasantly hot. Additionally, the tannins in the wine clash with the spices, creating a compounding effect (in a negative way).

We should note that in this pairing you do feel a hint of heat given the level of alcohol and the spice, but it is not detracting in the slightest. In fact, it is alluring and kept us coming back for more.

SUMMARY	Brokenwood Hunter Valley Shiraz	Chablis	Moscato d'Asti	Zinfandel
Matching	+		+	
Complementing	+			
Contrasting	+		+	+
Compounding				(–)
Complexing				
Cleansing			(–)	
Covering		(–)	(–)	
Clashing				(–)

Sous Vide Duck Breast with Cardamom, Thyme, and Duck Jus

DUCK

There are several varieties of duck available on the market today: Moulard, Muscovy, and Pekin, with the latter being the most popular. Pekin are often referred to as Long Island duck. They have dark flesh that is very rich with a thick layer of fat. If the skin is being served it is important to render the fat properly to achieve crispy skin.

SOUS VIDE DUCK BREAST WITH CARDAMOM, THYME, AND DUCK JUS

Yield: 10 portions

Cooking Method: Sous Vide

Ingredients	Amounts - US	Volume	Metric
For the Duck Breasts			
Duck breast, Pekin, scored		10 each	
Salt, kosher		as needed	
Black pepper, fresh ground		as needed	
Cardamom, ground		as needed	
Shallots, minced	1 ¼ oz.	¼ cup	34 grams
Juniper berries, crushed		50 each	
Thyme sprigs		20–30 each	
Duck fat, rendered	1 ½ fl. oz.	3 Tbl.	45 ml
Duck jus	24 fl. oz.	3 cups	740 ml
Thyme, chopped		1 Tbl.	
Parsley, Italian, chopped		1 tsp.	
Lemon juice, fresh		½ tsp.	
Butter, unsalted, cubed	½ oz.	1 Tbl.	14 grams
For the Duck Jus			
Roasted duck stock	32 fl. oz.	1 qt.	1 liter
Duck fat, rendered	1 fl. oz.	2 Tbl.	30 ml
Carrots, brunoise	2 oz.	½ cup	56 grams
Celeriac, brunoise	2 oz.	½ cup	56 grams
Leeks, brunoise	1 ½ oz.	½ cup	42 grams
Cornstarch		as needed	
Roasted duck stock		as needed	

Sous vide is a cooking technique in which the main item is vacuum-sealed in a plastic bag and cooked in a temperature-controlled water bath for a long period of time. This technique can be used effectively for tender and more exercised cuts, portions, and whole muscles as well as vegetables utilizing a shorter cook time.

(Continues on next page)

Duck Jus

1. Preheat a sauce pan over medium heat, add the duck fat and then the leeks, carrots, and celeriac.
2. Sweat until the vegetables begin to soften.
3. Add the roasted duck stock and bring to a simmer.
4. Simmer gently for 15 minutes.
5. Thicken with a cornstarch slurry to achieve a light nappe consistency. The amount of slurry needed will vary based on the consistency of the roasted duck stock.

Duck Breasts

1. Season the chilled duck breast on both sides with salt, pepper, and cardamom; place in a vacuum-seal bag.
2. Combine the room temperature duck fat, shallots, and juniper berries; evenly coat the flesh side of the duck breasts with this mixture. Place the thyme sprigs on top and bottom of the duck.
3. Seal the bags with a vacuum sealer and refrigerate for a minimum of 4 hours.
4. Set a thermal circulator or temperature-controlled water bath to 140 F (60 C) degrees.

5. Place the duck in the thermal circulator water bath and cook for 25 minutes.
6. Remove the duck from the bags, drain well, and pat the skin dry.
7. Preheat a sauté pan over medium-low heat; add enough duck fat to coat the bottom of the pan and add the duck breasts, skin-side-down.
8. Sauté until the skin is very crisp and the fat is rendered; turn the duck breasts briefly to slightly color the flesh side. Remove to a rack and allow to rest briefly.
9. Remove the excess fat from the pan. Deglaze the pan with duck jus; add the parsley, thyme, lemon juice, and mount with butter.
10. Taste and adjust the seasoning.
11. Slice the duck breast thinly, sauce, and serve.

Duck breasts often are served rare and sliced thin. I am not fond of this approach as the meat will be very chewy. When duck breasts are cooked as a single muscle they should be cooked to medium.

When working with products that will be cooked sous vide it is critical to ensure that the proteins are well chilled through the process of fabrication, marinating, and sealing. It is very important to research this technique completely and understand the potential sanitation concerns before proceeding.

Image © Cengage Learning 2013

WINE SELECTED with Sous Vide Duck Breast with Cardamom, Thyme, and Duck Jus

Wine: Guigal Côtes du Rhône Rouge ($14)
Origin: Côtes du Rhône, Rhône Valley, France

Taste and Texture Comparisons

Dish: Rich, Spice, Earthy, Sweet
Wine: Fairly Generous Body, Spice, Earthy, Herbal, Mineral, Raspberry Fruit, Low Acidity, Slightly Warm Alcohol

This wine is a blend of grapes, but is predominantly Syrah, whereas many Côtes du Rhônes are Grenache dominated. This one tastes a little richer, with more black pepper spice notes (from the Syrah) than a typical Côtes du Rhône.

Why This Is a Good Pairing

- ***Matching Weight and Intensity*** – Duck is fairly rich and this wine is also relatively rich. Thus, they match in intensity.
- ***Complementing*** – The herbs, earthiness, and spice from the dish connect with the slightly herbal and earthy nature of this wine.
- ***Contrasting*** – The rich flavor of the duck makes the fruit in the wine more vibrant.

Alternatives: Chinon and Chianti Classico—Both of these red wines have an herbal and earthy element that complement the dish's flavors and match the weight and intensity of the dish. They work well too.

Wines That Didn't Work

Dry White Sparkling – The acidity and effervescence of the wine strip the dish of the duck and herb flavors. The flavors fight one another rather than dance.

California Fumé Blanc – While the fresh fig notes in the wine contrast with the dish (making its flavors come out more), the cardamom clashes with the alcohol, warming the palate and cutting off the flavors of the dish and the wine.

New Zealand Pinot Noir – The flavor of the duck contrasts with the cherry flavor of the wine and makes the fruit pop too much. This makes the wine shout, but does absolutely nothing for the dish—a one-way pairing.

SUMMARY	Guigal Côtes du Rhône Rouge	Dry White Sparkling	California Fumé Blanc	New Zealand Pinot Noir
Matching	+			
Complementing	+			+
Contrasting	+			
Compounding				
Complexing				
Cleansing		(–)	(–)	
Covering				(–)
Clashing			(–)	

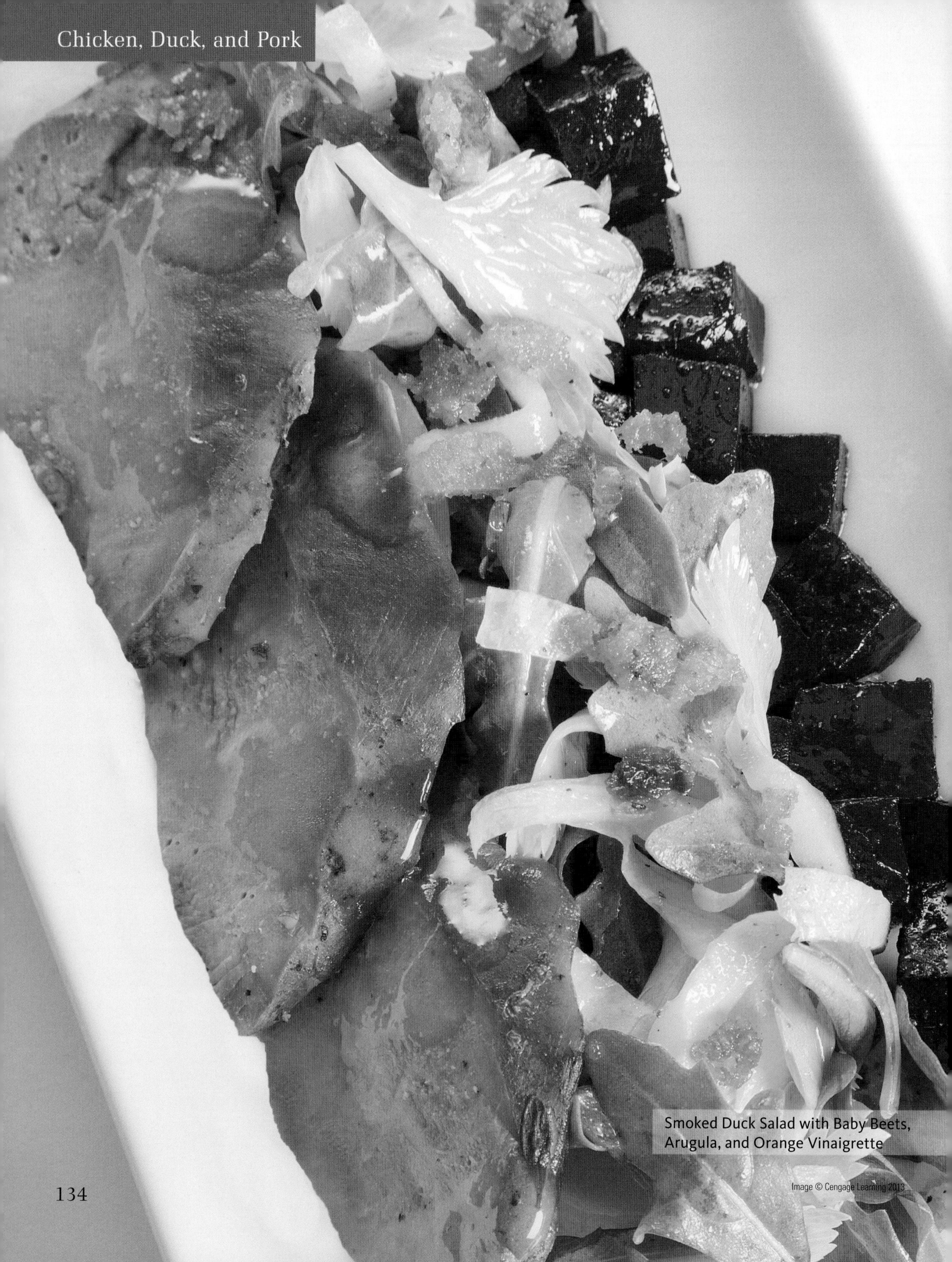

Smoked Duck Salad with Baby Beets, Arugula, and Orange Vinaigrette

SMOKED DUCK SALAD WITH BABY BEETS, ARUGULA, AND ORANGE VINAIGRETTE

Yield: 10 portions

Cooking Method: Pan-Smoke/Roast

Ingredients	Amounts - US	Volume	Metric
For the Duck			
Duck breast, Pekin		10 each	
Duck fat	2 ½ oz.	⅓ cup	70 grams
Wood chips, cherry		½ cup	
Belgian endive, chiffonade	5 oz.	2 ¼ cups	140 grams
Arugula, baby, stems trimmed	5 oz.	7 cups	170 grams
Watercress, trimmed	2 oz.	3 cups	56 grams
Celery leaves		½ cup	
Orange vinaigrette	8 fl. oz.	1 cup	240 ml
Salt, kosher		to taste	
Black pepper, fresh ground		to taste	
For the Brine			
Water	64 fl. oz.	2 qts.	2 liters
Salt, kosher	3 oz.	½ cup	84 grams
Black peppercorns, cracked	¼ oz.	2 tsp.	8 grams
Thyme sprigs		12 each	
TCM	⅜ oz.	1 ½ tsp.	10 grams
Honey	2 ½ oz.	3 Tbl.	64 grams
Brandy	2 fl. oz.	¼ cup	60 ml
For the Roasted Baby Beets			
Baby beets	16 oz.	454 grams	
Olive oil, pure		as needed	
Extra virgin olive oil		as needed	
Salt, kosher		to taste	
Black pepper, fresh ground		to taste	

Choose wood chips that are approximately ½- to 1-inch pieces that are ⅛-inch thick. For this type of pan smoking it isn't necessary to soak the chips, as the heat will cause them to smoke but not flame.

(Continues on next page)

Ingredients	Amounts - US	Volume	Metric
For the Orange Vinaigrette			
Orange juice	24 fl. oz.	3 cups	740 ml
White balsamic vinegar	2 fl. oz.	¼ cup	60 ml
Lemon juice, fresh	¾ fl. oz.	1 ½ Tbl.	22 ml
Shallots, minced	¼ oz.	1 Tbl.	8 grams
Dijon mustard	½ oz.	2 tsp.	14 grams
Thyme, chopped		1 tsp.	
Salt, kosher		1 tsp.	
Black pepper, fresh ground		½ tsp.	
Olive oil, pure	6 fl. oz.	¾ cup	180 ml
Extra virgin olive oil	2 fl. oz.	¼ cup	60 ml
Salt, kosher		as needed	
Black pepper, fresh ground		as needed	

Brining and Smoking

1. Combine the brine ingredients and bring to a simmer; remove from the heat and chill under refrigeration until cold.
2. Remove the skin from the duck breasts and reserve.
3. Brine the duck breasts, completely covered, for 6 hours under refrigeration. Remove the duck from the brine and place on a sheet pan lined with a rack, uncovered, in the refrigerator overnight.
4. Set up a pan smoker with a 4-inch hotel pan, four 4 oz. aluminum cups, a rack, and a 2-inch hotel pan as a lid. See illustration page 114.
5. Place the wood chips in the bottom center of the 4-inch hotel pan with the aluminum cups in the 4 corners, and place the rack with the duck breasts on top of the cups; cover with a 2-inch pan.
6. Turn the heat on medium high until chips begin to smoke. Monitor and control the heat and amount of smoke (the smoke should be a sliver-gray and relatively heavy in the smoker). Look for the flesh to pick up the smoke. It will begin to turn a pinkish-gray (approximately 3–5, minutes depending on the smoke). This step will determine how much smoke the duck picks up and ultimately will impact the flavor.
7. Remove from the pan and place in a 300 F (148 C) degree convection oven until 150 F (65 C) degrees internal temperature.
8. Chill overnight in the refrigerator.

Roasted Baby Beets

1. Preheat an oven to 300 F (150 C) degrees convection.
2. Cut the tops off of the beets, leaving 1 inch attached; wash the beets very well.
3. Place the beets in a deep pan, wrap in aluminum foil, and roast until fork tender, approximately 2 hours.

4. Allow the beets to cool to room temperature; working with gloves, cut the top and bottom off and peel the beets.
5. Cut the beets into medium dice.

Orange Vinaigrette

1. Place the orange juice in a saucepan and gently reduce by two-thirds; remove from the heat and chill under refrigeration.
2. Place the orange-juice reduction, vinegar, lemon juice, shallots, and Dijon mustard in a stainless steel mixing bowl and whisk well to combine.
3. Slowly drizzle in the oils while whisking constantly.
4. Add the thyme, season with salt and pepper, taste, and adjust the seasoning.

Plating

1. Place the skin on a parchment-lined sheet pan and bake at 350 F (176 C) degrees until completely rendered and crisp. Carefully pour off the rendered fat as necessary. Rough chop the crisp skin and reserve for garnish. Reserve the rendered fat for cooking.
2. Coat the beets with extra virgin olive oil and season with salt and pepper.
3. Place the greens in a stainless steel bowl and add the orange vinaigrette to taste, not all of the dressing will be used. Salt and pepper to taste and adjust the dressing and seasoning.
4. Slice the duck breast thin against the grain.
5. Plate the beets, salad and garnish with the crisp duck skin; drizzle the duck breast with a small amount of dressing.

Belgian endive is very delicate and will oxidize if cut in advance. Mix the salad greens with the dressing just prior to serving as they wilt quickly.

WINE SELECTED with Smoked Duck Salad with Baby Beets, Arugula, and Orange Vinaigrette

Wine: Dr. Loosen Erdener Treppchen Riesling Kabinett ($23)
Origin: Mosel, Germany

Taste and Texture Comparisons

Dish: Sweet, Smoky, Rich, Earthy, Acid, Slight Bitterness
Wine: Sweet, Fruity, Mineral, Crisp, Moderately Low Alcohol

This wine is a Kabinett, which generally means it is less sweet and has higher alcohol than a Spätlese or an Auslese.

Why This Is a Good Pairing

- ***Matching Intensity*** – The sweetness of the dish matches the sweetness of the wine. The acidity in the wine and in the vinaigrette prevents the sweetness from compounding.
- ***Complementing*** – The citrus flavors in the wine complement the orange vinaigrette. The smoke from the duck focuses the palate on the minerality in the Riesling.
- ***Contrasting*** – The richness of the duck contrasts with the light, delicate nature of the wine. This creates a refreshing, cleansing sensation without acidity.
- ***Complexing*** – The complementing and contrasting create a *complexing* reaction where you taste all the flavors in the dish and in the wine.
- ***Dance*** – When you taste this wine with this dish and get a bit of the crispy skin of the duck, the fat elongates the flavors on the palate even longer.

Wines That Didn't Work

Oregon Pinot Gris – The slightly citrus and spice character of the wine compounds with the orange in this dish. Then, the smoke overpowers the wine, making the wine disappear.

California Chardonnay – Although the smoked nature of the duck complements the oak flavor in the wine, the smoke contrasts too much with the fruit, making the wine taste candied (like cotton candy).

Red Burgundy – We tried several red burgundies with this dish. In each case, the acidity cleanses, but the tannins are too astringent (even though the tannins aren't that high).

Alternative: Beaujolais Nouveau—There is a contrast between the sweet candy-like fruit in the wine (which it's supposed to have) and the smokiness of the duck. This makes the flavors of the dish pop and complexes the wine. The Beaujolais Nouveau is a red wine and a less expensive alternative.

SUMMARY	Dr. Loosen Erdener Treppchen Riesling Kabinett	Oregon Pinot Gris	California Chardonnay	Red Burgundy
Matching	+			
Complementing	+		+	
Contrasting	+		(–)	
Compounding		(–)		
Complexing	+			
Cleansing	+			+
Covering		(–)		
Clashing				(–)

SAUTÉED DUCK BREAST WITH SUN-DRIED CHERRY SAUCE

Yield: 10 portions

Cooking Method: Sauté

Ingredients	Amounts - US	Volume	Metric
For the Duck Breast			
Duck breasts, boneless, skin scored		10 each	
Salt, kosher		as needed	
Black pepper, fresh ground		as needed	

(Continues on next page)

Ingredients	Amounts - US	Volume	Metric
For the Duck Sauce			
Roasted duck stock	32 fl. oz.	1 qt.	1 liter
Duck fat, rendered	¾ oz.	2 Tbl.	20 grams
Onions, medium dice	½ oz.	2 Tbl.	14 grams
Parsnips, medium dice	2 oz.	½ cup	56 grams
Celery, medium dice	2 oz.	½ cup	56 grams
Sachet		1 each	
Salt, kosher		as needed	
Black pepper, fresh ground		as needed	
Cornstarch		as needed	
Roasted duck stock		as needed	
For the Cherry Sauce			
Kirshwasser	3 fl. oz.	⅓ cup	90 ml
Sun-dried cherries	5 ½ oz.	1 cup	156 grams
Tarragon, chopped	⅛ oz.	1 Tbl.	2 grams
Sherry vinegar		1 tsp.	
Butter, unsalted, cubed	1 oz.	2 Tbl.	28 grams
Salt, kosher		to taste	
Black pepper, fresh ground		to taste	

Duck Sauce

1. Preheat a saucepan over medium high heat; add the duck fat and then the onions, parsnips, and celery.
2. Sauté until they begin to caramelize.
3. Add the duck stock and the sachet, bring to a simmer and cook for 20 minutes.
4. Combine the cornstarch and duck stock to make a slurry, it should be the consistency of heavy cream. The amount of slurry needed will vary based on the viscosity of the duck stock. With the sauce simmering slowly add the slurry while whisking. Strain through a chinois.

Duck Breast

1. Allow the duck to come to room temperature and season with salt and pepper on both sides.
2. Preheat a sauté pan over medium heat and add enough duck fat to coat the bottom of the pan; add the duck breasts skin-side-down and cook until the skin is very crisp and rendered. Turn the duck breasts over and cook to 140 F (60 C) degrees. Remove to a rack and allow to rest for 5 minutes.

Cherry Sauce

1. Degrease the pan, deglaze with the Kirshwasser, and reduce by two-thirds. Add the duck sauce and the cherries. Simmer gently for 6–8 minutes until the sauce has a deep cherry flavor.
2. Add the tarragon, sherry vinegar, mount with butter, and taste and adjust the seasoning.
3. Slice the duck breast thin, on a bias, and plate with the cherry sauce.

WINE SELECTED with Sautéed Duck Breast with Sun-Dried Cherry Sauce

Wine: Wildekrans Pinotage ($15)

Origin: Bot River, Walker Bay, South Africa

Taste and Texture Comparison

Dish: Richness, Sweet, Tart

Wine: Earthy, Fruity, Moderate Alcohol, Tannin, and Acidity

Pinotage is the flagship grape of South Africa. It has a few different styles, and this one falls closer to the "coffee camp" with obvious oak influence. It is aged in 80% medium-toast French barrels and 20% heavy-toast American barrels.

Why This Is a Good Pairing

- ***Matching Weight and Intensity*** – This is one of the richer dishes we profile in this section, and the duck as well as the sauce match the weight of the Pinotage. The intensity of flavors is also evenly matched.
- ***Complementing*** – The sun-dried cherries in the sauce pull out the rich cherry flavor in the wine. The *Maillard reaction* on the duck also complements the vanilla and toasty flavors of the oak in the wine.
- ***Contrasting*** – The flavor of the duck and the Maillard reaction also focuse the palate even more on the fruit. However, the fruit in the wine does not overpower the dish.
- ***Complexing*** – The Pinotage has earthy complexities that are brought out by the flavor of the duck, and this reaction helps you taste all the flavors of the dish and the wine. It's a great dance.

Wines That Didn't Work

Mosel Kabinett Riesling – The acidity cleanses slightly, but the sweetness of the wine compounds the sweetness of the cherry sauce, which ultimately covers the flavor of the duck.

Côtes du Rhône – Instead of complementing, the cherry flavor in the wine cancels out the flavor of the sauce. Additionally, the alcohol stands out like a sore thumb, wiping away some of the flavor of the dish and cutting the finish short.

Alternative: Russian River Pinot Noir—Similar to the Pinotage, the cherry flavor in the Russian River Pinot Noir sings, given the complement of the cherry sauce. The acidity cleanses the palate and, because the tannins are soft, they don't become astringent.

SUMMARY	Wildekrans Pinotage	Russian River Pinot Noir	Mosel Kabinett Riesling	Côtes du Rhône
Matching	+	+		
Complementing	+	+		
Contrasting	+	+		
Compounding			(–)	
Complexing	+			
Cleansing				(–)
Covering			(–)	
Clashing				(–)

Sous Vide Pork Tenderloin with Spicy Pineapple Salsa

PORK

Pork tenderloin is a minimally exercised cuts of protein and thus quite tender. It is low in fat and a good source of protein. Typically it is marketed whole, which can also be fabricated into individual portion cuts such as medallions, scaloppine, cutlets, sliced, and diced.

SOUS VIDE PORK TENDERLOIN WITH SPICY PINEAPPLE SALSA

Yield: 10 portions

Cooking Method: Sous Vide

Ingredients	Amounts - US	Volume	Metric
For the Pork			
Pork tenderloin, trimmed	3 lbs.	4 each	1.4 kilograms
Sage, leaves		40–50 each	
Salt, kosher		as needed	
Black pepper, course ground		as needed	
Extra virgin olive oil	2 fl. oz.	¼ cup	60 ml
For the Spicy Pineapple Salsa			
Pineapple, small dice	8 oz.	1 ½ cups	228 grams
Red pepper, small dice	3 oz.	¾ cup	84 grams
Jicama, small dice	2 ½ oz.	½ cup	70 grams
Red onion, small dice	1 oz.	¼ cup	28 grams
Extra virgin olive oil	1 ½ fl. oz.	3 Tbl.	45 ml
Lime juice	½ fl. oz.	1 Tbl.	15 ml
Parsley, Italian, chopped		1 Tbl. plus 1 tsp.	
Jalapeño, minced	¼ oz.	2 tsp.	6 grams
Salt, kosher		as needed	
Black pepper, fresh ground		as needed	

(Continues on next page)

Pineapple Salsa

Combine all of the ingredients for the salsa, mix well to evenly incorporate. Taste and adjust the seasoning. Allow the flavors to develop under refrigeration for 2 hours.

Pork

1. Season the pork tenderloins liberally with salt and black pepper and place in a vacuum-seal bag.
2. Lay the sage leaves flat on the surface of the pork and pour the olive oil over the pork.
3. Seal the bags appropriately with a vacuum sealer. Refrigerate for 4 hours.
4. Set up a thermal circulator or temperature-controlled water bath and set to 140 F (60 C) degrees.
5. Place the pork in the thermal circulator bath and cook for 30 minutes.
6. Remove the pork from the bag and drain well on a rack.
7. Preheat a sauté pan over medium-high heat.
8. Add the oil and then the pork, and sauté briefly until all sides are light golden brown. Adjust the heat as necessary.
9. Allow the pork to rest briefly and then slice thinly on a bias.
10. Serve with the Spicy Pineapple Salsa.

When working with products that will be cooked sous vide it is critical to ensure that the proteins are well chilled through the process of fabrication, marinating, and sealing. It is very important to research this technique completely and understand the potential sanitation concerns before proceeding.

WINE SELECTED with Sous Vide Pork Tenderloin with Spicy Pineapple Salsa

Wine: Ken Forrester "Petit" Chenin Blanc ($10)
Origin: Stellenbosch, South Africa

Taste and Texture Comparisons

Dish: Medium Body, Sweet/Tropical, Tender, Slight Acidity, Savory
Wine: Medium Body, Citrus, Tropical Notes, Soft Texture, Medium Alcohol, Crisp Acidity

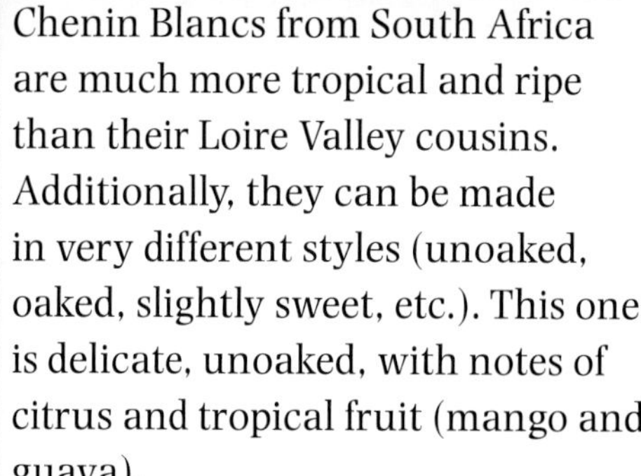
Chenin Blancs from South Africa are much more tropical and ripe than their Loire Valley cousins. Additionally, they can be made in very different styles (unoaked, oaked, slightly sweet, etc.). This one is delicate, unoaked, with notes of citrus and tropical fruit (mango and guava).

Why This Is a Good Pairing

- ***Matching Weight and Texture*** – The sous vide technique allows for a more delicate texture that matches quite well with the wine, which also has a soft weight and texture.
- ***Complementing*** – The tropical fruit in the salsa creates a bridge to some of the tropical fruit flavors in the wine (although the fruit in the wine is more in the mango/guava family than pineapple). The acidity from the fruit in the salsa also creates a bridge to the citrus flavors in the wine, creating a compounding effect, but in a way that does not cover the flavor of the pork.
- ***Cleansing*** – The acidity from the wine and the salsa is refreshing and cleansing. This softens the intensity of the sweetness from the pineapple and the peppers.

Wines That Didn't Work

Clare Valley Riesling – The wine is a bit austere in its structure and acidity. While with some dishes this is a great wine for cleansing, this dish's sweetness clashes, making the wine taste sour. Additionally, the lime notes in the wine and the dish compound unpleasantly.

Austrian Grüner Veltliner – The sweetness of the pineapple makes the Grüner Veltliner taste sour. There is also a bridge between the jalapeños and the white pepper of the wine, but not in a good way.

New Zealand Pinot Noir – As with the Grüner Veltliner, the sweetness of pineapple makes this wine taste sour. The spice in the dish also shortens the finish of the wine.

We tasted this dish with two different salsas: mango and pineapple salsa. The pineapple salsa has more success with the wine given its higher acidity. This made the dish more wine-friendly.

SUMMARY	Ken Forrester "Petit" Chenin Blanc	Clare Valley Riesling	Austrian Grüner Veltliner	New Zealand Pinot Noir
Matching	+			
Complementing	+		(–)	
Contrasting			(–)	(–)
Compounding	+	(–)		
Complexing				
Cleansing	+	(–)		
Covering				
Clashing				

Pork Schnitzel with Lemon

PORK SCHNITZEL WITH LEMON

Yield: 10 portions

Cooking Method: Pan-Fry

Ingredients	Amounts - US	Volume	Metric
Pork tenderloin, trimmed	2 ½ lbs	3 each	0.9 kilograms
Salt, kosher		as needed	
Black pepper, course ground		as needed	
Flour, all-purpose, unbleached		as needed	
Egg wash		as needed	
Panko bread crumbs, ground fine	6 oz.	2 cups	168 grams
Parsley, Italian, chopped		1 Tbl.	
Extra virgin olive oil		as needed	
Butter, unsalted, room temperature	3 oz.	⅓ cup	85 grams
Lemon wedges, ends trimmed, seeds removed		20 each	

Pork Schnitzel

1. Cut the pork into 2 ½-oz (62-gram) medallions. Place the medallions between plastic wrap and pound gently with a mallet until an even thickness of ¼ inch.
2. Combine the bread crumbs and parsley, mix well to evenly incorporate. Set up a standard breading procedure—flour, egg wash, bread crumbs.
3. Season the pork with salt and pepper. Bread the pork and place on a parchment lined sheet pan that has been lightly dusted with bread crumbs. Allow the breading to set under refrigeration for 2–4 hours.
4. Place enough oil in a sautoir so that when the pork is added it will come halfway up the side of the pork; allow for expansion of the oil and displacement when the pork is added. Preheat the oil over medium heat.
5. When the oil is hot (test by sprinkling a few bread crumbs in the oil; when it bubbles and they brown, the oil is ready), add the medallions, gently laying them away from you. Adjust the amount of oil as necessary.
6. Pan-fry the pork until it is evenly golden brown, approximately 1 ½ minutes, turn, and repeat. Take care when turning the cutlet not to break up the breading. Turn the pork away from you to avoid splattering in your direction.
7. Remove the pork, drain the oil, and add the butter to the pan. When the butter begins to foam, replace the pork and baste with the butter.
8. Drain on absorbent towels and serve immediately with lemon wedges.

WINE SELECTED with Pork Schnitzel with Lemon

Wine: Craggy Range Pinot Noir ($35)
Origin: Martinborough, North Island, New Zealand

Taste and Texture Comparisons

Dish: Crispy, Toasted, Medium Body, Sweet, Acidity
Wine: Aromatic, Fruity, Medium Bodied, Modest Tannins, Complex, Crisp Acidity

There are several styles of Pinot Noir in New Zealand. Many people are familiar with Central Otago on the South Island, where Pinot Noirs are more rich and opulent. This one from Martinborough on the North Island is known for its delicacy and finesse.

Why This Is a Good Pairing

- ***Matching*** – The weights of both the dish and wine are fairly equal.
- ***Contrasting in Textures and Flavors*** – The crisp acid from the Pinot Noir cuts through the richness from the frying of the schnitzel. This adds a refreshing character to the dish without covering up the dish's flavors. The toastiness from the frying and the breading contrasts with the ripe wild strawberry fruit, making the fruit pop. Additionally, the flavor of the pork comes through and contrasts with the earthy notes in the wine. This creates a *complexing* reaction where you taste all the layers of flavors of both the dish and the wine.
- ***Dance*** – The butter used to finish the pork elongates the flavors on your palate. The length of the flavors is quite long and finishes clean, preparing you for that next delicious bite.

Wines That Didn't Work

Prosecco – The wine's crisp acidity and the bubbles are refreshing and cleansing, and focus your palate on the flavors of the schnitzel, but this is a one-way pairing where the dish comes out on top. It does nothing for the wine.

Zweigelt – This Austrian red wine's blackberry fruit popped, but the wine's acidity is a bit neutralizing. The pairing clashes and the wine's earthiness is overpowering.

Alternative: Grüner Veltliner is a great white alternative. The white pepper flavors in the wine contrasts with the flavor of the pork. The wine's fresh, crisp acidity also cuts through the richness in the dish.

SUMMARY	Craggy Range Pinot Noir	Grüner Veltliner	Prosecco	Zweigelt
Matching	+			
Complementing				
Contrasting	+	+		+
Compounding				
Complexing	+			
Cleansing	+	+	+	(–)
Covering			(–)	
Clashing				(–)

GRILLED PORK TENDERLOIN WITH CARAMELIZED APPLE COMPOTE

Yield: 10 portions

Cooking Method: Grill

Ingredients	Amounts - US	Volume	Metric
For the Pork			
Pork tenderloin, trimmed	3 lbs.	4 each	1.4 kilograms
Balsamic vinegar	1 fl. oz.	2 Tbl.	30 ml
Extra virgin olive oil	2 fl. oz.	¼ cup	60 ml
Garlic clove, medium, crushed	1 oz.	8 each	28 grams
Parsley, Italian, leaves	¼ oz.	¼ cup	4 grams
Tarragon, sprigs	¼ oz.	4 sprigs	4 grams
Black pepper, course ground		as needed	
Salt, kosher		as needed	

(Continues on next page)

Ingredients	Amounts - US	Volume	Metric
For the Caramelized Apple Compote			
Extra virgin olive oil	1 ½ fl. oz.	3 Tbl.	45 ml
Honeycrisp apples, small dice	8 ¾ oz.	2 each	250 grams
Granny Smith apples, small dice	8 ¾ oz.	2 each	250 grams
Butter, unsalted, cubed	1 ½ oz.	3 Tbl.	42 grams
Brown sugar, light	¾ oz.	2 Tbl.	20 grams
Cinnamon, ground		¼ tsp.	
Nutmeg, fresh ground		⅛ tsp.	
Allspice, ground		pinch	
Ginger, ground		pinch	
Tarragon, chopped		1 ½ tsp.	
Salt, kosher		to taste	
Black pepper, fresh ground		to taste	
Cayenne pepper		small pinch	

Caramelized Apple Compote

1. Preheat a sauté pan over medium high heat.
2. Add the oil and then the apples, sauté until the apples begin to caramelize. Work in batches if necessary as not to overcrowd the pan and drop the heat.
3. Add the butter and allow it to melt; toss to mix evenly.
4. Add the remaining ingredients and mix well to thoroughly combine.
5. Taste and adjust the seasoning. The apples should be tender, maintain their shape, and be well-caramelized.
6. Remove from the heat and reserve under refrigeration until needed.

Pork

1. Season the pork with salt and black pepper.
2. Combine the balsamic vinegar, extra virgin olive oil, garlic, parsley, and tarragon and mix well to combine.
3. Place the pork in a non-reactive container (or zip-lock bag) and coat evenly with the marinade. Marinate under refrigeration for 4 hours.
4. Preheat a charbroiler/grill.
5. Grill the pork evenly on all sides to an internal temperature of 140 F (60 C) degrees. Allow to rest 10 minutes on a rack before slicing thinly on a bias.
6. Serve with the apple compote.

WINE SELECTED with Grilled Pork Tenderloin with Caramelized Apple Compote

Wine: Domaine Wachau Grüner Veltliner ($15)
Origin: Wachau, Austria

Taste and Texture Comparisons

Dish: Grilled/Smoky, Maillard Reaction, Sweet, Slightly Tart, Bold

Wine: Fairly Delicate, White Nectarines, White Pepper Spice, Crisp

Wachau has a few styles of Grüner Veltliner. This is a Federspiel-style wine (meaning not as light-bodied as a Steinfeder and not as rich or ripe as a Smaragd). Grüner is known for citrus (particularly grapefruit) and white pepper aromas/flavors.

Why This Is a Good Pairing

- ***Contrasting Intensity*** – The dish is quite flavorful while the wine is delicate. However, given the other complementing and contrasting reactions, this pairing works.
- ***Complementing*** – The spice component in the dish bridges with the white pepper spice element in the wine. Additionally, the white nectarine flavor in the wine connects with the sweetness of the balsamic vinegar and apples.
- ***Contrasting*** – The fresh, crisp acidity in the wine makes the apple flavors pop. Additionally, the fruit in the wine and with the apples contrasts with the Maillard reaction and grilled smokiness, creating a *complexing* reaction whereby the flavors of both the dish and the wine come through.

Wines That Didn't Work

Alsatian Gewürztraminer – The alcohol (14%+ abv) stands out too much and there is an unpleasant compounding of spice. Additionally, the floral perfumed aromas clash with this dish, making it taste too perfumy, or like soap.

Savennières – The classical bruised apple flavors of the wine compound with the apples in this dish and overpower the flavor of the pork. All you get is apples. (But, if you really like apples, this is the pairing for you.)

Alternative: A lightly oaked New Zealand Chardonnay creates a nice bridge between the apple flavor in the wine and apples in the dish. New Zealand has that New World ripeness while retaining an Old World crisp acidity. A similar complementing between the Maillard reaction in grilling and the slight toastiness of the oak occurs that creates a long finish.

SUMMARY	Domaine Wachau Grüner Veltliner	New Zealand Chardonnay	Alsatian Gewürztraminer	Savennières
Matching		+		+
Complementing	+	+		
Contrasting	+	+		
Compounding			(–)	(–)
Complexing	+			
Cleansing				
Covering				(–)
Clashing			(–)	

CHICKEN, DUCK, AND PORK PAIRING SUMMARY AND CONCLUSIONS

Chicken Breast

Dish	Method	Wine
Chicken Salad	Poach	Tavel Rosé, Domaine Pélaquié
Hot Smoked Chicken Breast	Brine–Smoke/Roast	Pinot Noir, Yabby Lake
Stuffed Chicken Breast	Stuff/Roast	Chardonnay, Gloria Ferrer

- ***Main ingredient tendencies:*** Chicken breast is a versatile protein, fairly mild in flavor, and medium-bodied. This allows for a variety of techniques and ingredients, which yield a wide range of wine pairings.
- ***Specific techniques that changed the pairing:*** Poaching keeps the chicken's delicate flavors and would be overpowered by a red wine. Smoking contrasts with the red berry fruit and connects with the oak tones in the Pinot Noir. Roasting provides for more intense flavor, which allows for more full bodied whites and a low-tannin red.
- ***Specific ingredients that changed the pairing:*** The salad's mayonnaise increases the richness and allows for a rosé to pair, while the cranberries create a bridge to the red berry notes in the Tavel. The richness of the mustard and the sauce with the smoked chicken breast yields a pairing with a red wine with some acid. Stuffing with cheese allows for a richer Chardonnay with buttery tones.

Chicken Legs

Dish	Method	Wine
Buttermilk Fried Chicken	Pan-Fry	Chardonnay, Chablis Christian Moreau
Chicken Cacciatore	Braise	Gewürztraminer, Willm
Tandoori Chicken	Roast	Shiraz, Brokenwood

- ***Main ingredient tendencies:*** Chicken legs have a bit more richness to them than chicken breast, which suggests a slightly richer pairing range.
- ***Specific techniques that changed the pairing:*** Pan-Frying yields a richness that allows a high-acid wine to provide cleansing without stripping the flavor of the dish. Roasting adds more intense flavor and the caramelization matches with a medium-plus-bodied Shiraz.
- ***Specific ingredients that changed the pairing:*** The richness in the Buttermilk Fried Chicken contrasts well with high acid in the Chablis. The low acidity of the Gewürztraminer contrasts well with the acid from the tomatoes in the Cacciatore. Lastly, the spice in the Tandoori complements the spice in the Shiraz (provided that the alcohol is moderate).

Duck

Dish	Method	Wine
Sous Vide Duck Breast	Sous Vide	Grenache, Guigal Côtes du Rhône Rouge
Smoked Duck Salad	Smoke	Riesling Kabinett, Dr. Loosen Erdener
Sautéed Duck Breast	Sauté	Pinotage, Wildekrans, Walker Bay

- ***Main ingredient tendencies:*** In comparison to chicken breast, duck breast has dark flesh that is very rich, with a thick layer of fat. This extends the range of wine pairings to the fuller end of the spectrum than chicken in general. Duck's more intense flavor contrasts well with fruit in sauces and wines, particularly citrus and red fruit.

- ***Specific techniques that changed the pairing:*** Smoking creates flavors that complement the mineral terroir notes in German Riesling.

- ***Specific ingredients that changed the pairing:*** The cardamom and thyme in the duck jus complemented the earthy and herbal notes in the Côtes du Rhône Rouge. The smoked duck's orange vinaigrette complemented the citrus notes in the Riesling, and the sun-dried cherry sauce with the sautéed duck breast complemented the rich red berry flavors of the Pinotage.

Pork

Dish	Method	Wine
Sous Vide Pork Tenderloin	Sous Vide	Chenin Blanc, Ken Forrester
Pork Schnitzel	Pan-Fry	Pinot Noir, Craggy Range
Grilled Pork Tenderloin	Grill	Grüner Veltliner, Domaine Wachau

- ***Main ingredient tendencies:*** Pork tenderloin is low in fat, quite tender, and mild in flavor. This allows for a wine pairing range of light whites to medium-bodied fruity reds.

- ***Specific techniques that changed the pairing:*** Sous Vide showcases the delicate flavor of the pork tenderloin and allows for a light white to pair well. Pan-Frying adds a richness that the Pinot Noir's high acid cleanses without stripping flavor. Grilling yields notes that complement the mineral terroir notes in the Grüner Veltliner.

- ***Specific ingredients that changed the pairing:*** The spicy pineapple salsa creates a bridge to the more tropical fruits in the delicate-bodied South African Chenin Blanc. The schnitzel's toasty bread crumbs contrast with the red berry fruit of the Pinot Noir, making the flavor of the pork and wine pop. The spice of the apple compote with the grilled pork tenderloin connects with the white pepper spice element in the Grüner Veltliner.

7
Beef, Lamb, and Venison

Beef, lamb, and venison are rich proteins with full flavor. They typically lend themselves well to robust cooking techniques: sauté, grill, stir-fry, braise, and stew. Yet they do offer some variety. Typically, it is red wines that pair best with these dishes.

The food and wine pairing cliché of "red wine with red meat" holds true for many of the dishes in this chapter; however, white wine has a strong presence in pairings with 6 of the 15 dishes. This dramatic shift in pairings is due to the changes in cooking techniques and/or accompanying ingredients.

Dish	Wine
Beef Tenderloin	
Beef Tartare	Au Bon Climat Chardonnay, Santa Barbara, California USA ($20)
Sautéed Tournedos of Beef with Cognac Peppercorn Sauce	Agua de Piedra Gran Reserva Malbec, Mendoza, Argentina ($12)
Gorgonzola Dolcelatte-Topped Beef Tournedos	Château La Bienfaisance St. Emilion, Bordeaux, France ($35)
Beef Flank Steak	
Beef and Broccoli Sitr-Fry	Ponzi Pinot Gris Willamette Valley, Oregon, USA ($18)
Grilled Flank Steak with Chimichurri Sauce	Craggy Range Sauvignon Blanc, Martinborough, New Zealand ($21)
Grilled Flank Steak Sandwich with Manchego Cheese, Grilled Peppers, Oven-Dried Tomatoes, and Pimenton Mayonnaise	Root 1 Carmenère Colchagua, Chile ($10)
Beef Shank	
BBQ Pulled Beef	Dr. Konstantin Frank Semi-Dry Riesling, New York, USA ($12)
Beef Bourguignon	Bodega Chacra Barda Pinot Noir, Patagonia, Chile ($27)
Thai Beef with Massaman Curry	Michele Chiarlo Moscato d'Asti Nivole, Piedmont, Italy (half bottle) ($14)
Lamb	
Rosemary Roasted Rack of Lamb with Lamb Jus	Guigal Côtes du Rhône Blanc, Rhône, France ($13)
Grilled Lamb Chops with Mint Emulsion	Cantravelli Taurasi Riserva, Campania, Italy ($24)
Chinese Five Spice Sautéed Lamb Chops	Atteca Old Vines, Calatayud, Spain ($16)
Venison	
Venison Burgers	Bodegas Alejandro Fernandez Tinto Pesquera, Ribera del Duero, Spain ($30)
Roasted Venison with Sauce Grand Veneur	Motes Alpha Cabernet Sauvignon, Chile ($20)
Venison Chili	Bogle Petite Sirah, California, USA ($10)

Below is a temperature chart outlining doneness based on the desired internal temperature. Remember that most cuts will continue to cook after they have been removed from the heat source, the larger the cuts the more heat they will hold and *carry over*.

Temperature Doneness Chart

Blue	Rare	Medium Rare	Medium	Medium Well	Well
95–100 F (35–37 C)	115–120 F (46–48 C)	125–130 F (51–54 C)	135–140 F (57–60 C)	145–150 F (62–65 C)	155–160 F (68–71 C)

Beef Tartare

Cooking red meats to a desired temperature can be tricky. There are two common methods to assess doneness. The first method is to insert an instant-read meat thermometer into the middle of the thickest part of the meat (taking care not to touch the thermometer probe to a bone). The second method is by touch. Success using the later method will be determined by repetition and experience.

BEEF TENDERLOIN

Tenderloin is known as one of the most tender and prized cuts of beef, thus the most expensive. It is classically used for Chateaubriand, Filet Mignon, Medallions, and Beef Wellington.

Beef Tartare is a classic recipe that calls for minced beef tenderloin (traditionally cut from the head of the tenderloin) mixed with raw egg yolks. Because these proteins are not cooked it is important that they are as fresh as possible and always handled with proper sanitation in mind.

BEEF TARTARE

Yield: 10 portions

Cooking Method: Raw

Ingredients	Amounts - US	Volume	Metric
Beef tenderloin, Prime, minced	16 oz.		454 grams
Egg yolk, large	1 oz.	2 each	28 grams
Onion, sweet, minced	1 ½ oz.	¼ cup	42 grams
Dijon mustard	½ oz.	1 Tbl.	14 grams
Capers, salt packed, soaked, chopped	1 ½ oz.	¼ cup	42 grams
Parsley, chopped	¼ oz.	1 ½ Tbl.	4 grams
Worcestershire sauce		1 tsp.	
Extra virgin olive oil		1 tsp.	
Tabasco sauce		⅛ tsp.	
Salt, sea		to taste	
Black pepper, fresh ground		to taste	
Baguette, sliced ⅛"		60 each	
Extra virgin olive oil		as needed	

Beef Tartare

1. Brush both sides of the baguette slices (crostini) with extra virgin olive oil and bake at 350 F (175 C) degrees convection for 10–12 minutes until golden brown.
2. Mince the beef as close to serving as possible; ensure that your cutting board and knife have been sanitized.
3. Combine the beef, egg yolks, onions, mustard, capers, parsley, Worcestershire sauce, extra virgin olive oil, Tabasco, salt, and pepper; mix well with a rubber spatula to evenly combine. Taste and adjust the seasoning.
4. Form the tartare into 2-oz. round patties; serve with the toasted baguette.

Today there are health concerns regarding the consumption of raw beef and eggs. If you prefer to reduce the threat of bacteria, the beef can be seared and then well chilled. In addition, a pasteurized egg product can be substituted for the yolks.

WINE SELECTED with Beef Tartare

Wine: Au Bon Climat Chardonnay ($20)
Origin: Santa Barbara County, California, USA

Taste and Texture Comparisons

Dish: Soft Texture, Slight Sweet, Slight Salt and Umami
Wine: Soft Texture, Fruity Apple, Hint of Butter, Modest Acidity, Moderate Alcohol

This white wine is fermented and aged in French oak, a small percentage of which is new oak. This producer creates a lightly oaked style in comparison to some other California Chardonnays.

Why This Is a Good Pairing

- ***Matching Textures*** – Beef Tartare and Chardonnay have a soft texture. Chardonnay, particularly from California, is especially soft given its more modest acidity than other grape varieties and in the cooler climates in France. Additionally, the dish and the wine match in intensity.
- ***Complementing*** – The crostini's flavor creates a bridge to the light buttery and slightly toasty oak flavors in the Chardonnay.
- ***Contrasting*** – The beef flavor contrasts with the fruitiness of the apples in the wine. This reaction augments the flavors of both.
- ***Dance*** – The richness of the beef elongates the flavors on your palate. The beef, sweetness of the onion, sweet impression of the fruit of the wine, and the hint of butter in the wine are lovely!

Wines That Didn't Work

Chablis – Chablis is a classic region for Chardonnay (and, some argue, its birthplace). Chablis is generally high in acidity, much higher than the California versions, and it is unoaked. That high acidity cleanses the tongue of the richness of the beef and pretty much the entire flavor of the dish.

St. Emilion – In St. Emilion, Merlot has burly muscles and flexes them. It overpowers the Beef Tartare and covers the flavors. It puts the dish in a chokehold and doesn't let go, totally killing the pairing.

Alternative: Beaujolais Nouveau—This wine works very much for the same reasons the Chardonnay does. Both have a soft texture and the berry notes of the wine are augmented by the beef. Even if you are not a fan of Beaujolais Nouveau, you may be surprised by how good the pairing is with Beef Tartare.

SUMMARY	Au Bon Climat Chardonnay	Dubeouf Beaujolais Nouveau	Chablis	St. Emilion
Matching	+	+		
Complementing	+	+		
Contrasting	+	+		
Compounding				
Complexing				
Cleansing			(–)	
Covering				(–)
Clashing				

Sautéed Tournedos of Beef with Cognac Peppercorn Sauce

SAUTÉED TOURNEDOS OF BEEF WITH COGNAC PEPPERCORN SAUCE

Yield: 10 portions

Cooking Method: Sauté

Ingredients	Amounts - US	Volume	Metric
For the Beef Tournedos			
Beef tournedos, prime, 5 oz., 142 grams		10 each	
Salt, kosher		to taste	
Black pepper, fresh ground		to taste	
Olive oil, pure	3 fl. oz.	⅓ cup	90 ml
For the Cognac Peppercorn Sauce			
Shallots, minced	½ oz.	2 Tbl.	14 grams
Cognac	3 fl. oz.	⅓ cup	90 ml
Veal stock reduction/demi-glace	20 fl. oz.	2 ½ cups	620 ml
Heavy cream	8 fl. oz.	1 cup	240 ml
Black peppercorns, cracked	½ oz.	1 ½ Tbl.	12 grams
Parsley, Italian, chopped		1 ½ tsp.	
Salt, kosher		to taste	
Lemon juice, fresh		½ tsp.	
Butter, unsalted, cubed	1 ½ oz.	3 Tbl.	42 grams

Beef Tournedos

The addition of a small amount of acid, such as lemon juice or vinegar, to a sauce just prior to serving brightens the flavor. The veal reduction or demi-glace should be rich and bold in flavor and have a light nappe consistency.

1. Season the tournedos on both sides with salt and pepper.
2. Preheat a sauté pan over medium-high heat.
3. Add the oil and then the tournedos; sauté until cooked halfway and the surface has browned evenly (approximately 3 minutes). Adjust the cook time according to desired doneness and work in batches so that you don't overcrowd the pan.
4. Turn the tournedos and continue cooking until the desired temperature is reached. Remove to a rack and allow to rest.
5. Reduce the heat to low, add the shallots, and sauté until tender with little color.
6. Deglaze with the cognac and capture the fond with a wooden spoon; reduce by two-thirds.
7. Add the veal reduction or demi-glace and simmer gently for 2 minutes.
8. Add the heavy cream and reduce until a nappe consistency.
9. Add the peppercorns and parsley and season to taste.
10. Add the lemon juice, and mount with butter.
11. Plate the tournedos and sauce; serve immediately.

WINE SELECTED with Sautéed Tournedos of Beef with Cognac Peppercorn Sauce

Wine: Agua de Piedra Gran Reserva Malbec ($12)

Origin: Mendoza, Argentina

Taste and Texture Comparisons

Dish: Rich, Umami, Savory, Earthy, Spice

Wine: Rich, Dark, Sweet Obvious Black and Blue Fruit, Plush Texture

Malbec shows dark black and blue fruits in the wine. In this way it is similar to Merlot. This wine is aged for nine months in American oak, which yields a sweet and almost toasted coconut and tobacco flavor.

Why This Is a Good Pairing

- ***Matching Intensity*** – The wine and the dish match in terms of the intensity of the flavors.
- ***Complementing*** – Tobacco/spice notes from the oak in the wine creates a bridge with the black pepper and earthy notes in the dish, augmenting both in a way that focuses on layers of flavors (creating a *complexing* reaction).
- ***Contrasting*** – Savory notes of the beef contrast with the dark fruit, which makes the flavors of the fruit stand out even more. Although a dry wine, the sweet impression of the dark blueberry and blackberry fruit contrasts with the Maillard reaction on the beef, making the caramelized flavors come out more.

Wines That Didn't Work

Bordeaux – Originally we had high hopes for a Bordeaux, so we sampled a left-bank Bordeaux, predominantly made with Cabernet Sauvignon (from Pauillac) and a right-bank Bordeaux predominantly made with Merlot (St. Emilion). Both wines are fairly youthful vintages of very good quality Bordeaux (2004/2005), which means they are quite powerful in their fruit and tannins. However, both of these wines overpower the dish, covering its flavors.

Alternative: Duoro Red—We tested a red wine from the Duoro Valley in Portugal that yielded similar reactions, complementing and contrasting like the Malbec. Touriga Nacional is the wine's main grape, which has a hint of licorice spice. The spice elements slightly compound (in a good way) with the spice from the peppercorns. It makes for a more "spicy" kick from your pairing if that's what you are looking for.

SUMMARY	Agua de Piedra Gran Reserva Malbec	Quinta do Quatro Ventos Duoro	Bordeaux Pauillac	Bordeaux St. Emilion
Matching	+	+		
Complementing	+	+		
Contrasting	+	+		
Compounding		+		
Complexing	+	+		
Cleansing				
Covering			(–)	(–)
Clashing				

Gorgonzola Dolcelatte-Topped Beef Tournedos

GORGONZOLA DOLCELATTE-TOPPED BEEF TOURNEDOS

Yield: 10 portions

Cooking Method: Grill

Ingredients	Amounts - US	Volume	Metric
For the Beef Tournedos			
Beef tournedos, prime, 5 oz., 142 grams		10 each	
Olive oil, pure	2 fl. oz.	¼ cup	60 ml
Salt, kosher		as needed	
Black pepper, fresh ground		as needed	
For the Gorgonzola Dolcelatte Topping			
Beurre noisette	1 fl. oz.	2 Tbl.	30 ml
Gorgonzola Dolcelatte, 1-oz. pieces	10 oz.	⅞ cup	284 grams
Panko bread crumbs, toasted	¼ oz.	2 Tbl.	6 grams
Parsley, Italian, chopped		1 Tbl.	
Thyme, fresh leaves, chopped		1 ½ tsp.	

Beef Tournedos and Gorgonzola Dolcelatte Topping

1. Preheat a charbroiler/grill.
2. Season the tournedos with salt and pepper on both sides, coat lightly with oil.
3. Lightly oil the surface of the grill with an appropriate towel, and then place the tournedos on the grill.
4. Cook for 2 minutes and then turn the tournedos 90 degrees to achieve cross-hatch marks and continue cooking for another 2 minutes. Adjust the cook time according to desired doneness.
5. Turn over the tournedos and repeat the above process until slightly below the desired temperature.
6. Brush the tournedos with beurre noisette and then top with the blue cheese. Continue cooking until the cheese has melted (note that this cheese melts very quickly), and the desired doneness is reached.
7. Garnish with the thyme, parsley, and Panko bread crumbs.

WINE SELECTED with Gorgonzola Dolcelatte-Topped Beef Tournedos

Wine: Château La Bienfaisance St. Emilion ($35)
Origin: St. Emilion, Bordeaux, France

Taste and Texture Comparisons

Dish: Bold, Rich, Grilled/Smoky, Umami, Sweet
Wine: Bold, Dark Fruit, Sweet Spice, Gripping Tannins, Moderate Alcohol

Bordeaux is where some dense and intense Merlots originate. This wine is 85% Merlot and 15% Cabernet Franc and aged for 15 months in French oak barrels (30% new oak).

Why This Is a Good Pairing

- ***Matching Intensity*** – Bold meets bold! The wine and the dish are intense, especially with the blue cheese.
- ***Mix and Match Textures*** – The wine has a rich chocolaty texture that has gripping tannins that match the rich texture of the grilled medallions, yet slightly contrast with the creamy blue cheese for a textural *complexing* effect.
- ***Contrasting*** – Because the flavors are so different, the bold black fruit in the wine contrasts with the savory meaty flavors and the smoky character from grilling. This makes the fruit stand out more.
- ***Complementing*** – Toasty and spicy vanilla notes in the wine (from the new French oak) create a bridge with the Maillard reaction of the beef.
- ***Complexing*** – The tannin of the wine is softened by the flavors of the grilled beef and the beurre noisette, making the wine more supple. The acidity in the wine cuts through the intense richness of the blue cheese, which enhances the flavors of both the meat and the cheese, creating a *complexing* effect.

Wines That Didn't Work

Dry Whites – We tried many dry white wines with the dish and they were just swallowed up by the dish's intensity. It even overpowers bold whites, such as heavily oaked California Chardonnay.

Argentinean Malbec – The dish's savory notes does contrast with the blackberry fruit of the wine. However, it makes the fruit stand out so much that it makes the dish taste as though it has blackberry jam poured on top of it.

Alternative: Sauternes—Interestingly, Sauternes is lovely with this dish and for some similar reasons as the St. Emilion. Sauternes is a sweet white wine so its fruit character is different; however, it contrasts and complements the intensity of the dish just as well. It may be odd to think of drinking a sweet wine during dinner, but it is something to consider when you want to make a bold statement.

SUMMARY	Chateau La Bienfaisance St. Emilion	Sauternes	Dry Whites	Argentinean Malbec
Matching	+	+		
Complementing	+	+		
Contrasting	+	+		(–)
Compounding				(–)
Complexing	+			
Cleansing	+			
Covering			(–)	
Clashing				

Beef and Broccoli Stir-Fry

BEEF FLANK STEAK

Flank steak is a very popular cut of beef that is seen in many cuisines around the globe. It is characterized by the long prominent grain that runs the length of the steak and is quite rich in flavor. It is important to slice against the grain for tenderness.

BEEF AND BROCCOLI STIR-FRY

Yield: 10 portions

Cooking Method: Stir-Fry

Ingredients	Amounts - US	Volume	Metric
Beef flank steak, trimmed	3 lbs.	2 each	1.4 kilograms
Broccoli, florets	2 lbs.		0.9 kilogram
Peanut oil	4 fl. oz.	½ cup	120 ml.
Ginger, chopped	¾ oz.	3 Tbl.	22 grams
Garlic, chopped	⅝ oz.	1 ½ Tbl.	16 grams
Marinade			
Soy sauce	3 fl. oz.	⅓ cup	90 ml
Rice wine or sherry	3 fl. oz.	⅓ cup	90 ml
Oyster sauce	2 fl. oz.	¼ cup	60 ml
Sesame oil	1 fl. oz.	2 Tbl.	30 ml
Cornstarch	¾ oz.	3 Tbl.	20 grams
Sauce			
Soy sauce	4 fl. oz.	½ cup	120 ml
Soy sauce, dark	1 fl. oz.	2 Tbl.	30 ml
Hoisin sauce	10 fl. oz.	1 ¼ cups	300 ml
Chicken stock	8 fl. oz.	1 cup	240 ml
Sesame oil		2 tsp.	
Cornstarch	⅝ oz.	2 ½ Tbl.	16 grams
Garnish			
Scallions, bias sliced thin	¾ oz.	3 Tbl.	22 grams

Stir-Fry

Grain

1. Cut the flank lengthwise, with the grain, into strips 1-inch wide; then cut 1-inch pieces on a slight bias against the grain.
2. Combine the marinade ingredients and whisk well to evenly incorporate. Marinate the flank in a non-reactive container (or Ziplock bag) for 1 hour and then drain well.
3. Combine the sauce ingredients and whisk well to evenly combine.
4. Blanch or steam the broccoli for 2 minutes, until it turns bright green and softens slightly. Shock immediately in ice water and *drain very well.*
5. Preheat a wok over high heat for 45 seconds.
6. Working in batches, depending on the size of your wok, add the oil and spread to coat the sides of the wok with the spatula.
7. Add the beef and spread evenly; allow to brown without stirring.
8. Add the ginger and garlic and stir-fry until the garlic turns light golden brown and the other side begins to color, approximately 45 seconds.
9. Add the broccoli and stir-fry for 45 seconds to heat.
10. Whisk the sauce to combine evenly. Make a well in the center of the wok with the spatula and add the sauce. Stir with the spatula until the sauce comes to a simmer and thickens. Not all of the sauce may be needed.
11. Mix all of the ingredients with the spatula and the wok ladle to coat evenly.
12. Plate immediately and garnish with scallions.

Depending on the size of the wok, you will need to work in batches so you don't overcrowd the pan and drop the heat. A large heavy-bottomed pan can be substituted for a wok if necessary.

WINE SELECTED with Beef and Broccoli Stir-Fry

Wine: Ponzi Pinot Gris, Willamette Valley ($18)
Origin: Willamette Valley, Oregon, USA

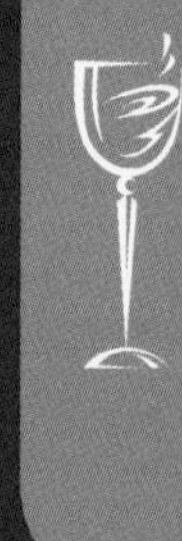

This is an unoaked, medium-bodied, medium-acid white wine with fresh, floral, and white peach notes. In general, Oregon Pinot Gris sits somewhere in between an Italian Pinot Grigio and an Alsace Pinot Gris in terms of flavor and style.

Taste and Texture Comparisons

Dish: Rich, Umami, Vegetal, Sweet
Wine: Fruity, Floral, Hint of Spice, Moderate Body, Acidity, and Alcohol

Why This Is a Good Pairing

- ***Complementing*** – The ginger in the dish complements and creates a bridge to the Pinot Gris's hint of spice.
- ***Contrasting*** – The beef in the dish augments the wine's fruit, making the fruit seem sweet even though it is a dry wine. This impression of sweetness does a nice dance with the umami in the soy/beef and the vegetal character of the broccoli.
- ***Cleansing*** – The acidity of the wine creates a slight cleansing sensation that is refreshing and does not strip the flavor of the dish.

Wines That Didn't Work

Oaked California Chardonnay – The flavors of the wine clash with the dish. The dish exaggerates the fruit in the wine but brings out an orange-like note, making the dish taste like "orange beef."

Alsatian Gewürztraminer – The dish compounds the spice in the wine. The wine's intense flavor also covers up the dish. Same is true for Alsatian Pinot Gris.

Barolo – Although the contrast of the beef makes the wine's fruit stand out, the wine overpowers the dish. Additionally, the salt in the dish clashes with the tannins in the wine, making the wine taste bitter.

SUMMARY	Ponzi Pinot Gris	Oaked California Chardonnay	Alsatian Gewürztraminer	Barolo
Matching				
Complementing	+			
Contrasting	+			+
Compounding			(–)	
Complexing				
Cleansing	+			
Covering			(–)	(–)
Clashing		(–)		(–)

Grilled Flank Steak with Chimichurri Sauce

GRILLED FLANK STEAK WITH CHIMICHURRI SAUCE

Yield: 10 portions

Cooking Method: Grill

Grilled beef and chimichurri sauce are specialties of Argentina. Typically the meats are grilled over high heat and well charred on the exterior. The sauce should have a bright fresh and slightly spicy flavor.

Ingredients	Amounts - US	Volume	Metric
For the Flank Steak			
Beef flank steak, trimmed	3 lbs.	2 each	1.4 kilograms
Salt, kosher		as needed	
Black pepper, fresh ground		as needed	
Olive oil, pure		as needed	
For the Chimichurri Sauce			
Red wine vinegar	3 fl. oz.	⅓ cup	90 ml
Garlic cloves, crushed	1 oz.	8 each	28 grams
Serrano chili, rough chopped	½ oz.	1 ½ Tbl.	14 grams
Extra virgin olive oil	6 fl. oz.	¾ cup	180 ml
Parsley, Italian, rough chopped	¾ oz.	1 cup	22 grams
Oregano, rough chopped	⅜ oz.	¼ cup	12 grams
Salt, kosher		1 ½ tsp.	
Black pepper, fresh ground		¾ tsp.	

Chimichurri Sauce

1. Combine the vinegar, garlic, and serrano chili in a blender and process until smooth. Do not over process/heat.
2. Add the oil, parsley, oregano, salt, and pepper and blend lightly to combine. The sauce should have a medium texture and not be a completely smooth puree.
3. Taste and adjust the seasoning, refrigerate until needed. This sauce is best made and used the same day; after 24 hours the vinegar will begin to turn the herbs brownish green.

Flank Steak

1. Preheat a charbroiler/grill.
2. Season the flanks on both sides and lightly coat with oil. Place the flank steaks on the grill and cook for approximately 4 minutes. Then rotate 90 degrees to achieve crosshatch marks and continue cooking for another 4 minutes. Adjust the cook time for thickness and desired doneness.
3. Turn over the flanks and repeat the above process until they are cooked to your desired doneness.
4. Remove from the grill and place on a rack to rest. Allow the steaks to rest for 10 minutes before carving. Slice the flank steak thinly against the grain.
5. Plate the sliced flank steak and sauce with the chimichurri.

WINE SELECTED with Grilled Flank Steak with Chimichurri Sauce

Wine: Craggy Range Sauvignon Blanc ($21)
Origin: Martinborough, North Island, New Zealand

Taste and Texture Comparisons

Dish: Aromatic, Acidic/Racy, Herbal, Fresh/Bright, Spice, Rich, Umami

Wine: Aromatic, Fruity, Bright/Crisp, Delicate Texture

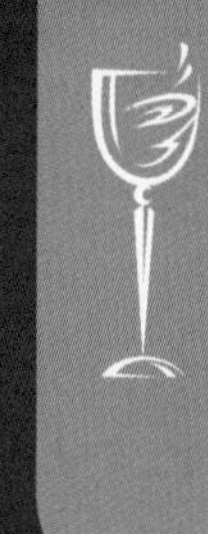

Sauvignon Blanc in New Zealand is the New World classic for this grape. In general, it is a very fresh, unoaked white with pungent aromas of citrus and passion fruit with grassy notes and marked crisp acidity.

Why This Is a Good Pairing

- ***Matching*** – The dish and the wine match in terms of intensity of flavor.
- ***Complementing*** – The acidity from the vinegar in the Chimichurri Sauce creates a bridge and complements the citrus notes in the wine.
- ***Contrasting*** – The tropical notes in the wine contrast with the garlic and spice in the dish, making both stand out.
- ***Cleansing*** – The high acid of the Chimichurri Sauce makes the dish very bright and refreshing and softens some of the acidity in the wine.

Wines That Didn't Work

Oregon Pinot Gris – The wine softens the power of the Chimichurri, but the sauce wins and the wine disappears.

Chilean Carmenère – The Maillard reaction connects with the grilled meat flavors (this grape is known for having a "meaty" aroma). However, the alcohol in the wine (14.5%+ abv) stands out like a sore thumb and clashes with the serrano chili as well as with the vinegar.

Alternative: Rioja Reserva—The weight of the wine and the dish match. The contrast between the beef and the wine makes the fruit in the wine pop. The Maillard reaction of the beef connects with some of the oak and spice tones of the wine.

SUMMARY	Craggy Range Sauvignon Blanc	Rioja Reserva	Oregon Pinot Gris	Chilean Carmenère
Matching	+	+		
Complementing	+	+		+
Contrasting	+	+		
Compounding				
Complexing				
Cleansing	+			
Covering			(–)	
Clashing				(–)

Grilled Flank Steak Sandwich with Manchego Cheese, Grilled Peppers, Oven-Dried Tomatoes, and Pimenton Mayonnaise

GRILLED FLANK STEAK SANDWICH WITH MANCHEGO CHEESE, GRILLED PEPPERS, OVEN-DRIED TOMATOES, AND PIMENTON MAYONNAISE

Yield: 10 portions

Cooking Method: Grill

Ingredients	Amounts - US	Volume	Metric
Beef flank steak, trimmed	3 lbs.	2 each	1.1 kilograms
For the Marinade			
Olive oil, pure	1 ½ fl. oz.	3 Tbl.	45 ml
Sherry vinegar	1 fl. oz.	2 Tbl.	30 ml
Garlic clove, crushed, medium	⅝ oz.	5 each	16 grams
Chili powder		1 tsp.	
Salt, kosher		as needed	
Black pepper, fresh ground		as needed	
Rosemary, sprigs		2 each	
For the Pimenton Mayonnaise			
Mayonnaise	5 ½ oz.	¾ cup	142 grams
Cumin, toasted		1 tsp.	
Lime juice, fresh		1 tsp.	
Pimenton		½ tsp.	
Black pepper, fresh ground		⅛ tsp.	
For the Italian Frying Peppers			
Italian frying peppers	8 oz.	1 cup	288 grams
Extra virgin olive oil		as needed	
For the Oven-Dried Plum Tomatoes			
Plum tomatoes, cut in half		30 pieces	
Extra virgin olive oil	2 ½ fl. oz.	4 ½ Tbl.	75 ml
Garlic clove, chopped	½ oz.	1 ½ Tbl.	14 grams
Oregano, chopped	¼ oz.	1 ½ Tbl.	7 grams
Salt, kosher		¾ tsp.	
Black pepper, fresh ground		½ tsp.	
For the Sandwich Components			
Ciabatta rolls		10 each	
Extra virgin olive oil		as needed	
Manchego cheese	10 oz.	10 slices	284 grams
Oven-dried plum tomato, halves		30 each	
Italian frying peppers, grilled, julienne	8 oz.	1 cup	228 grams
Spinach, baby	3 ½ oz.	3 cups	98 grams
Pimenton mayonnaise		as needed	

(Continues on next page)

Pimenton Mayonnaise

Combine all ingredients and mix well until evenly blended. Taste and adjust the seasoning. Reserve under refrigeration.

Italian Frying Peppers

1. Split the peppers in half lengthwise. Remove the stem and seeds.
2. Lightly coat with extra virgin olive oil. Season with salt and pepper.
3. Grill on both sides until the peppers begin to soften.
4. Reserve under refrigeration until needed.

Oven-Dried Plum Tomatoes

1. Place the tomatoes in a stainless steel bowl and drizzle with oil; add the garlic, oregano, salt, and pepper evenly over the surface of the tomatoes.
2. Gently mix to coat evenly.
3. Place on a sheet pan lined with a rack and roast at 275 F (135 C) degrees convection for 4 hours (depending on the moisture content), until the tomatoes are shriveled on the ends, moist in the center, and approximately one-third of their original size.
4. Reserve under refrigeration until needed.

Flank Steak

1. Combine the marinade ingredients and mix well. Coat the flank steak evenly on both sides. Place in a non-reactive container (or a Ziplock bag) and marinate for 8 hours.
2. Preheat a charbroiler/grill.
3. Place the flank steak on the grill and cook for 4 minutes. Then turn 90 degrees to achieve crosshatch marks and continue cooking for another 4 minutes. Adjust the cook time for thickness and desired doneness.
4. Turn the flanks and repeat the above process until they are cooked to your desired doneness.
5. Remove from the grill and place on a rack to rest. Allow the steaks to rest for 10 minutes before carving. Slice the flank steak thinly against the grain. (See page 167.)

Sandwich

1. Cut the ciabatta rolls in half, widthwise, and lightly brush the cut surfaces with extra virgin olive oil and toast on a griddle or in a sauté pan until golden brown.
2. Place a slice of cheese on the top buns and place under a salamander or broiler to melt.
3. Spread 1 Tbl. of the Pimenton Mayonnaise on the bottom buns. Add the spinach, peppers, sliced flank steak, tomatoes, and the top bun. Cut the sandwiches in half on an angle.

WINE SELECTED with Grilled Flank Steak Sandwich with Manchego Cheese, Grilled Peppers, Oven-Dried Tomatoes, and Pimenton Mayonnaise

Wine: Root 1 Carmenère Colchagua ($10)
Origin: Colchagua, Chile

Taste and Texture Comparisons

Dish: Sweet, Grilled/Smoky, Rich,Umami
Wine: Red and Black Fruit, Savory/Meaty/Grilled Notes, Soft Texture, Moderate Acidity and Alcohol

Carmenère is the flagship grape of Chile and sometimes has a meaty flavor all its own that can create fabulous "bridges" to beef dishes.

Why This Is a Good Pairing

- ***Matching*** – The dish and the wine match in terms of intensity of flavor and weight.
- ***Complementing*** – The grilled notes on the meat connect with the grilled meat/savory character that Carmenère is sometimes known for. There's also a connection between the sweetness of the tomatoes and the grilled peppers and the sweetness of the fruit in the wine.
- ***Contrasting*** – The beef contrasts with the fruit in the wine, making the wine's fruit stand out as well.
- ***Complexing*** – This food and wine combination allows you to taste all of the delicious layers of flavors in the dish and the wine—smoke, sweet peppers, red/black fruit, Manchego cheese, the toasted bread, etc. The richness from the mayonnaise helps all of the flavors do a long, delicious dance on your palate.

Wines That Didn't Work

Oregon Pinot Gris – Initially, the beef focuses your palate on the fruit of the wine, but the wine is ultimately covered by the intensity of the dish.

New Zealand Sauvignon Blanc – The wine's powerful fruit flavors slightly cover the dish. Additionally, the intensely floral and herbaceous flavors clash and fight with the dish.

Grenache (Côtes du Rhône/Gigondas) – Contrast between the beef and the fruit makes the fruit stand out more. However, this is a one-way pairing. The dish makes the wine taste better, but the wine does nothing for the sandwich.

SUMMARY	Root 1 Colchagua Carmènere	Oregon Pinot Gris	New Zealand Sauvignon Blanc	Grenache (Côtes du Rhône/Gigondas)
Matching	+			
Complementing	+			
Contrasting	+	+		+
Compounding				
Complexing	+			
Cleansing				
Covering		(–)	(–)	
Clashing			(–)	

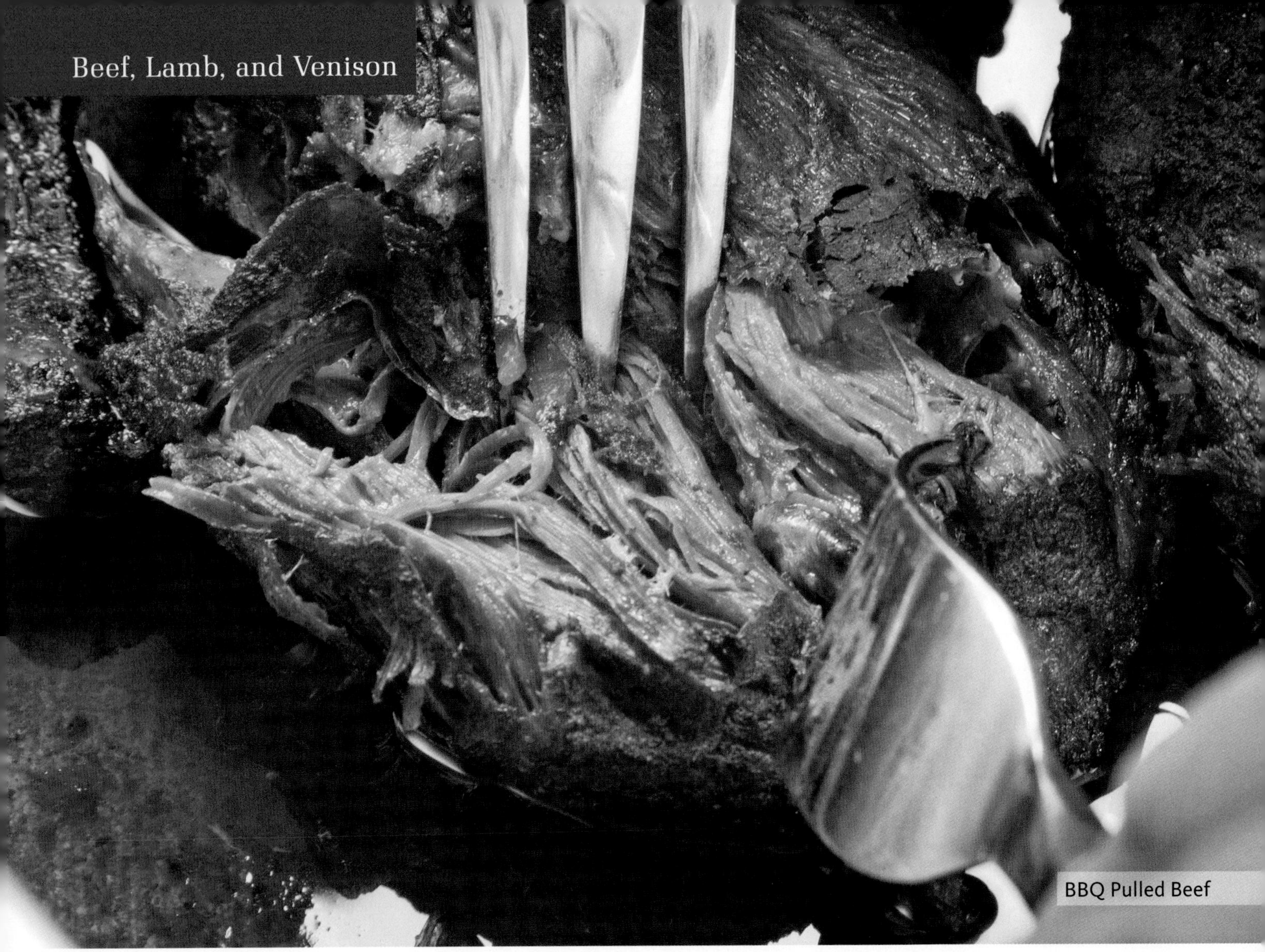

BBQ Pulled Beef

BEEF SHANK

Beef shank is a cut of meat that is relatively underutilized today. This very flavorful cut has a fair amount of connective tissue and requires a combination of moist and dry heat for cooking. As one of the more exercised cuts, it lends itself well to soups, stews, braising, and barbecue-style cooking.

You can substitute beef brisket or chuck if shank is unavailable. Adjust cook times accordingly for tenderness.

BBQ PULLED BEEF

Yield: 10 portions

Cooking Method: Roast

Ingredients	Amounts - US	Volume	Metric
Beef shank, boneless	4 lbs.		1.8 kilograms
Olive oil, pure		as needed	
Beef stock, hot		as needed	
For the Dry Rub Seasoning Mix	**Yield: 1 ¼ cups**		
Brown sugar	3 ⅜ oz.	½ cup	96 grams
Salt, kosher	1 ½ oz.	3 Tbl.	42 grams
Paprika	¾ oz.	3 Tbl.	24 grams
Cumin	¼ oz.	1 Tbl.	6 grams
Garlic powder	⅜ oz.	1 Tbl.	10 grams
Chili powder, dark	⅜ oz.	1 Tbl.	10 grams
Celery salt	¼ oz.	2 tsp.	8 grams
Onion powder		2 tsp.	
Oregano, dried		2 tsp.	
Pimenton		1 tsp.	
Allspice		½ tsp.	
Cayenne		¼ tsp.	
For the Mango BBQ Sauce	**Yield: 2 cups**		
Extra virgin olive oil	1 ½ fl. oz.	3 Tbl.	45 ml
Butter, unsalted	½ oz.	1 Tbl.	14 grams
Red onion, small dice	4 oz.	1 cup	114 grams
Red pepper, small dice	3 oz.	¾ cup	108 grams
Garlic, rough chopped	⅜ oz.	1 Tbl.	12 grams
Mango, ripe, chopped	8 oz.	1 ½ cups	214 grams
Chicken stock	6 fl. oz.	¾ cup	180 ml
Tomato puree	4 fl. oz.	½ cup	120 ml
Espresso	2 fl. oz.	¼ cup	60 ml
Brown sugar	1 ⅝ oz.	¼ cup	46 grams
Red wine vinegar	1 fl. oz.	2 Tbl.	30 ml
Chili powder, dark	¾ oz.	1 ½ Tbl.	21 grams
Worcestershire sauce	½ fl. oz.	1 Tbl.	15 ml
Chipotle pepper, chopped		½ tsp.	
Sage, ground		⅛ tsp.	
Salt, kosher		to taste	
Black pepper, fresh ground		to taste	

(Continues on next page)

Dry Rub Seasoning Mix

Combine all of the dry rub ingredients and mix well.

Mango BBQ Sauce

1. Preheat a saucepan over medium heat. Add the oil and butter, then the onion, and sauté until the onion begins to soften and color on the edges.
2. Add the red pepper and garlic. Continue cooking until the garlic is very aromatic and begins to color.
3. Add the remaining ingredients and bring to a simmer; cook gently for 20 minutes. Remove from the heat and puree the sauce in a blender until it is smooth. Taste and adjust the seasoning as well as the consistency with chicken stock.
4. Refrigerate until needed.

Beef Shank

1. Coat both sides of the beef shank with the dry rub seasoning mix and rub in well. Allow to marinate under refrigeration for 8 hours.
2. Preheat an oven to 275 F (135 C) degrees convection.
3. Preheat a sauté pan over medium heat. Add the oil and then the beef shank and sear on both sides until light brown.
4. Place the shanks in a roasting pan, or suitable pan for braising. Add enough hot beef stock to a depth of ½ inch in the bottom of the pan. Cover with foil and cook for 4–5 hours until fork tender. Gently turn the shank every hour. Add beef stock as necessary during cooking to keep the shank moist.
5. Remove from the oven and allow to cool slightly. Using two forks, gently pull the beef shank until it shreds evenly.
6. Serve with the Mango BBQ Sauce.

It is important to select fresh, ripe mangos for this sauce as the flavor and sweetness will have a big impact on the final product. When the sauce is initially puréed it will lighten in color, but it will darken slightly once chilled.

WINE SELECTED with BBQ Pulled Beef

Wine: Dr. Konstantin Frank Semi-Dry Riesling ($12)
Origin: Finger Lakes, New York, USA

Taste and Texture Comparisons

Dish: Sweet, Aromatic, Umami, Rich, Spice
Wine: Slightly Sweet, Aromatic, Light Body, High Acidity, Moderate Alcohol

If you like German-style Rieslings and a little New World fruitiness, Finger Lakes Rieslings are up your alley. They have less Old World minerality, but they are very "user-friendly" wines with some complexity.

Why This Is a Good Pairing

- ***Matching Sweetness and Complementing*** – The sweetness of the BBQ sauce matches and creates a bridge to the sweetness in the wine.
- ***Contrasting*** – The rich flavor of the beef and the spice contrasts with the fruit in the wine, which makes the fruit stand out a bit more (making it taste fruitier and a bit more tropical, like mango).
- ***Cleansing*** – The wine's high acidity prevents the sweetness from being cloying and makes the dish seem a bit lighter.

Wines That Didn't Work

New World Pinot Noir – We tried several New World Pinot Noirs. The dish's weight overpowers the wine and the dish's spice focuses your palate on the wine's alcohol.

Shiraz – Bold wine and bold dish, but because of the dish's spice the wine's alcohol (14.5%+ abv) stands out and strips some of the dish's flavor.

Washington Merlot – The spice contrasts with the intense oak flavor in the wine, which makes the wine taste like coconut candy, and the tannins are exaggerated.

SUMMARY	Dr. Konstantin Frank Semi-Dry Riesling	New World Pinot Noir	Australian Shiraz	Washington Merlot (American Oak)
Matching	+	(–)	+	
Complementing	+			
Contrasting	+	(–)	(–)	(–)
Compounding				
Complexing				
Cleansing	+			
Covering				
Clashing		(–)	(–)	(–)

Beef Bourguignon

BEEF BOURGUIGNON

Yield: 10 portions

Cooking Method: Stew

Ingredients	Amounts - US	Volume	Metric
Beef shank, boneless, large dice	4 lbs.		1.8 kilograms
Burgundy wine	28 fl. oz.	1 bottle	750 ml
Peppercorns, crushed		1 tsp.	
Thyme, sprigs		10 each	
Salt, kosher		as needed	
Black pepper, fresh ground		as needed	
Olive oil, pure	3 fl. oz.	⅓ cup	90 ml
Bacon, lardons	4 ½ oz.	3 thick slices	126 grams
Garlic, chopped		1 Tbl.	
Veal reduction, light nappe	40–48 fl. oz.	5–6 cups	1240–1500 ml
Bay leaf		1 each	
Onions, medium dice	8 oz.	2 cups	228 grams
Carrots, oblique cut	8 oz.	2 cups	228 grams
Pearl onions, cooked, peeled	10 oz.	60 each	280 grams
Butter, unsalted	1 oz.	2 Tbl.	28 grams
Chicken stock		as needed	
Button mushrooms, quartered	1 lb.	6 cups	0.5 kilogram
Olive oil, blended	1 ½ oz.	3 Tbl.	45 ml
Salt, kosher		as needed	
Black pepper, fresh ground		as needed	
For the Garnish			
Parsley, curly, chopped	¼ oz.	2 Tbl.	4 grams

(Continues on next page)

Beef Bourguignon

1. Combine the beef, wine, peppercorns, and thyme in a non-reactive container (or Ziplock bag) and marinate for 12 hours.
2. Drain the beef well, pat dry, and reserve the marinade.
3. Preheat the oven to 275 F (135 C) degrees convection.
4. Season the beef with salt and pepper.
5. Preheat a rondeau over medium-high heat, add 1 oz. of oil and the bacon, and cook until the bacon is light brown; remove the bacon with a slotted spoon and reserve.
6. Working in batches, as not to overcrowd the pan, add oil as needed and then the beef; cook until lightly browned on all sides. Remove the beef from the pan and reserve. Place in a suitable pan as not to stack the beef and allow it to steam. Control the heat as to not burn the fond.
7. Add the onions to the pan and cook until they begin to soften. Add the garlic and sauté until aromatic.
8. Add the reserved marinade and reduce by half. Add the veal reduction and bring to a simmer.
9. Place the veal reduction, beef, and bay leaf in a suitable pan for stewing; cover the pan with plastic and then aluminum foil. This can also be cooked in a rondeau with a lid. The liquid should be just covering the beef.
10. Place in the oven and cook for 2 hours. Add the carrots and continue cooking until the beef is tender, approximately 1 ½ hours. Stir the beef gently during cooking, every 30–40 minutes.
11. Preheat a sauté pan over medium heat and add the butter and the pearl onions. Season with salt and pepper and sauté until they are golden brown and heated throughout. Remove from the heat and reserve.
12. Preheat a sauté pan over medium-high heat and add the oil and the mushrooms. Sauté until they are caramelized and tender and season with salt and pepper.
13. Once the beef is tender, check the sauce consistency. If it is too thin, drain into a saucepan and reduce until a light nappe.
14. Taste and adjust the seasoning. Add the hot pearl onions and mushrooms to the beef and garnish with the bacon lardons and parsley.

One simple rule when it comes to cooking wine—if you wouldn't drink it, don't cook with it! This is a classic dish from the Burgundy region in France. For the marinade, I used a basic Bourgogne Rouge. Cook the stew the day before and allow the flavors to develop. Reheat in the oven the following day, prepare the mushrooms and onions, garnish, and serve.

WINE SELECTED with Beef Bourguignon

Wine: Bodega Chacra Barda Pinot Noir ($27)
Origin: Rio Negro, Patagonia, Argentina

Taste and Texture Comparisons

Dish: Rich/Bold, Slight Sweet, Earthy, Smoky, Umami
Wine: Aromatic, Fruity, Medium-Bodied, Soft Texture, Moderate Alcohol, Complexities (Earth, Mineral, Toast)

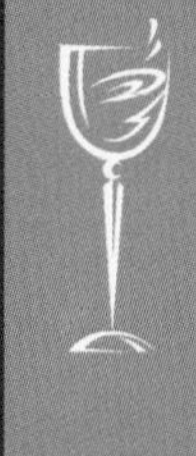

This wine comes from Patagonia, 620 miles south of Buenos Aires. Although showing New World ripe fruit, it also has a touch of the Old World with earthy, mineral nuances. It is also unfined and unfiltered, which adds to the wine's texture.

Why This Is a Good Pairing

- ***Matching Flavor Intensity*** – The dish is a bit heavier than the wine, but the flavor intensities match. The wine has rich strawberry and red cherry fruit, while the dish is rich with meaty flavor.
- ***Complementing*** – The earthy, mineral, and toast nuances are bridged by the mushrooms and Maillard reaction of the meat in the dish.
- ***Contrasting*** – The rich flavor of the stew meat and the earthiness of the mushrooms contrast with the rich red berry flavors of the wine, making the fruit pop even more.
- ***Cleansing*** – The wine's acidity cuts through the richness of the dish, creating a cleansing, refreshing sensation.

Wine That Didn't Work

Châteauneuf-du-Pape – The Grenache-based blend is a bit too low in acid and high in alcohol (14.5%+ abv), making the dish seem heavier and the heat from the alcohol more obvious.

Alternatives: Premier Cru Red Burgundy—As the name of the dish suggests, the traditional wine pairing favorite is red Burgundy. Many Beef Bourguignon recipes vary in their use of stock and wine. This recipe is classic in its ratio. The earthy notes in the dish create a connection to the richer, earthy flavors in the wine. We tried a basic Bourgogne Rouge to pair with the dish, but it was too simple and did not provide enough bridges to this dish. Therefore, in choosing a red Burgundy, go with a higher quality one as the complementing is increased and the complexities of both come out more. Langhe Nebbiolo also works for all the reasons the Argentina Pinot Noir works. Nebbiolo is much more tannic than the Pinot Noir, but the beef's protein combines with the tannin, making it seem softer on the palate. We should note though that the Langhe Nebbiolo's high acidity is almost too cleansing and it strips some of the flavors of the dish.

SUMMARY	Bodega Chacra Pinot Noir	Premier Cru Red Burgundy	Langhe Nebbiolo	Châteauneuf-du-Pape
Matching	+	+	+	
Complementing	+	+	+	
Contrasting	+	+	+	
Compounding				
Complexing	+	+	+	
Cleansing	+	+	(–)	
Covering				(–)
Clashing				(–)

Thai Beef with Massaman Curry

THAI BEEF WITH MASSAMAN CURRY

Yield: 10 portions

Cooking Method: Stew

Massaman Curry is traditionally served with steamed jasmine rice. Cinnamon sticks vary greatly in intensity and the amount can be adjusted while cooking. Before serving, remove the cinnamon sticks, cardamom seeds, and pods from the tamarind, if desired.

Ingredients	Amounts - US	Volume	Metric
Beef shank, boneless, large dice	3 lbs.		0.9 kilograms
Coconut milk	32 fl. oz.	4 cups	1 liter
Ginger, chopped	¾ oz.	3 Tbl.	21 grams
Peanut oil	2 fl. oz.	¼ cup	60 ml
Shallots, sliced ¼"	4 ½ oz.	¾ cup	126 grams
Massaman curry paste	3 ½ oz.	⅓ cup	98 grams
Cinnamon sticks	¾ oz.	4 each	24 grams
Cardamom seeds	¼ oz.	12 each	4 grams
Star anise		3 each	
Coconut cream	10 ½ oz.	1 ½ cups	294 grams
Palm sugar*	2 ½ oz.	3 Tbl.	68 grams
Tamarind paste	2 oz.	3 Tbl.	56 grams
Fish sauce	1 ½ fl. oz.	3 Tbl.	45 ml
Red potatoes, large dice	1 ¼ lb.	4 each	0.7 kilogram
Peanuts, roasted, unsalted	3 oz.	½ cup	84 grams
Salt, kosher		to taste	
Black pepper, fresh ground		to taste	

*If palm sugar is unavailable you can substitute brown sugar.

Thai Beef with Massaman Curry

1. Preheat the oven to 275 F (135 C) degrees convection.
2. Combine the beef, coconut milk, and ginger in a rondeau. Bring to a simmer, cover, and place in the oven. Stir gently every 30–40 minutes and allow to cook for approximately 2 hours, until the beef begins to soften but is not completely tender.
3. While the beef is cooking preheat a saucepan over medium heat, add the oil, and then the shallots, and sauté for 3–4 minutes until they are lightly caramelized.
4. Add the curry paste, cinnamon, cardamom, and star anise. Mix well and reduce the heat; toast this spice mixture lightly until it is very aromatic.
5. Add the coconut cream, palm sugar, tamarind paste, and fish sauce and bring to a gentle simmer; make sure to break up both the paste and the sugar. Simmer gently until the mixture thickens.
6. Once the beef has softened, add the coconut cream mixture and potatoes to the beef and continue cooking until the beef and potatoes are tender, approximately 30–40 minutes.
7. Taste and adjust the seasoning, garnish with peanuts.

WINE SELECTED with Thai Beef with Massaman Curry

Wine: Michele Chiarlo Moscato d'Asti Nivole ($14 half bottle)

Origin: Asti, Piedmont, Italy

Taste and Texture Comparisons

Dish: Rich, Spice, Bold, Creamy, Slight Sweetness

Wine: Aromatic, Soft Bubbles, Low Acidity, Low Alcohol, Sweet

The Muscat grape is one of the most aromatic and versatile on the planet. In Asti, it is very fragrant, light-bodied, delicately effervescent, and sweet, with low acid and low alcohol (5% abv).

Why This Is a Good Pairing

- ***Matching Intensity*** – The dish and the wine are intense in their aromas and flavor. The effervescence of the wine may make it seem light, but its sweetness adds to the weight.
- ***Complementing*** – The spice in the dish creates a link to the ginger spice sometimes found in Moscato d'Asti.
- ***Contrasting*** – For the most part, this pairing works because "opposites attract." The sweetness from the wine softens the spice of the dish. The wine's orange blossom notes contrast with the peanut and the coconut. These reactions create a complexity where you taste the many layers of flavors in the wine and the dish.
- ***Dance*** – The wine's low acid and the coconut cream allow the dish's spice and flavor to shine, creating a long finish.

Wines That Didn't Work

Dry Sparkling – The high acid of these wines and the lack of sweetness exacerbate the spice to where it overpowers the dish and the wine.

Riesling (Semi-Sweet) – Although the sweetness does soften the spice, the high acid of the wine slightly strips the flavor of the dish. Additionally, the weight of the dish is heavier than the wine; thus, it makes the wine seem thinner than it is.

Red Zinfandel – This was a disaster. The spice in the wine compounds with the spice in the dish and makes the wine's high alcohol (14.8% abv) very hot and unpleasant. The tannins of the wine and the spices in the dish also compound for a bitter taste.

SUMMARY	Nivole Moscato d'Asti	Dry Sparkling	Semi-Sweet Riesling	Red Zinfandel
Matching	+		(–)	
Complementing	+			
Contrasting	+			
Compounding				(–)
Complexing	+			
Cleansing		(–)	(–)	
Covering		(–)		
Clashing				(–)

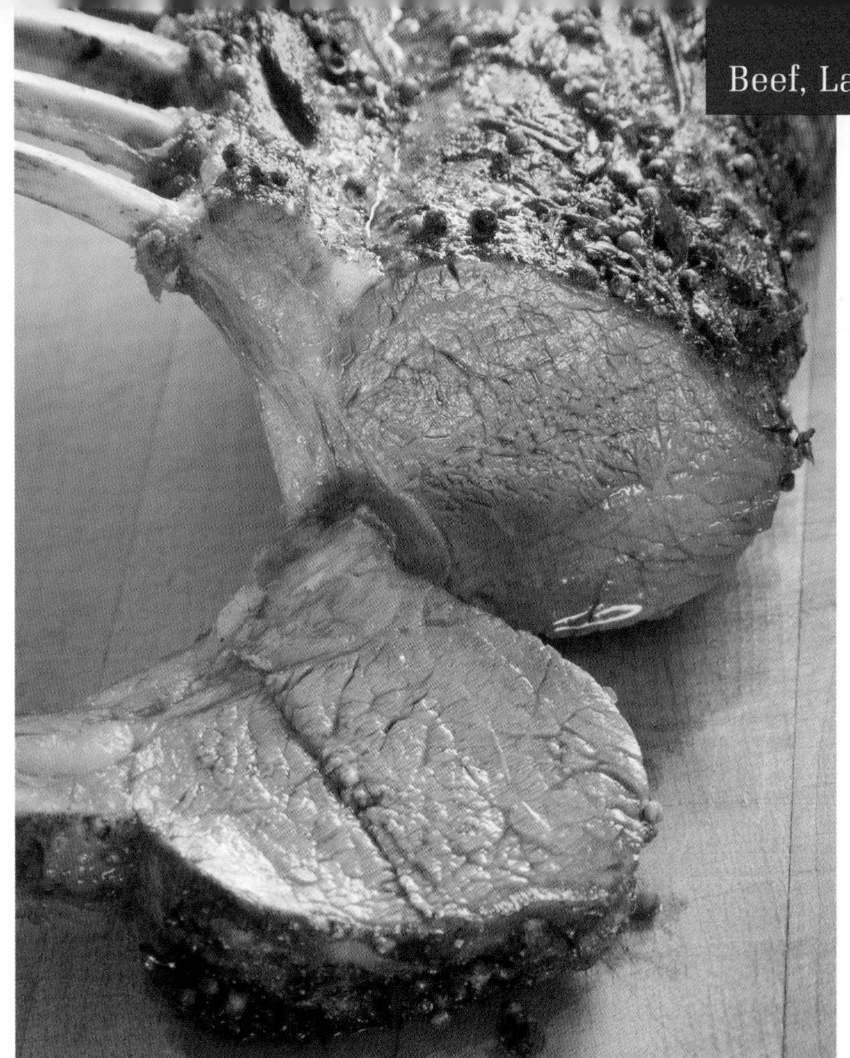

LAMB

ROSEMARY ROASTED RACK OF LAMB WITH LAMB JUS

Yield: 10 portions

Cooking Method: Roast

Ingredients	Amounts - US	Volume	Metric
For the Lamb			
Lamb racks, frenched, cap-off		3 each	
Salt, kosher		as needed	
Olive oil, pure	2 fl. oz.	¼ cup	60 ml
For the Marinade			
Olive oil, blended	8 fl. oz.	1 cup	240 ml
Rosemary, leaves	¾ oz.	⅔ cup	20 grams
Garlic cloves, crushed	¾ oz.	6 medium	20 grams
Mustard seeds, crushed	¾ oz.	2 Tbl.	20 grams
Parsley, rough chopped	½ oz.	1 cup	14 grams
Salt, kosher	¼ oz.	2 tsp.	8 grams
Black pepper, fresh ground		2 tsp.	

(Continues on next page)

Ingredients	Amounts - US	Volume	Metric
For the Lamb Jus			
Lamb jus, light nappe	24 fl. oz.	3 cups	740 ml
Rosemary, sprigs		as needed	
Lemon juice		1 tsp.	
Butter, unsalted	½ oz.	1 Tbl.	14 grams

Marinade

Combine the marinade ingredients and mix well.

Rack of Lamb

1. Coat the lamb racks evenly with the marinade and place in a non-reactive container (or Ziplock bag) and marinate under refrigeration for 4–6 hours.
2. Preheat an oven to 350 F (176 C) degrees convection.
3. Remove the lamb from the refrigerator and allow it to come to room temperature. Remove most of the herb leaves and season with salt.
4. Preheat a sautoir over medium-high heat; add the oil and the lamb. Sear to brown on all sides evenly.
5. Place the racks in a roasting pan, flesh facing up, and cook to an internal temperature of 125 F (52 C) degrees.
6. Allow the racks to rest for 10 minutes before carving.

Lamb Jus

1. Degrease the sautoir, add the lamb jus, and capture the fond with a wooden spoon.
2. Bring to a simmer. Add the rosemary sprigs and simmer gently for 10 minutes.
3. Strain out the rosemary, add the lemon juice, mount the butter, and taste and adjust the seasoning.
4. Carve the lamb rack into individual chops, plate and sauce with the lamb jus.

Lamb racks on the market today are typically from the United States, Australia, or New Zealand. Each country's lamb differs with respect to the size of the muscle, fat content, and flavor. American lamb typically has a larger muscle, fat cap, and bones. The average weight for a frenched rack, cap-off, is approximately 1¾ lbs. (0.8 kilogram). American lamb flavor is rich and bold, which is what was used in all recipes tested.

Australian and New Zealand lamb typically have a smaller muscle and less fat with smaller bones. The average weight for a frenched rack, cap-off, is approximately 12–20 oz. (340–568 grams). Australian lamb is slightly larger than New Zealand lamb. The lamb flavor is delicate and more mild than American lamb.

WINE SELECTED with Rosemary Roasted Rack of Lamb with Lamb Jus

Wine: Guigal Côtes du Rhône Blanc ($13)
Origin: Côtes du Rhône, Rhône Valley, France

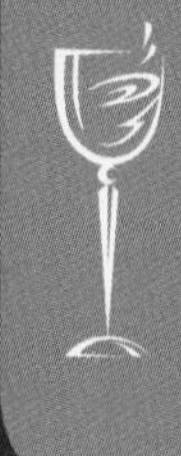

This wine is a blend of white grape varieties (Viognier, Roussane, Marsanne, Clairette, and Bourboulenc). It is predominantly Viognier that yields a more intense body, floral flavor, and modest acidity.

Taste and Texture Comparisons

Dish: Rich, Earthy, Herbal, Spice, Gamey
Wine: Aromatic, Floral, Fruity (White Peach), Low Acidity, Oily Texture, Full Body, Moderate Alcohol

Why This Is a Good Pairing

- ***Matching Flavor Intensity*** – Viognier is intense with its floral and peachy flavors while the dish is intense in its flavors of lamb, rosemary, and the soft spice of the mustard.
- ***Matching Body*** – Although you may not think a white wine could match the body of lamb, this one does. White Rhone blends tend to be fuller-bodied, which is why the lamb does not overpower them.
- ***Contrasting*** – The floral and fruity nature of the wine contrasts with the earthiness and the spice of the dish and makes the flavors of both the dish and the wine stand out. The richness of the dish also contrasts with the wine.
- ***Complexing*** – The contrast of flavors creates a *complexing* reaction that makes this $13 wine taste more expensive.

Wines That Didn't Work

Smaragd Grüner Veltliner – The theory behind testing this wine is that the white spice element Grüner Veltliner is known for would complement the spices in the dish. Although the Smaragd is a richer style of Grüner Veltliner, it is not big enough for this dish. The fairly crisp acidity also strips some of the flavor of the dish.

Red Burgundy – We tried several red Burgundies and, in each case, the Pinot Noirs are overpowered by this dish. The crisp acidity in the wines also strips the flavor of the dish.

Alternative: Crozes-Hermitage—The wine's toasty and dried-herb character complements the Maillard reaction and herbs in the dish. The contrast of the flavor of the lamb brings forth the raspberry fruit in this Syrah, and the complexity of the black pepper stands out.

Through the testing of this dish, we tasted several racks of lamb. One point we thought worth mentioning is that when we tasted a chop that had a bit more fat, it lengthened the finish of the pairing and enhanced it even more.

SUMMARY	Guigal Côtes du Rhône Blanc	Crozes-Hermitage	Smaragd Grüner Veltliner	Red Burgundy
Matching	+	+		
Complementing		+		
Contrasting	+	+		
Compounding				
Complexing	+			
Cleansing			(–)	(–)
Covering			(–)	(–)
Clashing				

Grilled Lamb Chops with Mint Emulsion

GRILLED LAMB CHOPS WITH MINT EMULSION

Yield: 10 portions

Cooking Method: Grill

Lamb has a fair amount of fat and may cause flare ups during grilling. Regulate the heat and/or move the chops as necessary to prevent burning; they should also be cooked on all sides to allow for even cooking.

Ingredients	Amounts - US	Volume	Metric
For the Lamb			
Lamb racks, frenched, cap-off		3 each	
Salt, kosher		as needed	
Black pepper, fresh ground		as needed	
Olive oil, pure		as needed	
For the Mint Emulsion Yield: 1 cup			
Brown sugar	1 ½ oz.	¼ cup	40 grams
Mint, leaves	¾ oz.	1 ½ cups	21 grams
Cider vinegar		2 tsp.	
Veal reduction, room temperature, medium nappe	6 fl. oz.	¾ cup	180 ml
Extra virgin olive oil	1 fl. oz.	2 Tbl.	30 ml
Mint, chiffonade		¼ cup	
Salt, kosher		to taste	
Black pepper, fresh ground		to taste	
Cayenne		pinch	

Mint Emulsion

1. Place the brown sugar and mint in a mortar. Using a pestle, grind the sugar and mint into a paste.
2. Place the mint paste in a stainless steel bowl; add the cider vinegar, and whisk well.
3. Add the veal reduction and whisk well.
4. Add the extra virgin olive oil while whisking constantly.
5. Add the mint chiffonade; season with salt, pepper, and cayenne; taste and adjust the seasoning.

Lamb Chops

1. Cut the lamb racks into 2-bone chops.
2. Preheat a charbroiler/grill.
3. Season the lamb chops with salt and pepper and lightly coat with oil.
4. Grill for 2 minutes, and then turn the chops 90 degrees to achieve crosshatch marks and continue cooking for another 2 minutes.
5. Cook the lamb evenly on all sides until the desired temperature is reached.
6. Plate the chops and drizzle with the mint emulsion.

WINE SELECTED with Grilled Lamb Chops with Mint Emulsion

Wine: Cantravelli Taurasi Riserva ($24)
Origin: Taurasi, Campania, Italy

Taste and Texture Comparisons

Dish: Full-Bodied, Rich, Herbal, Sweet ,Grilled Meat, Gamey
Wine: Full-Bodied, Dark Fruit (Blackberry), Earthy, Grilled Meat Flavor, Gripping Tannin, Slightly Rustic

This wine is made from a black grape called Aglianico, which is known for its dark color, black plum fruit flavors, earthy and grilled meat flavors, as well as its density.

Why This Is a Good Pairing

- ***Matching Intensity*** – The wine and the dish are fairly full-bodied and their intensity of flavors is evenly matched. This allows the flavors of both the wine and the dish to come through.
- ***Complementing*** – The earthy notes found in the wine are augmented by the grilled/Maillard reaction of the lamb as well as its earthy/savory flavors.
- ***Contrasting*** – The rich flavor of the grilled lamb contrasts with the fruit in the wine, making the fruit flavor and the grilled flavors pop.
- ***Balance*** – The mint emulsion is not too sweet and does not interfere with the wine. In fact, everything is quite balanced.

Wines That Didn't Work

California Chardonnay – There is a cleansing with the wine's acidity and the slightly warm alcohol. However, the dish and the wine end up canceling each other out.

Washington Merlot – Oak in this wine completely overpowers the dish. Additionally, there is a compounding of the sweetness from the American oak (coconut) and the brown sugar in the dish. The dish ends up tasting a bit too sweet and out of balance.

Coonawara Shiraz – The richness of the wine overpowers the dish. We thought that the grilling flavor would contrast with rich fruit and that the slight minty complexities in the wine would complement the sauce. But the wine is too bold and the oak too intense, overpowering the dish. In addition, the tannins become astringent.

Alternative: Victoria Shiraz—Australian Shiraz sometimes has an element of eucalyptus, which complements nicely with the mint emulsion. Additionally, the boldness of the fruit contrasts well with the lamb. Victoria is a cooler region than some other parts of Australia and, as a result, it yields a wine that is less overpowering and less tannic than some others (see Coonawara Shiraz above).

SUMMARY	Cantravelli Taurasi Riserva	Victoria Shiraz	California Chardonnay	Washington Merlot	Coonawara Shiraz
Matching	+				
Complementing	+	+			
Contrasting	+	+			
Compounding				(–)	
Complexing					
Cleansing			(–)		
Covering				(–)	(–)
Clashing			(–)		

CHINESE FIVE SPICE SAUTÉED LAMB CHOPS

Yield: 10 portions

Cooking Method: Sauté

Ingredients	Amounts - US	Volume	Metric
Lamb racks, frenched, cap-off		3 each	
Salt, kosher		as needed	
Olive oil, pure		as needed	
For the Marinade			
Peanut oil	2 fl. oz.	¼ cup	60 ml
Soy sauce, low sodium	1 ½ fl. oz.	3 Tbl.	45 ml
Scallions, sliced thin	1 oz.	½ cup	28 grams
Ginger, chopped	⅜ oz.	1 ½ Tbl.	12 grams
Garlic, chopped	⅜ oz.	1 ½ Tbl.	12 grams
Sesame oil		2 tsp.	
For the Chinese Five Spice			
Szechuan peppercorns	⅜ oz.	1 Tbl. plus 1 tsp.	8 grams
Fennel seeds, lightly toasted	¼ oz.	1 Tbl.	6 grams
Star anise		6 each	
Cinnamon, ground		1 Tbl.	
Ginger, ground		1 tsp.	
Cloves		8 each	
For the Garnish			
Cilantro, rough chopped		2 Tbl.	

(Continues on next page)

Chinese Five Spice

Combine the ingredients for the Chinese Five Spice and grind in a spice blender until finely ground.

Marinade

Combine the marinade ingredients and mix well.

Lamb Chops

1. Cut the lamb racks into individual chops.
2. Coat the lamb chops with the marinade and place in a nonreactive container (or Ziplock bag) and marinate under refrigeration for 2 hours.
3. Remove the lamb from the refrigerator and allow it to come to room temperature. Wipe off the excess marinade.
4. Preheat a sauté pan over medium-high heat.
5. Liberally season both sides of the lamb chops with the Chinese Five Spice and salt.
6. Add the oil to the pan and then the lamb chops, working in batches as to not overcrowd the pan. Once the chops have cooked halfway and are deep brown, turn and repeat. The lamb should be medium rare when cooked and takes approximately 2 minutes per side.
7. Plate and garnish with cilantro.

WINE SELECTED with Chinese Five Spice Sautéed Lamb Chops

Wine: Bodega Atteca Old Vines Calatayud ($16)
Origin: Calatayud, Spain

This wine is 100% Garnacha (aka Grenache in France). Calatayud is one of the rare places that Garnacha is generally not blended. It is fairly full-bodied with modest acidity and warm alcohol (14.5% abv).

Taste and Texture Comparisons

Dish: Rich, Spice, Earthy, Gamey
Wine: Fruity, Spice, Slightly Earthy, Generous Body, Modest Acidity, Warm Alcohol

Why This Is a Good Pairing

- ***Matching Intensity*** – The dish is fairly rich and spicy and the wine is fairly full-bodied with spice and earth tones as well. Neither overpowers the other or fights for dominance.
- ***Complementing*** – The spices in the wine (licorice, black pepper, and slight Asian spices) complement and bring out the cinnamon and the star anise in the Chinese Five Spice.
- ***Contrasting*** – The earthy/gamey flavor of the lamb contrasts with the cherry flavors of the wine, making the fruit in the wine come alive.

Wines That Didn't Work

Châteauneuf-du-Pape – At first, similar reactions happened as with the Calatayud. However, the tannin from the wine becomes drying and astringent.

Aglianico – The tannins from the cinnamon and Chinese Five Spice compounds with the tannins and earthiness in the wine. This yields a very earthy taste with quite astringent tannins.

Zinfandel – The wine overpowers the dish in its weight and in tannin, which clashes and becomes astringent.

SUMMARY	Bodega Atteca Old Vines Calatayud	Châteauneuf-du-Pape	Aglianico	Zinfandel
Matching	+			
Complementing	+			
Contrasting	+	+		
Compounding			(–)	
Complexing				
Cleansing				
Covering				(–)
Clashing		(–)	(–)	(–)

Venison Burgers

VENISON

Venison is classified as a game meat that was traditionally available in the fall. We utilize farm-raised venison for these recipes, which has a milder game flavor.

VENISON BURGERS

Yield: 10 portions
Cooking Method: Grill

Ingredients	Amounts - US	Volume	Metric
For the Burgers			
Venison leg, ground	3 ¾ lbs.		1.7 kilograms
Salt, kosher		as needed	
Black pepper, fresh ground		as needed	
Brie cheese	10 oz.	10 slices	284 grams
Brioche burger bun, split		10 each	
Butter, unsalted, melted		as needed	
Mustard spread		1 Tbl.	
Romaine lettuce, shredded	5 oz.	2 ½ cups	284 grams
Tomatoes, sliced ¼"		10 each	
For the Mustard Spread			
Grain mustard	2 ⅛ oz.	¼ cup	58 grams
Dijon mustard	1 oz.	2 Tbl.	28 grams
Mayonnaise	1 oz.	2 Tbl.	28 grams

Mustard Spread

Combine the mustards and the mayonnaise and mix well until fully combined.

Venison Burgers

1. Form the venison into 6-oz. patties; do not pack too tightly. Season on both sides with salt and pepper.
2. Preheat a charbroiler/grill.
3. Place the venison burgers on the grill and cook for 2 minutes and then rotate 90 degrees to achieve crosshatch marks. Adjust the cook time for thickness and desired doneness and continue cooking for another 2 minutes.
4. Turn the venison burgers and repeat the above process; after rotating the burgers, add the cheese. Continue cooking until they are cooked to your desired doneness. Recommended doneness is medium rare to medium.
5. Lightly brush the bun with butter on the cut surfaces and grill until heated and lightly colored.
6. Spread the mustard spread on the bottom bun, top with lettuce and then the burger, and place the tomatoes on top.

WINE SELECTED with Venison Burgers

Wine: Bodegas Alejandro Fernandez Tinto Pesquera Ribera del Duero ($30)
Origin: Ribera del Duero, Spain

This wine is made from the Spanish red grape Tempranillo. Rioja is where it is best known, but in Ribera del Duero, where the altitude is higher, Tempranillo becomes darker in its fruit character, richer, and more brooding.

Taste and Texture Comparisons

Dish: Rich Venison, Gamey, Grilled/Smoky, Maillard Reaction, Slight Sweet, Toasty

Wine: Full-Bodied, Balanced Acidity, Slightly Warm Alcohol, Complex

Why This Is a Good Pairing

- ***Matching Intensity*** – The wine and the dish are fairly concentrated in flavor and intensity, which makes for a well-balanced pairing.
- ***Contrasting*** – The gamey flavors of the venison contrast with the rich fruit in this wine and they both stand out.
- ***Complementing*** – The gamey flavors of the venison create a bridge to the grilled meat notes in the wine as well as bring out its earthy bramble and spice notes.
- ***Complexing*** – The wine has many layers of flavors (grilled meat, blackberry/raspberry, earth, bramble, and spice) as does the dish (venison, brie, mustard, brioche). The complementing and contrasting allow the palate to taste all the layers of flavors.
- ***Dance*** – The richness in the dish (from the venison, brie, and spread) elongates the flavors on the palate.

Wines That Didn't Work

Primitivo – The fruit contrasts too much with the game flavors and makes the wine taste too candied or like dried fruit.

Bierzo – The earthy character of the wine compounds with the earthy notes in the dish (in a negative way). There is also a clash, and the wine takes on a squid ink–brine like quality.

Napa Cabernet Sauvignon – The very obvious, up-front fruit in this Cabernet is a bit sweet with the dish and the predominant fruit character covers up some of the lovely complexities of the dish.

SUMMARY	Bodegas Alejandro Fernandez Tinto Pesquera	Primitivo	Bierzo	Napa Cabernet Sauvignon
Matching	+	+	+	+
Complementing	+			
Contrasting	+	(–)		(–)
Compounding			(–)	
Complexing	+			
Cleansing				
Covering				(–)
Clashing				

ROASTED VENISON WITH SAUCE GRAND VENEUR

Yield: 10 portions

Cooking Method: Roast

Ingredients	Amounts - US	Volume	Metric
Venison roasts, cut from the round	3 lbs.		1.4 kilograms
Salt, kosher		as needed	
Black pepper, course ground		as needed	
Olive oil, pure	2 fl. oz.	¼ cup	60 ml
For the Marinade			
Extra virgin olive oil	3 fl. oz.	⅓ cup	90 ml
Cider vinegar	1 ½ fl. oz.	3 Tbl.	45 ml
Juniper berries, crushed	⅜ oz.	1 ½ Tbl.	9 grams
Garlic cloves, crushed	⅜ oz.	3 each	9 grams
Thyme, sprigs, fresh	¼ oz.	15 each	6 grams

(Continues on next page)

Ingredients	Amounts - US	Volume	Metric
For the Sauce Grand Veneur			
Venison stock, reduction	24 fl. oz.	3 cups	740 ml
White wine, Pinot Gris	3 fl. oz.	⅓ cup	90 ml
Red currant jelly	½ oz.	1 Tbl.	28 grams
Cornstarch		1 ½ Tbl.	
Venison stock	1 ½ fl. oz.	2 ½ Tbl.	45 ml
Butter, unsalted, room temperature	1 oz.	2 Tbl.	28 grams
Thyme, fresh, chopped		1 ½ tsp.	
Parsley, Italian, chopped		1 tsp.	
Salt, kosher		to taste	
Black pepper, fresh ground		to taste	

Marinade

Combine the extra virgin olive oil, cider vinegar, juniper, garlic, and thyme; mix well.

Venison Roast

1. Tie the venison roasts with butcher twine. Season with salt and pepper; coat evenly with the marinade; marinate under refrigeration for 6–8 hours.
2. Preheat an oven to 300 F (150 C) degrees convection.
3. Preheat a sautoir over medium heat. Add the oil and then the venison and brown lightly on all sides.
4. Remove to a roasting pan lined with a rack and place in the oven.
5. Deglaze the pan with the wine, and reduce by three-quarters. Reserve this for the sauce.
6. Cook the roast until an internal temperature of 125 F (52 C) degrees. Allow it to rest for 15 minutes before slicing.

Sauce Grand Veneur

1. Deglaze the roasting pan with 4 oz (120 ml) of venison stock and combine with the wine reduction and the remaining venison stock. Bring the sauce to a simmer and reduce until the flavor is well developed.
2. Add the red currant jelly and whisk to fully incorporate.
3. Combine the cornstarch and venison stock and mix well to fully combine. While the sauce is simmering, slowly whisk in the slurry until the sauce is a light nappe.
4. Mount the sauce with butter, add the thyme, and parsley, and taste and adjust the seasoning.
5. Slice the venison thinly and serve with Sauce Grand Veneur.

The amount of time the sauce needs to reduce and the amount of slurry will be determined by the consistency of the venison reduction.

WINE SELECTED with Roasted Venison with Sauce Grand Veneur

Wine: Motes Alpha Cabernet Sauvignon ($20)
Origin: Colchagua Valley, Chile

Taste and Texture Comparisons

Dish: Rich Venison, Gamey, Earthy, Sweet
Wine: Fairly Full-Bodied, Moderate Acidity, Slightly Warm Alcohol, Complex Savory Notes

Chilean Cabernet Sauvignons generally have the up-front ripeness and fruit found in the New World, but also can have a touch of earthy and herbal complexities found in the Old World.

Why This Is a Good Pairing

- ***Matching Intensity and Texture*** – The intensity of flavor in both the wine and the dish are fairly equal and there is no risk of one overpowering the other. The rich texture of the venison and the tannin texture of the wine are also evenly matched.
- ***Contrasting*** – The meaty/gamey nature of the venison contrasts with the rich, ripe fruit of the Chilean Cabernet, making the flavor of the fruit pop.
- ***Complementing*** – The red currant fruit in the sauce complements the black currant fruit in the wine. Additionally, the complexities in the wine (game, herbs) create a bridge to the same flavors in the dish.

Wines That Didn't Work

Ribera del Duero – The complexities of the wine augment the complexities in the dish, but the richness of the wine ultimately covers the dish.

Pinotage – Pinotage is known for some earthy flavors. Its earthiness and minerality compound with the earthiness and gaminess in the dish in an unpleasant way, Earth + Earth = Earth^2.

Nebbiolo – The game brings out the fruit in the wine, but the dish then overpowers the wine.

Alternative: Napa Cabernet Sauvignon—While the fruit of the wine is augmented, the toastiness and the spice are complemented by the maillard reaction and the spices in the dish.

SUMMARY	Motes Alpha Cabernet Sauvignon	Ribera del Duero	Pinotage	Nebbiolo
Matching	+			
Complementing	+			
Contrasting	+			
Compounding			(–)	
Complexing	+	+		
Cleansing				
Covering		(–)		(–)
Clashing				

Venison Chili

VENISON CHILI

Yield: 10 portions
Cooking Method: Stew

Ingredients	Amounts - US	Volume	Metric
Venison, leg, medium dice	2 lbs.		0.9 kilogram
Pork butt, medium dice	1 lb.		454 grams
Salt, kosher		as needed	
Black pepper, fresh ground		as needed	
Olive oil, pure	4 fl. oz.	½ cup	120 ml
Onions, small dice	8 oz.	2 cups	228 grams
Garlic, chopped	⅜ oz.	1 Tbl.	10 grams
Serrano chili, minced	¼ oz.	1 Tbl.	8 grams
Chili powder, dark		3 Tbl.	
Cumin, toasted		2 tsp.	
Oregano, dried		2 tsp.	
Tomatoes, plum, crushed	48 oz.	6 cups	1 ½ liters
Chicken stock	16 fl. oz.	2 cups	500 ml
Venison stock	8 fl. oz.	1 cup	240 ml
Cannellini beans, cooked	1 lb.	2 cups	454 grams
Salt, kosher		to taste	
Black pepper, fresh ground		to taste	
For the Garnish			
Sharp cheddar, grated	6 ¼ oz.	1 ¼ cups	175 grams
Red onion, minced	3 oz.	¾ cup	84 grams
Cilantro, chopped		3 Tbl.	

Chili

1. Preheat a rondeau over medium-high heat.
2. Season the venison and pork with salt and pepper. Add the oil to the rondeau and then the venison and pork. Work in batches to brown, take care not to overcrowd the pan. Remove the venison and pork when they are browned to an appropriate pan, do not stack, as they will steam and lose moisture.
3. Add the onions to the pan and sweat until tender. Add the garlic and serrano chilis and sauté until aromatic and the garlic begins to color lightly.
4. Add the chili powder, cumin, and oregano; mix well to coat evenly. Toast for 1 ½ minutes.
5. Add the tomatoes, stocks, venison, and pork; bring to a gentle simmer.
6. Simmer for approximately 2 ½ hours, until the venison and pork are almost tender; and then add the beans.
7. Simmer for an additional 20 minutes until the venison and pork are tender; taste and adjust the seasoning.
8. Plate and garnish with cheddar cheese, red onions, and cilantro.

WINE SELECTED with Venison Chili

Wine: Bogle Petite Sirah ($10)
Origin: California USA

Taste and Texture Comparisons

Dish: Rich Venison, Gamey, Sweet, Smokey, Spice
Wine: Rich Fruit, Very Ripe, Full-Bodied, Modest Acidity with Slightly Warm Alcohol

Petite Sirah is not Syrah, nor is it related (except that they're both red grapes). Petite Sirah has tiny (petite) berries, which gives it a lower juice-to-skin ratio. This yields rich, full black fruit flavor and dense tannins.

Why This Is a Good Pairing

- ***Matching Intensity*** – The flavor of the dish and the flavor of the wine are both fairly intense.
- ***Contrasting*** – The rich, dark fruit of the wine contrasts with the intense gamey flavor of the venison, making the flavor of the fruit pop.
- ***Complementing*** – There is a connection between the spice in the dish and the spice from the oak in the wine.
- ***Complexing*** – The contrasting and complementing allow the palate to focus on many layers of flavors in the wine (blackberry, black cherry, blue fruit, chocolate, coconut, spice) and the dish (game, tomatoes, cumin, cayenne, smoke, etc.).

Wines That Didn't Work

Ribera del Duero – Layers of spice and the venison are complemented; however, the earthiness of the wine compounds with the earthy/gamey flavors of the chili and is overpowering.

Chilean Cabernet Sauvignon – The spice augments the wine's alcohol, making the heat of the spices come out even more, losing some of the nuances of the dish.

Malbec – Spices clash and the wine is covered by the intense flavors of the dish.

SUMMARY	Bogle Petite Sirah	Ribera del Duero	Chilean Cabernet Sauvignon	Malbec
Matching	+	+		
Complementing	+	+		
Contrasting	+			
Compounding				
Complexing	+			
Cleansing				
Covering		(–)		(–)
Clashing			(–)	(–)

BEEF, LAMB, AND VENISON PAIRING SUMMARY AND CONCLUSIONS

Beef Tenderloin

Dish	Method	Wine
Beef Tartare	Raw	Chardonnay, Au Bon Climat
Sautéed Beef Tournedos	Sauté	Malbec Gran Reserva, Agua de Piedra
Gorgonzola Dolcelatte-Topped Beef Tournedos	Grill	Merlot, St. Emilion, Château La Bienfaisance

- ***Main ingredient tendencies:*** Beef in general is a rich protein that pairs well with full-bodied whites and reds and tends to overpower delicate wines. Beef's flavor contrasts with wine's fruit, making it pop.
- ***Specific techniques that changed the pairing:*** The tartare allows for a medium- to full-bodied Chardonnay (shared texture and weight) but was overpowered by reds. Grilling creates the most intense flavor of these recipes and so a more powerful red was needed.
- ***Specific ingredients that changed the pairing:*** The Gorgonzola Dolcelatte added further depth and richness, which changed the pairing to a richer, full-bodied, dense red wine.

Beef Flank Steak

Dish	Method	Wine
Beef and Broccoli Stir-Fry	Stir-Fry	Pinot Gris, Ponzi
Grilled Flank Steak with Chimichurri Sauce	Grill	Sauvignon Blanc, Craggy Range
Grilled Flank Steak Sandwich	Grill	Carmenère, Root 1 Colchagua

- ***Main ingredient tendencies:*** Flank steak is quite rich in flavor and fat, which makes it gravitate towards sweetness, acidity, and potentially richness, pointing to a wide range of wine pairing possibilities.
- ***Specific techniques that changed the pairing:*** Stir-frying has less of an impact on the protein and therefore is not a surprise match with a medium-bodied white wine. We employed the same technique for the last two recipes in this section to demonstrate how the ingredients can change the pairing.
- ***Specific ingredients that changed the pairing:*** The stir-fry's ginger notes paired with the hint of spice in the Pinot Gris. The refreshing citrus and herbal notes in the Chimichurri connect to similar notes in the Sauvignon Blanc, and the Carmenère's gamey notes created a bridge to the sandwich's flavors.

Beef Shank

Dish	Method	Wine
BBQ Pulled Beef	Roast	Semi-Dry Riesling, Dr. Konstantin Frank
Beef Bourguignon	Stew	Pinot Noir, Bodega Chacra Barda
Thai Beef with Massaman Curry	Stew	Moscato d'Asti, Nivole Michele Chiarlo

- ***Main ingredient tendencies:*** Beef shank is a very bold flavorful cut that requires a long cooking time.
- ***Specific techniques that changed the pairing:*** Techniques such as roasting and stewing typically are characterized by intense flavors, and the wines that pair with these dishes have pronounced aromas/flavors.
- ***Specific ingredients that changed the pairing:*** The Pinot Noir had a bridge to the Beef Bourguignon given the wine used in the recipe, but its tannin clashed with the spice in the other two dishes. The spice in the BBQ and Thai Beef prompted fruity wines with a touch of sweetness.

Lamb

Dish	Method	Wine
Rosemary Roasted Rack of Lamb	Roast	Viognier, Guigal Côtes du Rhône
Grilled Lamb Chops with Mint Emulsion	Grill	Aglianico, Cantravelli Taurasi Riserva
Chinese Five Spice Sautéed Lamb Chops	Sauté	Garnacha, Atteca

- ***Main ingredient tendencies:*** Lamb's flavor contrasts very well with the fruit in Old World wines. The wines that paired well were on the weightier side, from a full-bodied white to a full-bodied red.
- ***Specific techniques that changed the pairing:*** The roasting and grilling techniques increase some of the earthy tones in the dish, which contrast well with the fruit and complement the earthy tones in the wines.
- ***Specific ingredients that changed the pairing:*** The mild sweetness and the purity of flavor of the mint emulsion created balance and complemented with the Aglianico. The Five Spice blend was too intense for a tannic wine like the Aglianico, but too bold for the Viognier.

Venison

Dish	Method	Wine
Venison Burgers	Grill	Tinto Pesquera, Bodegas Alejandro Fernandez
Roasted Venison with Sauce Grand Veneur	Roast	Cabernet Sauvignon, Motes Alpha
Venison Chili	Stew	Petite Sirah, Bogle

- ***Main ingredient tendencies:*** Venison's powerful and rich nature in general requires bolder and more structured red wines. Its intense flavor contrasts with wine's fruit flavor, making both the venison and the fruit shine.
- ***Specific techniques that changed the pairing:*** Grilling and roasting techniques can increase toasty and caramelized flavors that complement these elements in more richly oaked reds. Grilling allows for some complementing of the earthy and mineral terroir notes in the Tempranillo.
- ***Specific ingredients that changed the pairing:*** The herbs in the roasted venison marinade and Sauce Grand Veneur complemented the herbal notes in Cabernet Sauvignon. However, given venison's intense flavor, watch for elements in wine that can compound, such as earthy or gamey flavors.

8
Pasta and Pizza

In previous chapters we covered how to match wines with a variety of proteins and limited accompaniments. Pasta and pizza flavor profiles offer a combination and range of depth, intensity, weights, and textures. These factors are what make pasta and pizza so exciting.

In this chapter you will learn how flavor combinations are affected by changing temperature, altering ingredients, adding butter or wine, as well as the type of sauce chosen. All of these elements impact the pairing and your palate's perception of the wine. Each dish and wine has its own tastes and textures that interact with each other, leading to a successful pairing.

Dish	Wine
Ravioli	
Cheese Ravioli with Asparagus and Butter Sauce	Burgans Albariño, Rias Baixas, Spain ($14)
Meat Ravioli in Brodo	Château de Campuget Costières de Nimes Rosé, Rhone, France ($10)
Shrimp Ravioli with Tomato Coulis	Charles Heidsieck Brut Réserve, Champagne, France ($45)
Spaghetti	
Spaghetti con le Vongole	Nederberg Sauvignon Blanc, South Africa ($9)
Spaghetti alla Carbonara	Masi Costasera Amarone della Valpolicella, Veneto, Italy ($45)
Spaghetti alla Puttanesca	Azienda Agraria Le Rote Vernaccia di San Gimignano ($14)
Mezze Rigatoni	
Mezze Rigatoni with Broccoli Rabe and Sausage	Tedeschi Soave Classico, Veneto, Italy ($14)
Mezze Rigatoni Salad with Roasted Butternut Squash, Red Onions, Sage, and Pumpkin Seeds	Chateau St. Jean Chardonnay, California, USA ($15)
Mezze Rigatoni alla Sauce Bolognese	St. Francis Old Vines Zinfandel, California, USA ($19)
Pizza	
Margherita Pizza	Bearboat Pinot Noir, California, USA ($22)
Fennel Sausage and Porcini Mushroom Pizza	Domaine Wachau Terressen Federspiel Grüner Veltliner, Wachau, Austria ($14)
Ricotta, Taleggio, and Arugula Pizza	Barone Ricasoli Brolio Chianti Classico, Tuscany, Italy ($19)

PASTA

There are two basic ways to categorize pasta: fresh and dry. From there pasta is broken down into shapes: long (spaghetti), tubes (rigatoni), soup pasta (orzo), special shapes (orecchiette), and stuffed (ravioli). The shape of the pasta and the filling dictate the type of sauce used. For example, long pasta is best suited for olive oil, butter, cream, or tomato-based sauces that are smooth and coat the shape; while tubes are best suited for chunky-style sauces that can trap the ingredients in the pasta. It is important to consider this when pairing a sauce with a pasta shape as this will also determine how the pasta "eats" or is received on your palate. If the sauce doesn't coat the pasta or you keep searching for the chunks in the sauce, this diminishes the dish.

BASIC PASTA DOUGH

Yield: 60 ravioli

Ingredients	Amounts - US	Volume	Metric
Flour 00	13 oz.	2 ¾ cups	368 grams
Semolina durum	4 oz.	¾ cup	114 grams
Eggs, large	7 oz.	4 each	225 grams
Extra virgin olive oil	1 fl. oz.	2 Tbl.	30 ml
Salt, kosher	⅝ oz.	1 Tbl. plus 1 tsp.	18 grams

Pasta Dough

1. Using a stand mixer with a dough hook, combine the eggs, oil, and salt; mix on low speed for 30 seconds.
2. Add the flours and mix on low speed. Allow the dough to mix until a smooth ball has fully formed and has "cleaned" the sides of the bowl, approximately 4–6 minutes. Stop the mixer to scrape down the hook if needed. The dough should be smooth and elastic.
3. Remove and cover the dough with plastic wrap and allow the dough to rest for 1 hour before rolling out. Refrigerate the dough if not using within 1 hour.

Alternatively, the dough can be mixed by hand. Working on a large wooden cutting board or granite/marble surface, make a well in the center of the flour; add the eggs, oil, and salt in the center. Using a fork, begin whisking the eggs and slowly drawing the flour into the center to incorporate. Once the eggs are mixed with the flour, begin kneading with your hands and work the dough until it is smooth.

Basic Guidelines for Rolling Out Pasta Dough

- Divide the dough into small workable pieces; the size will vary depending on whether you are hand rolling or using a pasta machine.
- When using a machine, flatten the dough with your hand first so that the dough does not break apart on the initial roll-through.

- Begin rolling the dough on the thickest setting, folding it into thirds in the shape of a square and working to attain a rectangular sheet as the dough comes through the machine. Repeat this step two times on the first two settings. This will achieve a smooth texture as well as the best possible yield.
- Continue rolling the rectangular sheets through, moving only one setting at a time. Roll all sheets on one setting before changing to the next and thinner setting. Keep the dough sheets covered loosely with plastic wrap during the rolling process.
- For ravioli, the dough sheet should be thin enough to read newspaper print through. This will be one of the thinnest settings.
- Store the pasta sheets on parchment-lined sheet pans that have been lightly dusted with flour. Cover with plastic until ready to use. If not using immediately, store under refrigeration.

The dough should be used within 24 hours. After this time the dough will begin to discolor and absorb moisture. Once shapes are formed, fresh pasta can be frozen. Certain ravioli fillings will freeze better than others and have different shelf lives (cheese ravioli freezes well; meat ravioli doesn't freeze as well).

It is also important to note that when working with fresh dough one must pay close attention to several key factors: proper scaling and measurements, type of flour, how and where flour is stored, water, and moisture. All of these components will impact the texture and consistency of the dough; the amount of flour used may need to be adjusted.

Cooking One Pound of Dry Pasta

1. Add 2 Tbl. of salt to 6 qts. of water and bring to a simmer.
2. It is not necessary to add oil to the water as it sits on top of the water and the pasta cooks in the water.
3. Do not break long pasta when placing it in the water; the pasta maker worked hard to attain the shape and size!
4. Stir the pasta occasionally to prevent sticking, until it is al dente. Drain well and mix with the sauce as per the recipe.

One pound of dry pasta is sufficient for approximately 8 primi piatti portions (appetizer size) or 2 pounds cooked pasta.

It is best to cook dry pasta just prior to serving. Par-cooking in advance will compromise the texture and consistency of the final product as well as its ability to hold the sauce.

Cheese Ravioli with Asparagus and Butter Sauce

RAVIOLI

The following three recipes are for ravioli that are pasta ripiena (stuffed pasta).

CHEESE RAVIOLI WITH ASPARAGUS AND BUTTER SAUCE

Yield: 50 ravioli

Ingredients	Amounts - US	Volume	Metric
For the Ravioli			
Basic Pasta Dough		see recipe	
Egg wash, for sealing the ravioli		as needed	
For the Ravioli Filling			
Ricotta, fresh	1 ½ lb.	3 cups	680 grams
Parmigiano Reggiano, grated	4 ½ oz.	1 ½ cups	128 grams
Bread crumbs, toasted	1 ½ oz.	⅓ cup	42 grams
Parsley, Italian, chopped	⅜ oz.	3 Tbl.	9 grams
Salt, kosher		1 tsp.	
Black pepper, fresh ground		¼ tsp.	
Cayenne pepper		⅛ tsp.	
Egg yolk, large	1 ⅛ oz.	2 each	32 grams
For the Asparagus and Butter Sauce	**Yield: 10 portions**		
Asparagus, peeled, blanched, 1" pieces	10 oz.	1 bunch	284 grams
Chicken stock	20 fl. oz.	2 ½ cups	600 ml
Butter, unsalted, cubed	5 oz.	10 Tbl.	142 grams
Parmigiano Reggiano, grated	2 oz.	⅔ cup	56 grams
Salt, kosher		to taste	
Black pepper, fresh ground		to taste	
Parsley, Italian, chopped		1 Tbl.	
Tarragon, chopped		1 Tbl.	

Ravioli Filling

1. Combine all ingredients except the egg yolk; mix well to fully incorporate.
2. Taste and adjust the seasoning.
3. Add the egg yolk and mix to incorporate evenly.
4. Reserve under refrigeration until needed.

Ravioli

1. Roll out the pasta dough as discussed in the general guidelines for pasta dough, on page 209.
2. Place 1 ½ tsp. of filling along the center of a sheet of dough, allowing 1 inch between the filling and ½ inch at the top and bottom.
3. Lightly brush the exposed surface of the dough with egg wash.

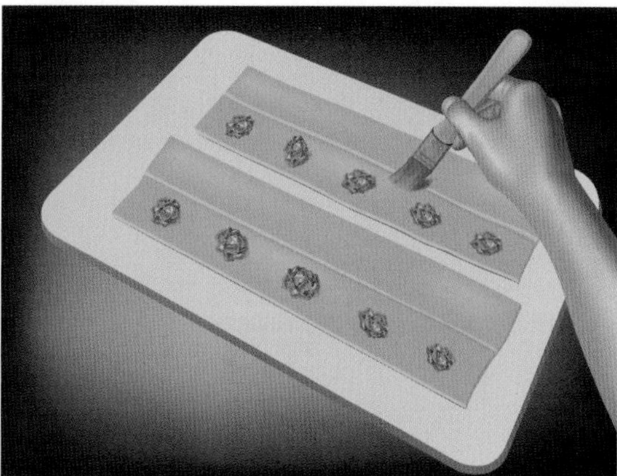

4. Fold the back edge of the dough forward to line up with the front edge. Using your finger, seal the dough between the filling first and then along the front edge.

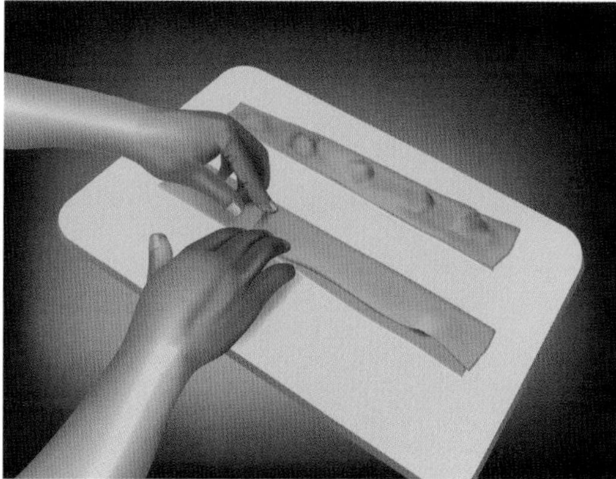

5. Using a ravioli wheel, cut along the long end of the sheet first and then between each ravioli.

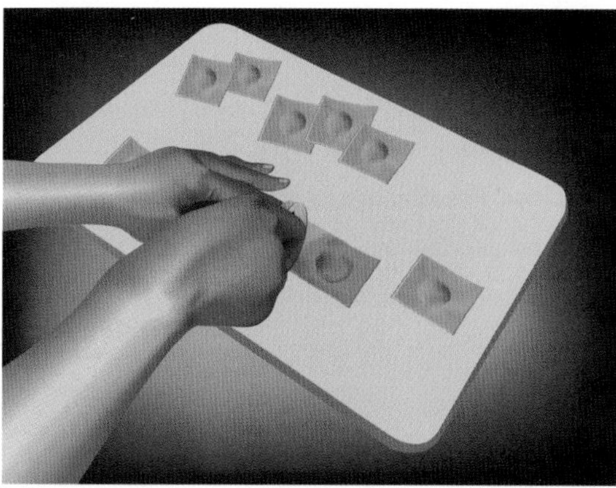

(Continues on next page)

6. Use your fingers to remove any air bubbles between the layers and around the filling as well as to fully seal the ends.

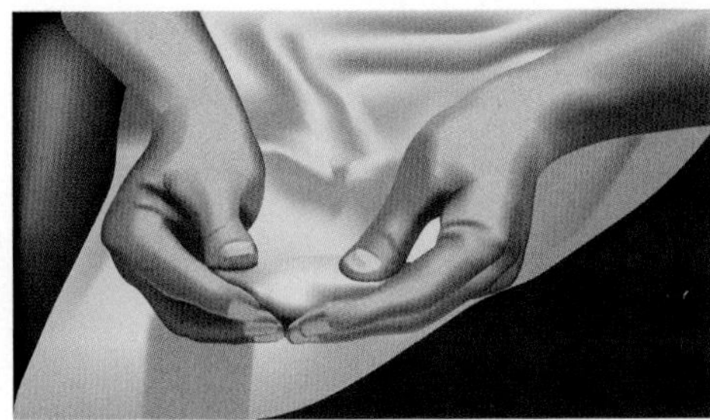

7. Place the ravioli on a parchment-lined sheet pan that has been lightly dusted with flour. Lightly dust the top of the ravioli with flour; cover with parchment paper and plastic wrap.
8. Refrigerate until needed. Use within 24 hours or the ravioli will begin to darken in color as well as stick to the paper.
9. Place the ravioli in salted simmering water (if the water is at a rapid boil the ravioli may break apart), for approximately 3 ½ minutes until cooked.
10. Drain the ravioli well and add to the sauce; proceed as indicated below.

Asparagus and Butter Sauce

1. Place the chicken stock in a large sauté pan and reduce by one-third, then lower the heat and add the butter; swirl the pan gently to fully incorporate.
2. Add the cheese, cooked ravioli, and the asparagus; swirl gently to coat with the sauce and melt the cheese. You may need to work in small batches so that you don't overcrowd the pan.
3. Add the herbs, taste, and adjust the seasoning.
4. Plate and serve immediately.

Asparagus can be quite difficult to pair with wine. It contains methionine, mercaptan, and thiols, which create a chemical reaction on your palate that makes wine taste green or metallic and overall can be a negative experience. However, when the asparagus is grilled, or served with a butter sauce, as in this recipe, its *bitterness* is diminished, making it more agreeable with wine.

Sometimes you can adjust a dish to make it more *wine-friendly* and enhance a pairing. The initial pairing was good, but not magical. The finish was relatively short. We made some minor adjustments to the sauce adding more butter and decreasing the stock. These changes make the dish more wine-friendly by increasing the depth of flavor and extending the finish on your palate.

WINE SELECTED with Cheese Ravioli with Asparagus and Butter Sauce

Wine: Burgans Albariño ($14)
Origin: Rias Baixas, Spain

Taste and Texture Comparisons

Dish: Soft Texture, Buttery, Creamy, Slightly Sweet, Slight Vegetal/Green

Wine: Soft Texture, Lightly Floral, Stone Fruit, Medium-Body, Crisp Acidity

Albariño is an increasingly popular white grape variety from northwestern Spain (in Portugual it's called Alvarinho). Albariño from Rias Baixas is medium-bodied with delicate floral, white peach, and mineral notes.

Why This Is a Good Pairing

- ***Matching Texture and Intensity*** – The wine and the dish are soft in texture and medium in their flavor intensity.
- ***Complementing*** – Tarragon and ricotta have a slight sweetness that connects with the sweetness of the fruit in the wine. Additionally, the creamy filling carries the flavors of the tarragon and the wine longer.
- ***Contrasting*** – The vegetal/green nature and flavor of the asparagus also focuses the palate on the fruit, which softens the impression of the asparagus (in a good way).
- ***Cleansing*** – The wine's crisp acidity cleanses the palate slightly, making the dish a bit fresher and lighter. However, the wine does not strip the fat or flavor of the cheese or butter (these fats are the vehicle of the dish's flavor across the palate).

Wines That Didn't Work

Oaked California Chardonnay – The wine overpowers the dish in weight and flavor, covering the dish. Additionally, the butter in the dish compounds with the butter flavor in the wine and makes both taste oily.

Bourgogne Rouge – The tarragon and the asparagus compound with some of the herbal/earthy notes in the wine. The acidity is also a bit too cleansing, which strips the dish of some of its flavor.

Alternative: Valpolicella—Although a red wine, it reacts with this dish are similar to the pairing with the Albariño. The wine's red fruit pops. The tarragon and ricotta have an inherently sweet and earthy tone that bring out the wine's fruit as well as create a *complexing* reaction, showing layers of flavors in the dish and the wine.

SUMMARY	Burgans Rias Baixas Albariño	Valpolicella	Oaked California Chardonnay	Bourgogne Rouge
Matching	+	+		
Complementing	+	+		
Contrasting	+	+		
Compounding			(–)	(–)
Complexing		+		
Cleansing	+			(–)
Covering			(–)	
Clashing				

MEAT RAVIOLI IN BRODO

Yield: 50 ravioli

Ingredients	Amounts - US	Volume	Metric
For the Ravioli			
Basic Pasta Dough		see recipe	
Egg wash, for sealing the ravioli		as needed	
For the Ravioli Filling			
Veal, ground	12 oz.	1 ½ cups	340 grams
Pork, ground	6 oz.	¾ cup	170 grams
Chicken, ground	6 oz.	¾ cup	170 grams
Mortadella, ground	4 oz.	½ cup	114 grams
Parmigiano Reggiano, grated	6 oz.	2 cups	170 grams
Eggs, large, whisked	7 oz.	3 each	198 grams
Parsley, Italian, chopped		2 Tbl.	
Extra virgin olive oil	½ fl. oz.	1 Tbl.	15 ml
Salt, kosher		1 tsp.	
Black pepper, fresh ground		½ tsp.	
Nutmeg, ground		⅛ tsp.	

Ingredients	Amounts - US	Volume	Metric
For the Veal Broth Yield: 1 quart			
Veal stock	48 fl. oz.	6 cups	1.4 liters
Veal trim, large dice	1 lb.		454 grams
Olive oil, pure	1 ½ fl. oz.	3 Tbl.	
Onions, large dice	3 oz.	¾ cup	84 grams
Carrots, large dice	1 ½ oz.	⅓ cup	42 grams
Celery, large dice	1 ½ oz.	⅓ cup	42 grams
Garlic clove, medium, chopped		1 each	
Tomatoes, Roma	3 oz.	1 each	86 grams
Sachet		1 each	
Salt, kosher		to taste	
Black pepper, fresh ground		to taste	
Egg whites, large, whisked well	2 oz.	2 each	56 grams
White wine, light, dry	½ fl. oz.	1 Tbl.	15 ml
For the Garnish			
Parsley, Italian, chopped		1 Tbl.	
Extra virgin olive oil		2 ½ tsp.	

Ravioli Filling

1. Combine all of the ingredients and mix well to fully incorporate.
2. Poach a tablespoon (quenelle) of the mixture to test, taste and adjust the seasoning.
3. Reserve under refrigeration until needed.

Veal Broth

1. Preheat a stockpot over medium-high heat.
2. Add the oil and the veal trim; cook until well browned on all sides.
3. Add the onions and the carrots; sauté until they are caramelized evenly.
4. Add the garlic and sauté until aromatic.
5. Add the stock, tomato, and the sachet.
6. Bring to a simmer and cook for 2 hours or until the broth is very flavorful. Do not boil the broth or the final product will be cloudy and have a greasy mouth feel. Taste and adjust the seasoning.
7. Strain the broth through a chinois lined with cheesecloth and cool in an ice bath to below 90 F (32 C) degrees.

(Continues on next page)

8. Whisk the egg whites until thin and fluid; add the wine and mix to combine.
9. Place the broth in a stockpot; add the egg white/wine mixture and begin heating over medium heat while stirring with a wooden spoon.
10. Stir until the egg whites begin to turn "white," at approximately 115 F (46 C) degrees.
11. Allow the "raft" to fully form—do not boil the broth.
12. Carefully ladle the broth through a cheesecloth-lined chinois.
13. Taste and adjust the seasoning.
14. Reserve hot for service.

Ravioli

1. Roll out the pasta dough as discussed in the general guidelines for pasta dough, on page 209.
2. Place 1 ½ tsp. of filling along the center line of a sheet of dough, allowing 1 inch between the filling and ½ inch at the top and bottom.
3. Lightly brush the exposed surface of the dough with egg wash.
4. Fold the back edge of the dough forward to line up with the front edge. Using your finger, seal the dough between the filling first and then along the front edge.
5. Using a ravioli wheel, cut along the long end of the sheet first and then between each ravioli.
6. Use your fingers to remove any air bubbles between the layers and around the filling as well as to fully seal the ends.

   See illustrations on pages 213–214.

7. Place the ravioli on a parchment-lined pan that has been lightly dusted with flour. Lightly dust the top of the ravioli with flour and cover with parchment and plastic wrap.
8. Refrigerate until needed. Use within 24 hours or the ravioli will begin to turn darker in color as well as stick to the paper.
9. Place the ravioli in simmering water (if the water is at a rapid boil they may break apart), for approximately 3 ½ minutes until cooked.
10. Drain the ravioli well and place in the service bowl. Add 3 oz. of clarified veal broth and garnish with parsley and olive oil.
11. Serve immediately.

WINE SELECTED with Meat Ravioli in Brodo

Wine: Château de Campuget Costières de Nimes Rosé ($10)
Origin: Rhône Valley, France

Taste and Texture Comparisons

Dish: Mixture of Textures (Rich and Light), Herbal, Bold, Umami
Wine: Light-Bodied, Delicately Fruity, Crisp, Slight Savory Herbal Note

This wine shares some elements with Provence rosés and is more delicate than Tavel rosé. It is delicately pink and dry with notes of strawberry, minerals, and hints of fresh herbs (herbs de Provence).

Why This Is a Good Pairing

- ***Matching Flavor Intensity*** – The flavor intensity of the meat filling matches the wine. This is why the wine does not overpower the dish and vice versa.
- ***Complementing*** – The wine's slight herbal notes complement some of the herbal notes in the savory meat filling.
- ***Contrasting*** – The savory, meaty character of the filling and brodo contrasts with the wine's delicate fruitiness, making the wine's fruit stand out a bit more.
- ***Cleansing*** – The crisp acidity of the wine is very refreshing and adds lightness to the dish.

Wines That Didn't Work

Languedoc Viognier – This white is a bit too big for this dish and the acid is too low, making the dish taste heavier and the flavors a bit flat or muted.

Chianti Classico – Surprisingly, the Chianti Classico is too rich in flavor intensity and weight and ultimately overpowers the dish.

Alternative: Bourgogne Rouge—A light, unoaked Bourgogne Rouge pairs quite well for the same reasons as the rosé. The Bourgogne Rouge has a little more earthy notes, which are complemented and create a *complexing* reaction. However, we found that richer Pinot Noirs (those with more oak character and a richer, more complex style) are augmented in their fruit and though the dish helps the wine, the wine overpowers the dish.

SUMMARY	Château de Campuget Costières de Nimes Rosé	Bourgogne Rouge	Languedoc Viognier	Chianti Classico
Matching	+	+		
Complementing	+	+		
Contrasting	+	+		
Compounding				
Complexing		+		
Cleansing	+	+		
Covering			(–)	(–)
Clashing			(–)	

Shrimp Ravioli with Tomato Coulis

SHRIMP RAVIOLI WITH TOMATO COULIS

Yield: 50 ravioli

Ingredients	Amounts - US	Volume	Metric
For the Ravioli			
Basic Pasta Dough		see recipe	
Egg wash, for sealing the ravioli		as needed	
For the Ravioli Filling			
Ricotta Impasta	10 oz.	1 ½ cups	284 grams
Shrimp, seared, chopped	10 oz.	1 ¼ cups	284 grams
Fontina cheese, grated	2 oz.	1 cup	56 grams
Tarragon, chopped		1 Tbl.	
Lemon zest, blanched		1 ½ tsp.	
Roasted garlic, paste		¾ tsp.	
Salt, sea		¾ tsp.	
Black pepper, fresh ground		½ tsp.	
Cayenne		⅛ tsp.	
For the Tomato Coulis **Yield: 2 ½ cups**			
Extra virgin olive oil	1 fl. oz.	2 Tbl.	30 ml
Onion, small dice	2 oz.	½ cup	58 grams
Garlic clove, medium, sliced		1 ½ tsp.	
White wine, Pinot Grigio	2 fl. oz.	¼ cup	60 ml
Tomatoes, San Marzano style, chopped	1 lb. 10 oz.	3 cups	736 grams
Chicken stock	6 fl. oz.	¾ cup	180 ml
Red pepper, crushed		¼ tsp.	
Salt, kosher		¾ tsp.	
Black pepper, fresh ground		¼ tsp.	
Heavy cream	3 fl. oz.	⅓ cup	90 ml
Butter, unsalted, cubed	1 oz.	2 Tbl.	28 grams
For the Garnish			
Parsley, Italian, chopped		1 Tbl.	

(Continues on next page)

Ravioli Filling

1. Combine all ingredients; mix well to fully incorporate.
2. Taste and adjust the seasoning.
3. Reserve under refrigeration until needed.

Ravioli

1. Roll out the pasta dough as discussed in the general guidelines for pasta dough, on page 209.
2. Place 1 ½ tsp. of filling along the center line of a sheet of dough, allowing 1 inch between the filling and ½ inch at the top and bottom.
3. Lightly brush the exposed surface of the dough with egg wash.
4. Fold the back edge of the dough forward to line up with the front edge. Using your finger, seal the dough between the filling first and then along the front edge.
5. Using a ravioli wheel, cut along the long end of the sheet first and then between each ravioli.
6. Use your fingers to remove any air bubbles between the layers and around the filling as well as to fully seal the ends.
   See illustrations on pages 213–214.
7. Place the ravioli on a parchment-lined pan that has been lightly dusted with flour. Lightly dust the top of the ravioli with flour; cover with parchment and plastic wrap.
8. Refrigerate until needed. Use within 24 hours or the ravioli will begin to turn darker in color as well as stick to the paper.

Tomato Coulis

1. Preheat a saucepan over medium heat.
2. Add the olive oil and the onions; sweat until tender.
3. Add the garlic and sauté until very aromatic.
4. Deglaze with the white wine and reduce by three-quarters.
5. Add the tomatoes, chicken stock, and the seasonings; bring to a simmer.
6. Cook gently for 30 minutes or until the acidity is cooked out and the tomatoes have a slightly sweet flavor.
7. Remove from the heat and pass through a food mill with a medium disc.
8. Return to a gentle simmer; add the cream and simmer gently for 5 minutes.
9. Add the butter and whisk to incorporate.
10. Taste and adjust the seasoning.
11. Place the ravioli in simmering water (if the water is at a rapid boil they may break apart), for approximately 3 ½ minutes until cooked.
12. Ladle 1 ½ oz. of Tomato Coulis in the bottom of the bowl.
13. Drain the ravioli well and place in the service bowl. Add an additional ¾ oz. of sauce on top of the ravioli.
14. Garnish and serve immediately.

WINE SELECTED with Shrimp Ravioli with Tomato Coulis

Wine: Champagne Charles Heidsieck Brut Réserve ($45)

Origin: Champagne, France

Taste and Texture Comparisons

Dish: Light Sweetness, Mild Spice, Rich, Soft Texture

Wine: Dry, Crisp, Toasty, Biscuity/Yeasty, Sparkling

This is a full-bodied, non-vintage Champagne given it has a higher level of reserve champagnes (about 40%) and is aged on lees for almost four years.

Why This Is a Good Pairing

- ***Matching Flavor Intensity*** – Although there is a contrast between the weight of the dish and the lightness of the Champagne, the flavor intensities of both are fairly evenly matched.
- ***Complementing*** – The cream in the dish connects with some of the slight creamy and nutty notes in the Champagne. Additionally, the flavor of the pasta connects with some of the biscuity autolytic notes of the Champagne.
- ***Contrasting*** – The tomatoes focus your palate on the biscuity autolytic tones of the Champagne.
- ***Cleansing*** – The effervescence is cleansing, but also the acidity in Champagne is quite high. Both of these cleanse the palate, cutting through the richness of the dish. This helps your palate focus on some of the delicate flavors of the shrimp.

Wines That Didn't Work

Barbera d'Asti – The acidity of the Barbera cuts through the cream; however, the weight of the wine is a bit much for this dish and covers up the delicate flavor of the shrimp.

California Pinot Noir – The tarragon connects with a slight earthy note in the wine; however, the wine covers some of the elements of the dish. Additionally, the dish's mild spice clashes with the wine's alcohol (14%+ abv), which makes both stand out and cuts the finish short.

Alternative: Fino Sherry—Understanding that this is a fortified wine, the alcohol stands out more than with other wines (and cuts the finish shorter than with the Champagne); yet, the salty almond nuttiness of the Fino Sherry contrasts with and brings out the sweetness of the shrimp and a bit of the tarragon. Additionally, the nuttiness of the sherry complements the butter/cream.

SUMMARY	Champagne Charles Heidsieck Brut Réserve	Fino Sherry	Barbera d'Asti	California Pinot Noir
Matching	+			
Complementing	+	+		+
Contrasting	+	+		
Compounding				
Complexing				
Cleansing	+	(–)	+	
Covering			(–)	(–)
Clashing				(–)

Spaghetti con le Vongole (Clam Sauce)

SPAGHETTI

SPAGHETTI CON LE VONGOLE (CLAM SAUCE)

Yield: 8 portions

Ingredients	Amounts - US	Volume	Metric
Spaghetti, dry	1 lb.		454 grams
For the Sauce			
Clams, little neck, purged*		7 dozen	
Extra virgin olive oil	2 fl. oz.	¼ cup	60 ml
Onion, small dice	3 oz.	¾ cup	84 grams
Garlic, sliced	1 oz.	2 Tbl.	28 grams
Clam juice, bottled	16 fl. oz.	2 cups	480 ml
White wine, Sauvignon Blanc	3 fl. oz.	⅓ cup	90 ml
Oregano, fresh chopped		1 Tbl. plus 1 tsp.	
Parsley, Italian, chopped		1 Tbl.	
Black pepper, fresh ground		¼ tsp.	
Crushed red pepper		¼ tsp.	
Butter, unsalted	1 oz.	2 Tbl.	28 grams
For the Garnish			
Parsley, Italian, chopped		1 Tbl.	

* To purge the clams of sand, combine 6 qts (6 liters) of water, 55 F (12 C) degrees, mixed with 2 Tbl. of salt and then add the clams. Place the bowl in a quiet place with no vibration for 30–40 minutes. Drain well and rinse the clams with cold water.

(Continues on next page)

Spaghetti con le Vongole

1. Set up a pasta pot and time the cooking of the pasta to add to the sauce in step 8. (See page 210.)
2. Preheat a sautoir/rondeau over medium heat.
3. Add the oil and the onion; sweat until the onions are tender.
4. Add the garlic and sauté until it is aromatic and begins to color lightly on the ends.
5. Add the white wine and reduce by half.
6. Add the clam juice, oregano, parsley, black pepper, and crushed red pepper; bring to a simmer.
7. Add the purged clams and cover with a lid. Remove the clams as they open and place them in a bowl to keep warm.
8. Once all of the clams are open and the pasta is very al dente (1 minute prior to being done), drain the pasta and add it to the sauce.
9. Gently simmer the pasta in the sauce until it is al dente and has absorbed some of the sauce.
10. Add the butter and return the clams; mix well.
11. Portion, garnish, and serve immediately.

This recipe has no salt added because clams typically provide enough salt for seasoning. Butter is optional in this preparation; it adds a velvety mouth feel and helps the sauce to coat the pasta. The amount of clam juice may be adjusted based on how much natural juice is released when the clams open. Discard any clams that do not open as they may be dead.

WINE SELECTED with Spaghetti con le Vongole

Wine: Nederberg Sauvignon Blanc ($9)
Origin: Paarl, South Africa

Taste and Texture Comparisons

Dish: Aromatic, Herbal, Briny, Bright
Wine: Aromatic, Herbal, Delicate, Crisp

Sauvignon Blanc from South Africa can be quite pungent. This one is a bit more restrained and more Old World-like with notes of gooseberry, delicate flowers, fresh-cut grass, and mineral tones.

Why This Is a Good Pairing

- ***Matching*** – The dish and the wine match in terms of flavor intensity.
- ***Complementing*** – The light herbal nature of the wine connects with some of the herbal notes in the dish. In this instance green + green was a pleasant green.
- ***Contrasting*** – The fruit and crisp acidity in the wine bring out the salty/briny character of the clams. It makes their flavors pop.
- ***Cleansing*** – The crisp acidity of the wine lightens the dish and makes it a more refreshing pairing.

Wines That Didn't Work

Chablis – The salty/briny nature of the dish makes the fruit flavors stand out in the wine initially, but then the dish cuts the flavor of the wine. The dish is slightly overpowering as the wine is more neutral in its flavor profile than is the South African Sauvignon Blanc.

Oaked California Chardonnay – Compounding of a small amount of butter in the dish and the buttery notes in the wine makes, this taste like one big butterball. The flavor of the oak also covers the flavor of the clams.

Chianti Classico – The dish completely overpowers the wine. The saltiness and the tannins clash, which makes the wine taste bitter.

SUMMARY	Nederberg South Africa Sauvignon Blanc	Chablis	California Chardonnay	Chianti Classico
Matching	+	(–)	(–)	
Complementing	+			
Contrasting	+			
Compounding			(–)	
Complexing				
Cleansing	+			
Covering		(–)	(–)	(–)
Clashing				(–)

Spaghetti alla Carbonara "Charcoal/Coal Miner's Style"

SPAGHETTI ALLA CARBONARA "CHARCOAL/COAL MINER'S STYLE"

Yield: 8 portions

Ingredients	Amounts - US	Volume	Metric
Spaghetti, dry	1 lb.		454 grams
For the Sauce			
Extra virgin olive oil	½ fl. oz.	1 Tbl.	15 ml
Pancetta or Guanciale, small dice	5 oz.	1 cup	140 grams
Egg yolks, large	4 ⅜ oz.	8 each	122 grams
Parmigiano Reggiano, grated	1 ½ oz.	½ cup	36 grams
Pecorino Toscano, grated	¾ oz.	¼ cup	18 grams
Black pepper, fresh, course ground		2 tsp.	
Heavy cream, warm	2 fl. oz.	¼ cup	60 ml
For the Garnish			
Parsley, Italian, chopped		as needed	

Spaghetti alla Carbonara

1. Set up a pasta pot and time the cooking of the pasta to add to the sauce in step 7. (See page 210.)
2. Preheat a saucepan over medium heat.
3. Add the oil and the pancetta or guanciale; sauté until it is light brown but not too crisp.
4. Remove from the heat and reserve.
5. Place the yolks in a stainless steel mixing bowl and whisk until fluid.
6. Add the cheeses, black pepper, and the pancetta with the rendered fat; whisk until fully combined. If using the heavy cream, add it to the yolks.
7. Once the spaghetti is al dente, drain well and add to the mixing bowl with the yolks and cheese. Add a small amount, approximately 2 Tbl., of pasta cooking water to the bowl to adjust the sauce consistency.
8. Taste and adjust the seasoning.
9. Garnish and eat immediately.

Traditional Pasta alla Carbonara is a very delicate preparation; it is intended to be cooked, mixed, and eaten immediately because the longer the pasta sits, the more the eggs will begin to thicken and the pasta will become very pasty. As listed above, it is optional to add 2 oz. of heavy cream to the yolks, which will hold the sauce consistency a bit longer after mixing.

WINE SELECTED with Spaghetti alla Carbonara

Wine: Masi Costasera Amarone della Valpolicella ($45)
Origin: Valpolicella Classico, Veneto, Italy

Taste and Texture Comparisons

Dish: Rich, Bold Flavor, Creamy, Salty, Umami
Wine: Rich, Bold Flavor, Bitter, Spice, High Alcohol

Amarone is a style of wine made from dried grapes from the region of Valpolicella Classico. Dried grapes have more concentration, and a higher sugar content, which leads to higher alcohol, and fuller body.

Why This Is a Good Pairing

- ***Matching*** – The dish and the wine are bold and rich. They match in flavor intensity and in weight.
- ***Complementing*** – The black pepper spice in the dish complements some of the spicy notes in the wine.
- ***Contrasting*** – The pancetta softens the tannins in the wine (making the wine softer and more approachable) and it also contrasts well with the fruit in the wine, making the fruit pop.
- ***Complexing*** – This is quite a magical pairing because the dish and the wine are both complex in their flavors and you taste each layer.

Wines That Didn't Work

Oaked California Chardonnay – Theoretically, the vanilla and spice of the oak would augment the flavor of the pancetta in the dish, but this didn't happen. There is also a compounding effect, making the wine and the dish very heavy and out of balance.

Argentinean Malbec – The flavor of the wine overpowers the dish, yet the weight of the dish overpowers the wine making the wine seem thinner than it is. Additionally, some of the flavors clash, making the wine taste slightly metallic.

Alternative: Zinfandel—This wine works well with this dish for some of the same reasons that the Amarone works. Many Zinfandels and most Amarones wines are generally above 15% abv, so you need to be careful with the amount of black pepper you add to the dish. If there is too much black pepper, it will make the wine taste "hot" or too alcoholic and out of balance.

SUMMARY	Masi Costasera Amarone della Valpolicella	St. Francis Old Vines Zinfandel	Oaked California Chardonnay	Argentinean Malbec
Matching	+	+		
Complementing	+	+		
Contrasting	+	+		
Compounding			(–)	
Complexing	+	+		
Cleansing	+			
Covering			(–)	(–)
Clashing				(–)

SPAGHETTI ALLA PUTTANESCA

Yield: 8 portions

Ingredients	Amounts - US	Volume	Metric
Spaghetti, dry	1 lb.		454 grams
For the Puttanesca Sauce			
Extra virgin olive oil	2 fl. oz.	¼ cup	60 ml
Onion, small dice	4 oz.	1 cup	112 grams
Garlic, rough chopped	1 oz.	2 Tbl.	28 grams
Anchovy filet, mashed	¼ oz.	3 each	8 grams
Tomatoes, canned, San Marzano style, chopped	3 lbs.	5 cups	1,360 grams
Olives, Kalamata, rough chopped	4 oz.	½ cup	114 grams
Capers, soaked, drained	¾ oz.	2 Tbl.	22 grams
Oregano, rough chopped		1 ½ Tbl.	
Parsley, Italian, chopped		1 Tbl.	
Salt, kosher	¼ oz.	1 tsp.	6 grams
Black pepper, fresh ground	¼ oz.	1 tsp.	6 grams
For the Garnish			
Oregano, chopped		1 ½ tsp.	
Parsley, Italian, chopped		1 ½ tsp.	

The word "puttanesca" literally translates to "in the style of the prostitute." It is a highly aromatic sauce that is said to attract customers. The pasta came on the scene in the late 1960s to early 1970s and comes from the town of Siracusa in Sicily. There's no documentation to prove this, but it's an interesting story.

Spaghetti alla Puttanesca

1. Set up a pasta pot and time the cooking of the pasta to add to the sauce in step 10. (See page 210.)
2. Preheat a saucepan over medium heat.
3. Add the oil and onions; sweat until the onions are tender.
4. Add the garlic and sauté until it is very aromatic and begins to color lightly.
5. Add the anchovy filets and mix well to break up.
6. Add the tomatoes and bring to a gentle simmer. Cook for 20 minutes.

(Continues on next page)

7. Add the olives, capers, oregano, and parsley and continue cooking for an additional 15–20 minutes or until the acidity is cooked out and the tomatoes have a slightly sweet flavor.
8. Add the salt and pepper, taste, and adjust the seasoning.
9. Cook the spaghetti al dente and drain well.
10. Mix the pasta with 2 ½ cups of the puttanesca sauce.
11. Place the pasta in a bowl and top with 2 oz. of additional sauce.
12. Garnish and serve immediately.

The salt content in the olives and capers can vary so it is important to taste and adjust the seasoning accordingly. This sauce can be made in advance and stored in the refrigerator. The flavor will deepen after 2 days but the sauce should be used within 4 days.

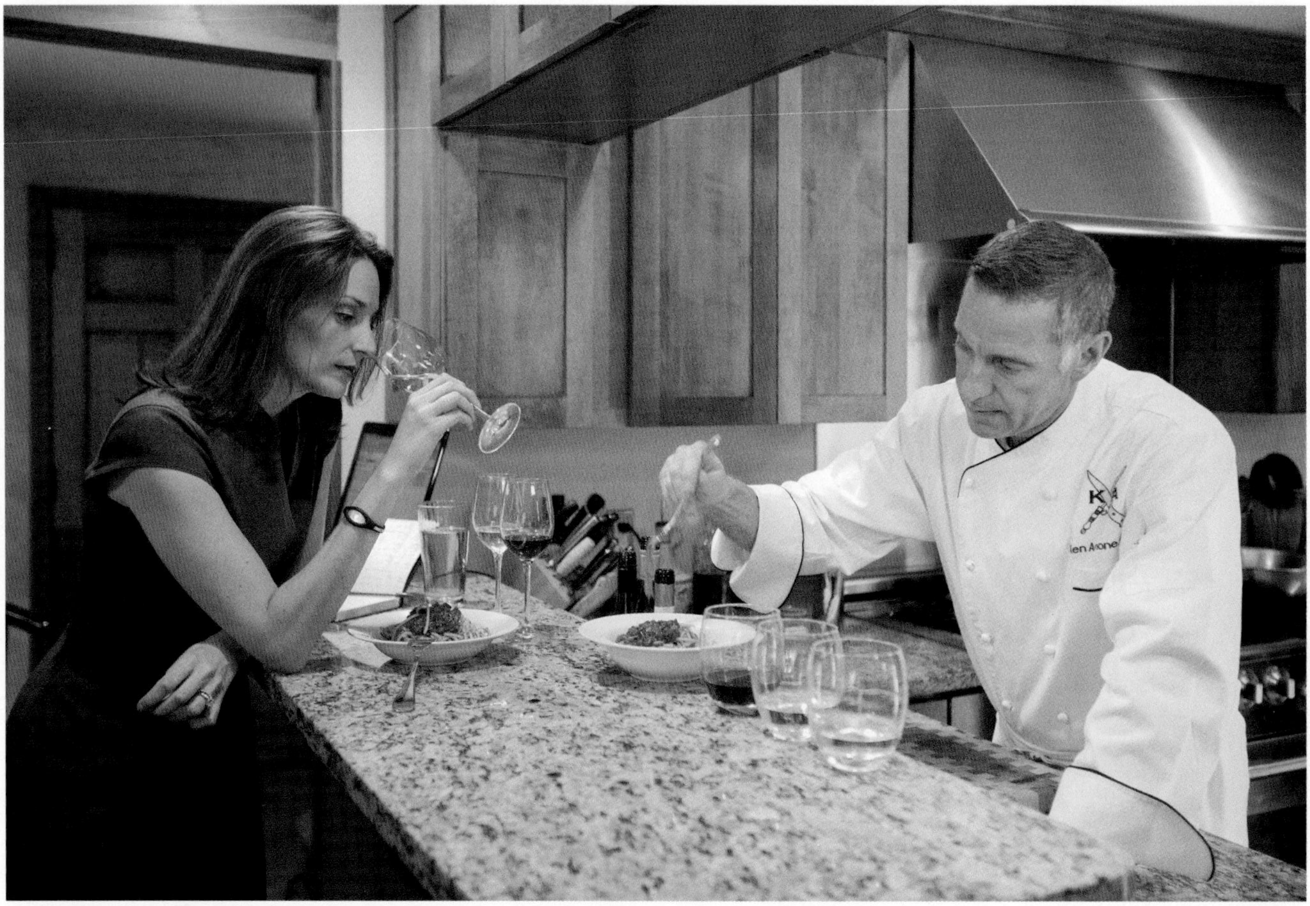

WINE SELECTED with Spaghetti alla Puttanesca

Wine: Azienda Agraria Le Rote Vernaccia di San Gimignano ($14)
Origin: San Gimignano, Tuscany, Italy

Taste and Texture Comparisons

Dish: Aromatic, Aggressive, Herbal
Wine: Moderate Acidity, Alcohol, Body, Soft Texture

Vernaccia is a medium-bodied white with a soft texture. It has citrus notes and, like many Italian whites, it has mineral and some delicate almond notes.

Why This Is a Good Pairing

- ***Contrasting Textures*** – The dish is racy, aggressive, and aromatic while the wine is much softer. The pairing is like falling into a pillow. The wine softens the raciness of the dish, while the herbs of the dish and the almond notes in the wine pop.
- ***Complementing*** – The soft almond tones in the wine connect with the flavor of the pasta.
- ***Contrasting*** – The wine's soft citrus flavor and the herbal notes in the dish contrast, which augments both even more.
- ***Cleansing*** – The dish creates a cleansing sensation with the wine, but not so much that it strips the flavor of the wine.

Wines That Didn't Work

Chianti Classico – The acidity is too cleansing and the herbal notes in the wine make the capers stand out too much.

Napa Cabernet Sauvignon – The Napa Cabernet we tried has some obvious oak tones (vanilla, spice, tobacco), which clash terribly with the dish. The racy and herbal notes make the oak flavors in the wine taste like laundry detergent. The intensity of the wine also covers the dish.

Alternative: Amarone—We tried two different Amarones with this dish to make sure it works as an alternative. The acidity in the wine and the dish match. The dried fruit in the wine makes the flavors of the tomatoes taste sweeter. There is also a *complexing* reaction in which we could taste all the layers in the dish and in the wine.

SUMMARY	Azienda Agraria Le Rote Vernaccia di San Gimignano	Amarone	Chianti Classico	Napa Cabernet Sauvignon
Matching		+		
Complementing	+	+		
Contrasting	+	+		
Compounding			(–)	
Complexing		+		
Cleansing	+	+	(–)	
Covering				(–)
Clashing				(–)

MEZZE RIGATONI

Mezze rigatoni is a half cut of rigatoni. This shape allows for pieces of broccoli rabe and sausage to be captured in the pasta.

MEZZE RIGATONI WITH BROCCOLI RABE AND SAUSAGE

Yield: 8 portions

Ingredients	Amounts - US	Volume	Metric
Mezze rigatoni, dry	1 lb.		454 grams
Extra virgin olive oil	3 fl. oz.	⅓ cup	90 ml
Fennel sausage, no casing	1 lb.	2 ¼ cups	452 grams
Onions, small dice	6 oz.	1 ½ cups	170 grams
Garlic, sliced thin	½ oz.	1 Tbl.	14 grams
Chicken stock	8–12 fl. oz.	1–1 ½ cups	240–360 ml
Broccoli rabe, blanched, rough chopped	12 oz.	2 bunches	342 grams
Salt, kosher		½ tsp.	
Crushed red pepper		¼ tsp.	
Black pepper, fresh ground		¼ tsp.	
Parmigiano Reggiano, grated	1 ½ oz.	½ cup	42 grams
Butter, unsalted, cubed	1 oz.	2 Tbl.	28 grams
Basil, chiffonade		3 Tbl.	
Parsley, Italian, chopped		1 Tbl.	
For the Garnish			
Parmigiano Reggiano, grated		2 Tbl.	
Pine nuts, toasted		1 ½ Tbl.	
Parsley, Italian, chopped		1 Tbl.	

Mezze Rigatoni

1. Set up a pasta pot and time the cooking of the pasta to add to the sauce in step 7. (See page 210.)
2. Preheat a sautoir/rondeau over medium-high heat.
3. Add the oil and the sausage. Allow the sausage to brown and then begin to break up/crumble with a wooden spatula or spoon. Cook until the sausage is evenly golden brown.
4. Lower the heat to medium and add the onions and garlic; sauté until the onions are tender and have started to brown on the ends. (If the sausage is very lean you may need to add additional oil for the onions and garlic.)
5. Add the chicken stock and bring to a simmer.
6. Add the broccoli rabe and the seasonings; return to a simmer.
7. Add the cooked al dente pasta and mix well to combine; return to a gentle simmer and allow the pasta to absorb some of the sauce and then remove from the heat.
8. Add the basil, parsley, butter, and Parmesan cheese; mix well to combine. Taste and adjust the seasoning.
9. Adjust the sauce consistency with the pasta water as needed.
10. Garnish with Parmigiano Reggiano, pine nuts, and parsley; serve immediately.

WINE SELECTED with Mezze Rigatoni with Broccoli Rabe and Sausage

Wine: Tedeschi Capitel Tenda Soave Classico ($14)
Origin: Soave Classico, Veneto, Italy

This wine is made with 100% Garganega. Soave has floral, pear, and mineral notes with a soft texture that makes it quite versatile with many dishes.

Taste and Texture Comparisons

Dish: Savory, Bold, Rich, Bitter, Spicy, Umami
Wine: Fresh Fruit, Soft Texture, Moderate Body, Acidity, and Alcohol

Why This Is a Good Pairing

- ***Contrasting Texture*** – The wine is soft-textured and moderate while the dish is more bold, bitter, and spicy. The wine softens the bitterness of the dish without covering any flavors or clashing.
- ***Complementing*** – The soft almond notes in the wine complement the pasta and pine nuts, highlighting their flavors.
- ***Contrasting*** – The fruit and floral notes of the wine contrast with the bitterness, Umami, and spice of the dish. This makes the flavors of both the dish and the wine pop.
- ***Complexing*** – The contrasting and complementing create a *complexing* reaction; you taste all the layers of each.
- ***Cleansing*** – The moderate acidity is crisp enough to create a soft, refreshing reaction on the palate without stripping any flavor from the dish or the wine.

Wines That Didn't Work

Sauvignon Blanc – We tried several Sauvignon Blancs. The herbaceousness of the wine along with the green flavor and bitterness of the broccoli rabe and the herbs compound for an unpleasant green character (Green + Green = $Green^2$).

Zinfandel – The wine is too overpowering and bold for this dish and covers up the flavors. Additionally, the bitterness in the broccoli rabe and the tannins in the wine compound, which makes both taste more bitter.

Alternative: Orvieto—Although some of the reactions are the same as the Soave Classico, there are differences. The Orvieto is not as soft in texture and has less obvious fruit, which makes the fennel and sausage stand out more, and perhaps taste a bit sweeter. Although the pairing is different than with the Soave, it is a very good pairing.

SUMMARY	Tedeschi Capitel Tenda Soave Classico	Orvieto	Sauvignon Blanc	Zinfandel
Matching				
Complementing	+	+		
Contrasting	+	+		
Compounding			(–)	(–)
Complexing	+			
Cleansing	+	+		
Covering				(–)
Clashing				

MEZZE RIGATONI SALAD WITH ROASTED BUTTERNUT SQUASH, RED ONIONS, SAGE, AND PUMPKIN SEEDS

Yield: 8 portions

Ingredients	Amounts - US	Volume	Metric
For the Salad			
Mezze rigatoni, cooked, chilled	1 lb.		908 grams
Butternut squash, roasted	12 oz.	2 ½ cups	336 grams
Red onions, roasted	4 oz.	1 cup	114 grams
Extra virgin olive oil	2 ½ fl. oz.	2 ½ Tbl.	75 ml
Parmigiano Reggiano cheese, grated	½ oz.	3 Tbl.	16 grams
Pumpkin seeds, toasted	¼ oz.	1 ½ Tbl.	10 grams
Pumpkin seed oil		1 ½ tsp.	
Sage leaves, sliced thin widthwise		10 each	
Parsley, Italian, chopped		1 Tbl.	
Salt, kosher		½ tsp.	
Black pepper, fresh ground		¼ tsp.	
For the Roasted Butternut Squash			
Butternut squash, peeled, medium dice	2 lbs.	1 each	906 grams
Extra virgin olive oil	1 fl. oz.	2 Tbl.	30 ml
Salt, kosher		¾ tsp	
Black pepper, fresh ground		½ tsp.	
For the Roasted Red Onions			
Red onion, medium dice	12 oz.	1 each	340 grams
Extra virgin olive oil	1 fl. oz.	2 Tbl.	30 ml
Salt, kosher		½ tsp.	
Black pepper, fresh ground		¼ tsp.	
For the Toasted Pumpkin Seeds			
Pumpkin seeds	2 oz.	3 Tbl.	20 grams
Extra virgin olive oil		as needed	
For the Garnish			
Parmigiano Reggiano, shaved	2 oz.	¾ cup	56 grams
Pumpkin seeds, toasted	¼ oz.	1 ½ Tbl.	10 grams

(Continues on next page)

Roasted Butternut Squash

1. Mix the butternut squash with the oil and seasoning.
2. Roast at 375 F (176 C) degrees convection for 20 minutes or until tender and lightly caramelized. The yield will be 55–60% of original weight.

Roasted Red Onions

1. Mix the red onions with the oil and seasoning.
2. Roast at 375 F (190 C) degrees convection for 25 minutes or until tender and lightly caramelized. The yield will be 35–40%.

Toasted Pumpkin Seeds

1. Coat pumpkin seeds very lightly with olive oil.
2. Toast at 325 F (165 C) degrees for approximately 10 minutes until crisp and lightly toasted.

Mezze Rigatoni Salad

1. Combine all ingredients and mix gently to fully incorporate.
2. Taste and adjust the seasonings. Allow the flavors to develop for 2 hours under refrigeration.
3. Garnish with Parmigiano Reggiano and pumpkin seeds and serve.

Pumpkin seed oil is very perishable and should be tasted before using. It is also very strong and will vary in intensity; start with a small amount and adjust to taste.

WINE SELECTED with Mezze Rigatoni Salad with Roasted Butternut Squash, Red Onions, Sage, and Pumpkin Seeds

Wine: Chateau St. Jean Sonoma County Chardonnay ($15)
Origin: Sonoma, California, USA

Taste and Texture Comparisons

Dish: Rich, Sweet, Earthy, Creamy Mouth Feel, Toasty, Nutty

Wine: Rich, Boldly Fruity, Medium Acidity, Vanilla, Spice, Butter Notes

Sonoma County is a relatively cool wine region within California. This leads to Chardonnays that are higher in acidity and lower in alcohol than in some of the warmer California regions. This Chardonnay has very ripe apple fruit and oak influence with 13.5% alcohol.

Why This Is a Good Pairing

- ***Matching*** – The dish and the wine match each other in flavor intensity and weight. The texture of the wine is slightly oily, but so is the dish, but this reaction is not compounded as there are other reactions occurring, such as complementing and contrasting.
- ***Complementing*** – The toasty, slightly nutty flavors from the oak in the wine create a bridge to the flavors of the pumpkin seeds and the butternut squash. The pumpkin seeds and the toasty notes of the butternut squash in the dish also bring out the buttery notes in the wine in a complementary, not compounding, way.
- ***Contrasting*** – The sage in the dish contrasts with the flavors of the apples and vanilla from the Chardonnay, which brings out the flavor of all of them.
- ***Complexing*** – There are a lot of flavor combinations within this dish, yet you taste the squash, pumpkin seeds, the pasta, the sage as well as all of the layers of flavors in the wine (apple, spice, butter, toast, vanilla, hint of nuts).

Wines That Didn't Work

Alsatian Gewürztraminer – The wine's intense flavors cover the dish and clash with the red onion, making the dish taste bitter.

Dolcetto – The sage complements some notes in the wine, but ultimately the dish overpowers this unoaked red wine.

Alternative: Sonoma Merlot—The wine and the dish match in intensity. The squash and pumpkin seeds contrast with the blackberry and plum fruit of the wine. The sweetness of the wine's fruit complements the squash and the red onions. The sage creates a *complexing* reaction as well.

SUMMARY	Chateau St. Jean Sonoma County Chardonnay	Sonoma Merlot	Alsatian Gewürztraminer	Dolcetto
Matching	+	+		
Complementing	+	+		+
Contrasting	+	+		
Compounding				
Complexing	+	+		
Cleansing				(–)
Covering			(–)	(–)
Clashing			(–)	

MEZZE RIGATONI ALLA SAUCE BOLOGNESE

Yield: 8 portions

Ingredients	Amounts - US	Volume	Metric
Mezze rigatoni, dry	1 lb.		454 grams
For the Sauce Bolognese			
Extra virgin olive oil	1 ½ fl. oz.	3 Tbl.	45 ml
Onion, small dice	4 oz.	1 cup	120 grams
Carrot, small dice	2 oz.	½ cup	66 grams
Celery, small dice	2 oz.	½ cup	66 grams
Garlic, sliced	¼ oz.	½ Tbl.	6 grams

Ingredients	Amounts - US	Volume	Metric
Beef, ground	6 oz.	1 cup	170 grams
Veal, ground	3 oz.	½ cup	84 grams
Pancetta, small dice	2 ½ oz.	½ cup	70 grams
White wine, Chardonnay	4 fl. oz.	½ cup	
Tomatoes, San Marzano Style, canned	3 lbs.	6 cups	1,360 grams
Bay leaf		1 each	
Salt		2 tsp.	
Black pepper, fresh ground		¼ tsp.	
Nutmeg, fresh ground		⅛ tsp.	
Sage leaves, chiffonade, widthwise		1 Tbl.	
For the Garnish			
Parmigiano Reggiano, grated	1 ½ oz.	⅓ cup	40 grams
Parsley, Italian, chopped		2 Tbl.	

Mezze Rigatoni

1. Set up a pasta pot and time the cooking of the pasta to add to the sauce in step 10. (See page 210.)
2. Preheat a saucepot over medium-high heat.
3. Add the oil and then the beef, veal, and pancetta. Sauté until the meat begins to brown lightly. Stir carefully to break up the ground meat while cooking.
4. Add the onion, carrot, and celery. Sauté until they begin to soften, approximately 6 minutes.
5. Add the garlic and cook until very aromatic.
6. Add the wine and reduce by three-quarters.
7. Add the tomatoes, bay leaf, salt, pepper, nutmeg, and bring to a simmer. Simmer gently for 2 ½–3 hours or until the meat is tender and the sauce is very flavorful. If the sauce becomes too thick, add a small amount of water to adjust the consistency.
8. Add the sage in the last 30 minutes of cooking.
9. Taste and adjust the seasoning.
10. Mix the al dente pasta with 2 ½ cups of sauce and combine well.
11. Plate the pasta and add an additional 1 ½ oz. of sauce on top.
12. Garnish with Parmigiano Reggiano and parsley; serve immediately.

"Alla Bolognese" means in the style of Bologna, a city in the Emilia-Romana region of Italy. There are many versions of this sauce and it is said that originally it didn't contain tomatoes. Variations include red or white wine, milk, and one to four types of ground meat. This sauce should be made 24 hours before using and will get better after 2 days.

WINE SELECTED with Mezze Rigatoni alla Sauce Bolognese

Wine: St. Francis Old Vines Zinfandel ($19)
Origin: Sonoma, California, USA

This Zinfandel comes from old vines, some of which are more than 100 years old. This makes the wine's flavor more concentrated and rich. Some of the wines are also aged in new American oak barrels, leading to sweet vanilla, coconut, and tobacco flavors.

Taste and Texture Comparisons

Dish: Rich, Meaty, Savory (Umami), Sweet
Wine: Bold, Ripe Red Fruit, Sweet Vanilla, Toast, Spice, High Alcohol

Why This Is a Good Pairing

- ***Matching*** – The dish and the wine are both quite bold and rich in their flavor intensity. They match in weight as well, which prevents them from overpowering each other.
- ***Complementing*** – The sweetness of the tomato and vegetables is complemented by the sweetness of the fruit in the wine (and vice versa).
- ***Contrasting*** – The umami and flavor of the meat in the Bolognese contrasts with the ripe raspberry, cranberry, and blackberry fruit of the wine, which makes the fruit stand out. The savory nature of the dish also contrasts with the sweetness of the oak (sweet vanilla and coconut), making all of them stand out more for a *complexing* reaction.
- ***Dance*** – The richness of the meat and the rich flavor of the wine do a nice dance and have a long finish.

Wines That Didn't Work

Amarone – Initially there is a complementing of the sweetness of the fruit of the wine and the tomatoes, but it then compounds, making the tomatoes taste like candy and the wine taste sour.

Barossa Shiraz – The Barossa Shiraz is too intense in flavor for this dish. The wine overpowers and covers the flavors, and the meat contrasts with the wine's fruit, making the wine taste too sweet and candied.

Alternative: Chianti Classico—Acidity from the Sangiovese brightens this dish. The meat contrasts with the bright cherry fruit of the wine, making it stand out. The fruit of the wine makes the tomatoes taste sweeter. The herbal notes in the wine connect with the savory nature of the dish and there is a *complexing* reaction. It shares similar reactions to the Zinfandel, yet is a very different and good pairing.

SUMMARY	St. Francis Old Vines Zinfandel	Chianti Classico	Amarone	Barossa Shiraz
Matching	+	+		
Complementing	+	+		
Contrasting	+	+	(–)	(–)
Compounding				
Complexing	+	+		
Cleansing				
Covering				(–)
Clashing			(–)	

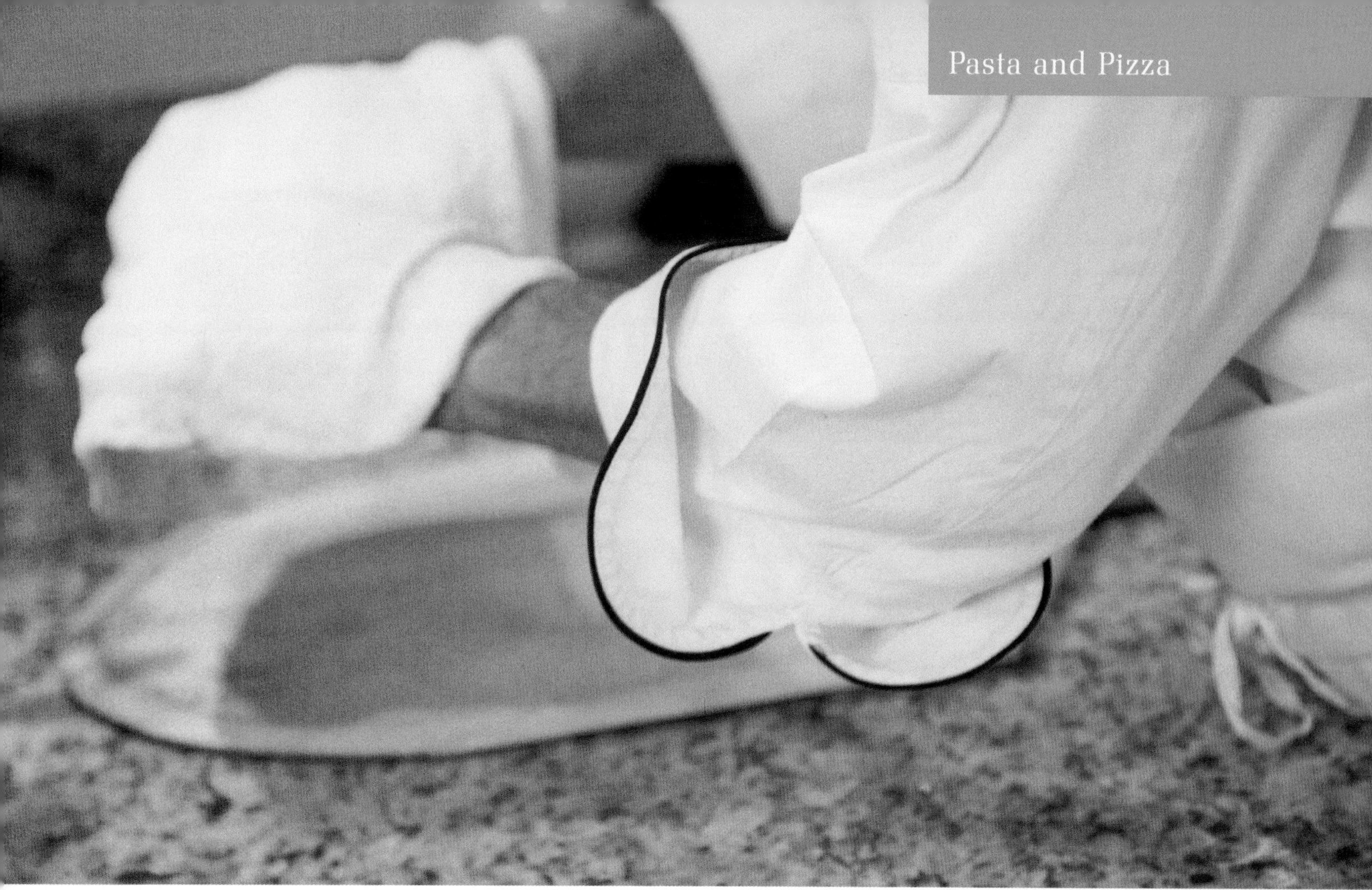

PIZZA

Naples, Italy, is the home of pizza. It is believed that an Italian baker, Raffaele Esposito, created the pizza margherita in the late 1800s for visiting royalty. Tomatoes, mozzarella, and basil were used to represent the colors of the Italian flag. Still today Neapolitans take their pizza very seriously. An organization called Associazione Verace Pizza Napoletana (VPN) was established in 1984 to protect the original Neapolitan pizza. Restaurants must meet specific pizza-making criteria in order to receive certification. Dough, tomatoes, oil, cheese, basil, oven, temperature, and cook time are all closely scrutinized.

BASIC PIZZA DOUGH

Yield: 6 each – 14-oz. dough balls

Ingredients	Amounts - US	Volume	Metric
Water, 90–100 F (32–38 C) degrees	24 fl. oz.	3 cups	740 ml
Honey	½ fl. oz.	1 Tbl.	30 ml
Yeast, dry active	¼ oz.	1 Tbl.	8 grams
Extra virgin olive oil	1 ½ fl. oz.	3 Tbl.	45 ml
Salt, kosher	½ oz.	1 Tbl.	14 grams
Flour, bread	26 oz.	5 cups	746 grams
Farina Flour "00"	13 oz.	2 ¾ cups	373 grams

(Continues on next page)

Pizza Dough

1. Combine the water, honey, and yeast; stir to dissolve. Allow this mixture to sit at room temperature for 10 minutes until foamy and the yeast has dissolved.
2. Add the olive oil and salt; stir to combine.
3. Using a stand mixer add the flour on top and begin mixing on low speed until the dough forms and pulls away from the sides of the bowl.
4. Continue mixing for 7–8 minutes until the dough is smooth and elastic. Alternately, the dough can be kneaded by hand on a lightly floured work surface.
5. Scale the dough into 14-oz. portions; round the dough portions gently by hand on a lightly floured work surface.
6. Place the dough on a sheet pan that has been lightly dusted with flour; lightly dust the top of the dough as well.
7. Cover loosely with plastic wrap and refrigerate until needed.
8. The dough should rest for 4 hours to allow the gluten to relax. If the dough is used too soon it will be difficult to stretch out and will create a tough crust.

Pizza dough should have a slightly tacky feel. The amount of flour needed will vary and can be adjusted as needed to achieve the proper texture and consistency. Fresh yeast, ¾ oz., can be substituted for ⅜ oz. of dry active yeast. All-purpose flour can be substituted for bread flour and the Farina "00."

BASIC PIZZA SAUCE

Yield: 3 cups

Ingredients	Amounts - US	Volume	Metric
Tomato, puree	1 lb. 12 oz.	3 ½ cups	794 grams
Extra virgin olive oil	1 fl. oz.	2 Tbl.	30 ml
Salt, kosher		1 tsp.	
Oregano, fresh, chopped		¾ tsp.	
Black pepper, fresh ground		½ tsp.	
Cayenne pepper		⅛ tsp.	

Pizza Sauce

1. Combine all ingredients and whisk to evenly incorporate.
2. Refrigerate until needed.

Margherita Pizza

MARGHERITA PIZZA

Yield: 2 each – 13 inch

Ingredients	Amounts - US	Volume	Metric
Dough, balls	14 oz.	2 each	396 grams
Pizza sauce	16 fl. oz.	2 cups	500 ml
Mozzarella, fresh, grated	10 oz.	2 ¼ cups	283 grams
For the Garnish			
Basil leaves, chiffonade		8 each	

Margherita Pizza

1. Preheat oven to 500 F (260 C) degrees convection with a pizza stone or tiles.
2. Stretch out the dough until it is approximately a 13-inch round, using as little flour as possible.
3. Lightly dust a pizza peel with cornmeal.

4. Place the dough on top of the cornmeal.
5. Spread the pizza sauce evenly over the surface of the dough, leaving a ¾-inch border for the crust.
6. Sprinkle the cheese evenly over the surface of the sauce.
7. Slide the pizza onto the stone by placing the tip near the back of the stone and tilting it on an angle while pulling back towards you.
8. Rotate the pizza after 4 minutes.
9. Total cook time will be approximately 8 minutes.
10. Remove from the oven and add basil garnish.
11. Cut the pizza into 8 pieces and serve immediately.

The pizza can also be cooked in a half-sheet pan or other appropriate pan if you do not have a pizza stone/tiles. Using a stainless steel pan that conducts heat evenly will result in a crispier crust.

WINE SELECTED with Margherita Pizza

Wine: Bearboat Russian River Pinot Noir ($22)
Origin: Russian River, California, USA

Taste and Texture Comparisons

Dish: Sweet, Herbal, Slightly Acidic, Crisp, Rich Cheese
Wine: High Acidity, Sweet Fruit Impression (Low Tannin)

Russian River Pinot Noir is more up front in its fruit than its Burgundian cousin and a bit richer than Carneros.

Why This Is a Good Pairing

- ***Matching Intensity and Weight*** – Both are aromatically intense and have a freshness to their aromas and both are moderate in weight; neither overpowers the other.
- ***Complementing*** – The sweetness of the tomatoes/basil and the sweet impression of the wine's red berry fruit are bridged. This has a slight compounding effect, in a positive way.
- ***Complexing*** – The basil on the pizza connects to a slight earthy tone in the Pinot Noir, making the wine taste more complex. Additionally, the light tannin in the Pinot Noir brings a textural dimension that adds depth.
- ***Cleansing*** – The mozzarella is cleansed slightly by the acidity of the wine, but not so much that it pulls the flavor away. It also makes the dish taste fresh and light.

Wines That Didn't Work

Sauvignon Blanc – We tried a few Sauvignon Blancs with this dish. They are all fresh and so is the dish, but unfortunately, the herbaceousness in the wine and the basil in the pizza compound (Green + Green = Green ^{2}). The acidity is too cleansing and strips some of the flavor; not a pleasant match.

Soave Classico – This Italian white wine matches the dish's intensity and weight, but it is a great neutralizer. Not only does the dish do nothing for the wine, but also the wine does nothing for the dish. They canceled each other out in flavor.

Chianti Classico – The freshness and sweetness of the tomatoes clash a bit with the wine. Additionally, the sweetness in the dish makes the wine taste a bit sour. This is not the reaction experienced with the Russian River Pinot Noir. Having said this, a youthful, fruity and light basic Chianti or Montepulciano will have a better chance.

SUMMARY	Bearboat Russian River Pinot Noir	Sauvignon Blanc	Soave Classico	Chianti Classico
Matching	+	+	+	
Complementing	+			
Contrasting				
Compounding	+	(–)		
Complexing	+			
Cleansing	+		(–)	
Covering				(–)
Clashing				(–)

Fennel Sausage and Porcini Mushroom Pizza

FENNEL SAUSAGE AND PORCINI MUSHROOM PIZZA

Yield: 2 each – 13 inch

Ingredients	Amounts - US	Volume	Metric
Dough, balls	14 oz.	2 each	396 grams
Pizza sauce	16 fl. oz.	2 cups	0.5 liter
Mozzarella, fresh	6 oz.	1 ½ cups	256 grams
Asiago, fresco, grated	4 oz.	1 cup	114 grams
Fennel sausage, cooked, crumbled	10 oz.	2 cups	282 grams
Porcini mushrooms, dry, reconstituted, drained, chopped	1 ¾ oz.	½ cup	50 grams
For the Garnish			
Oregano, fresh, chopped		1 tsp.	

Pizza

1. Preheat oven to 500 F (260 C) degrees convection with a pizza stone or tiles.
2. Carefully stretch out the dough until it is approximately a 13-inch round, using as little flour as possible.
3. Lightly dust a pizza peel with cornmeal.
4. Place the dough on top of the cornmeal.
5. Spread the pizza sauce evenly over the surface of the dough, leaving a ¾-inch border for the crust.
6. Sprinkle the cheeses evenly over the surface of the sauce.
7. Sprinkle the sausage and porcini over the surface of the cheeses.
8. Slide the pizza onto the stone by placing the tip near the back of the stone and tilting it on an angle while pulling back towards you.
9. Rotate the pizza after 4 minutes.
10. Total cook time will be approximately 8 minutes.
11. Remove from the oven and garnish with the oregano.
12. Cut the pizza into 8 pieces with a pizza wheel and serve immediately.

To reconstitute dried porcini mushrooms, place them in a bowl and cover with simmering water. Cover with plastic wrap for 1 hour to soften. Remove the mushrooms from the liquid and rinse them with cold water until the grit/sand is removed. Strain the liquid and reserve it for another use (stock, sauce, soup, or reduction). One ounce of dried porcinis yields 3 ounces of reconstituted mushrooms.

WINE SELECTED with Fennel Sausage and Porcini Mushroom Pizza

Wine: Domaine Wachau Terressen Federspiel Grüner Veltliner ($14)

Origin: Wachau, Austria

Taste and Texture Comparisons

Dish: Spice, Crunchy Texture, Earthy, Rich, Umami

Wine: Spice, Crisp, Fresh, Fairly Light-Bodied

Grüner Veltliner is an Austrian white grape known for citrus, white pepper spice, and (some say) lentil notes. This one is a "Federspiel" (a medium-bodied style designation in Wachau).

Why This Is a Good Pairing

- ***Contrasting Weight and Textures*** – The wine has a delicate structure in comparison to the dish. You might think the dish would overpower the wine, but the strong bond in flavors between the dish and the wine makes for a contrast in textures and weight that adds dimension and depth.
- ***Complementing*** – The spice from the fennel and earthiness from the mushrooms in the dish connect with the white pepper spice and hint of lentils in the Grüner Veltliner.
- ***Cleansing*** – The wine's crisp acidity cuts through some of the richness of the Asiago cheese and the sausage, adding freshness to the dish.

Wines That Didn't Work

Alsatian Gewürztraminer – They match in weight, spice, and earthiness, but the dish and the wine clash as though they are wrestling with each other rather than dancing.

Australian Shiraz – Another spicy wine, the Shiraz (Syrah) is known for black pepper spice. Unfortunately, the wine is too full-bodied, concentrated, and overpowers the dish. The wine's high alcohol (14.5%+ abv) also augments the dish's spice, making it "hot."

Rioja – The wine matches in weight and intensity to the dish; however, the flavors of the wine and the dish are compounded to an unpleasant level. The earthiness of the mushrooms and the sausage + the earthiness of the Rioja = mushroom and earth^2, making both the wine and the dish taste more literally like earth (dirt).

SUMMARY	Domaine Wachau Grüner Veltliner	Alsatian Gewürztraminer	Australian Shiraz	Rioja
Matching		+		+
Complementing	+			
Contrasting	+			
Compounding				(–)
Complexing				
Cleansing	+			
Covering			(–)	
Clashing		(–)		

Ricotta, Taleggio, and Arugula Pizza

RICOTTA, TALEGGIO, AND ARUGULA PIZZA

Yield: 2 each – 13 inch

Ingredients	Amounts - US	Volume	Metric
Dough, balls	14 oz.	2 each	396 grams
For the Ricotta Mixture			
Ricotta, fresh	12 oz.	1 ¾ cups	340 grams
Mozzarella, grated	2 oz.	½ cup	57 grams
Parmigiano Reggiano, grated	⅝ oz.	¼ cup	16 grams
Extra virgin olive oil	1 fl. oz.	2 Tbl.	30 ml
Parsley, Italian, chopped		1 ½ Tbl.	
Salt, kosher		¼ tsp.	
Black pepper, fresh ground		⅜ tsp.	
Taleggio, sliced ¼"	4 oz.	¾ cup	112 grams
Arugula, baby	2 oz.	3 cups	57 grams
Extra virgin olive oil	1 fl. oz.	2 Tbl.	30 ml
Black pepper, fresh ground		to taste	

Pizza

1. Preheat oven to 500 F (260 C) degrees convection with a pizza stone or tiles.
2. Combine the ingredients for the ricotta mixture and stir well to evenly incorporate.
3. Stretch out the dough until it is approximately a 13-inch round, using as little flour as possible.
4. Lightly dust a pizza peel with cornmeal.
5. Place the dough on top of the cornmeal.
6. Combine the ingredients for the ricotta mixture, taste and adjust the seasoning.
7. Spread the ricotta mixture evenly over the surface of the dough, leaving a ¾-inch border for the crust.
8. Tear the taleggio into small pieces and distribute evenly over the ricotta. (Taleggio cheese is greater than 40% butterfat and will soften quickly at room temperature; keep refrigerated until needed).
9. Slide the pizza onto the stone by placing the tip near the back of the stone and tilting it on an angle while pulling back towards you.
10. Rotate the pizza after 4 minutes.
11. Total cook time will be approximately 8 minutes.
12. Remove from the oven and place the arugula evenly over the surface, drizzle the extra virgin olive oil over the arugula and grind black pepper on top.
13. Cut the pizza into 8 pieces with a pizza wheel and serve immediately.

WINE SELECTED with Ricotta, Taleggio, and Arugula Pizza

Wine: Barone Ricasoli Brolio Chianti Classico ($19)
Origin: Chianti Classico, Tuscany, Italy

Taste and Texture Comparisons

Dish: Rich, Creamy, Bold, Herbal, Slightly Bitter, Smoky
Wine: Medium-Bodied, Herbal, Crisp Acidity, Moderate Tannin, Earthy

Chianti Classico is one of the most recognized wines in the world. Wineries are quite varied in their production methods from very traditional to modern. This producer uses both cask and new barrels, but also has a dash of Cabernet Sauvignon and Merlot.

Why This Is a Good Pairing

- ***Matching Intensity and Texture*** – The dish and the wine match in aroma and flavor intensity for this pairing.
- ***Complementing*** – The peppery character of the arugula complements and creates a bridge to the herbal notes in the wine, making the wine more savory and complex.
- ***Contrasting*** – The slight smoky/charred note to the pizza crust and the slight bitterness of the arugula contrast with the fruit in the wine, making the fruit in the wine pop and taste fresh.
- ***Cleansing*** – The wine's crisp acidity is slightly cleansing of the richness of the cheese, but not so much that it strips the flavor of the cheese or the pizza overall.
- ***Dance*** – The richness of the cheese is what carries the flavors through one of the longest dances and one of the most magical pairings described in this book.

Wines That Didn't Work

Soave Classico – Many might think "Italian white wine, Italian white pizza," and while the wine's pear fruit stands out initially, the wine is ultimately overpowered by the intensity of the dish. There is nothing offensive about the pairing, it just gets swallowed up.

Oaked Chardonnay – Although matching in weight and richness, the wine's flavors (vanilla and spice from the oak and butter from malolactic fermentation) are too intense for this dish. The wine overpowers the dish.

Vino Nobile di Montepulciano – This wine shares the same grape and region as the Chianti Classico, yet doesn't work with this dish. The producer we tested is very traditional with earthy, herbal (almost menthol) notes. These aspects for this wine are more intense and clash with the dish and the wine's slightly rustic tannins compound with the arugula.

SUMMARY	Brolio Chianti Classico	Soave Classico	Oaked Chardonnay	Vino Nobile di Montepulciano
Matching	+			
Complementing	+			
Contrasting	+			
Compounding				(–)
Complexing	+			
Cleansing	+			
Covering		(–)	(–)	
Clashing				(–)

PASTA AND PIZZA PAIRING SUMMARY AND CONCLUSIONS

The techniques used for the pasta and pizza dishes are predominantly the same. The ingredients are what is really driving these pairings.

Ravioli

Dish	Wine
Cheese Ravioli with Asparagus and Butter Sauce	Albariño, Burgans Rias Baixas
Meat Ravioli in Brodo	Rosé, Château de Campuget Costières de Nimes
Shrimp Ravioli with Tomato Coulis	Champagne Charles Heidsieck Brut Réserve

- ***Main ingredient tendencies:*** Ravioli offers a wide range of versatility with wines, given filling and sauce ingredients. We found sparkling, white, light-bodied reds, rosé, and white fortified whites wines pair with these dishes.

- ***Specific ingredients that changed the pairing:*** In general, the richer the filling ingredients, the bolder you can go with the wine pairing. The shrimp's slightly briny character complements the mineral notes in the champagne. The cheese ravioli's asparagus contrasts with the Albariño's stone fruit, making it pop. The meat ravioli in brodo contrasted with the berry fruit in the rosé, but was too delicate for a red.

Spaghetti

Dish	Wine
Spaghetti con le Vongole	Sauvignon Blanc, Nederberg
Spaghetti alla Carbonara	Amarone della Valpolicella, Masi Costasera, Veneto
Spaghetti alla Puttanesca	Vernaccia di San Gimignano, Azienda Agraria Le Rote

- ***Main ingredient tendencies:*** The range for pairing wine with pasta is vast, depending on preparation and the sauce, from light-bodied white to full-bodied red.

- ***Specific ingredients that changed the pairing:*** A common theme was the bolder the sauce, the richer the wine that paired. There were also potential derailing ingredients in some of these sauces (i.e., black pepper in the carbonara and the capers in the puttanesca). These ingredients require you to pay careful attention to balance.

Mezze Rigatoni

Dish	Wine
Mezze Rigatoni with Broccoli Rabe and Sausage	Tedeschi Soave Classico
Mezze Rigatoni Salad with Roasted Squash	Chateau St. Jean Chardonnay
Mezze Rigatoni alla Sauce Bolognese	St. Francis Old Vines Zinfandel

- ***Main ingredient tendencies:*** Mezze rigatoni can hold larger cut ingredients and sauce than spaghetti because of its shape. This provides for a variety of different textures and ingredients, which lends to a wide variety of wine pairings.

- ***Specific ingredients that changed the pairing:*** The butternut squash is sweet and caramelized, which complements the buttery and toast notes in the Chardonnay. The broccoli rabe can be quite bold and can clash with many wines yet worked well with a mild Soave. The meat in the Bolognese makes for the richest sauce of these recipes and calls for a bolder wine, and the dish's protein softens the Zinfandel's tannins.

Pizza

Dish	Wine
Margherita Pizza	Pinot Noir, Bearboat
Fennel Sausage and Porcini Mushroom Pizza	Grüner Veltliner, Domaine Wachau
Ricotta, Taleggio, and Arugula Pizza	Chianti Classico, Barone Ricasoli Brolio

- ***Main ingredient tendencies:*** Pizza offers a wide variety of tastes and textures given the variety of toppings and sauces.

- ***Specific ingredients that changed the pairing:*** The sweetness of the tomatoes complements the sweet impression of the Pinot Noir's red berry fruit, yet the Chianti Classico tastes sour with the Margherita Pizza. The fennel and mushrooms connect with the white pepper spice and hint of lentils in the Grüner Veltliner. The peppery character of the arugula complements and creates a bridge to the herbal notes in the Chianti Classico.

9
Desserts

Baking and pastry is a precise science where recipes typically call for a formula or ratio of ingredients. When executing a recipe, you should start by gathering all mise en place, preparing molds or pans, and then proceeding with the method of preparation. This is important as many recipes are time and temperature sensitive during preparation.

Desserts are an exciting category with which to pair wine. Most restaurants offer a dessert menu with wine options and it's a great way to take advantage the food and wine pairing opportunity.

Balancing key components—sweetness and acidity—is crucial. Sweet wines can vary widely in their sugar content. Your palate can perceive sweetness in wine generally above 5 grams per liter residual sugar. We tested wines from dry to more than 400 grams per liter residual sugar. The acidity in the wine and the dish creates balance for this sugar content and makes all the difference.

The range of wines that pair well with desserts is wide, from sparkling dry rosé champagne to Pedro Ximenez. You will also notice that within each section, complementing and contrasting become very important.

Dish	Wine
Lemon	
Lemon Sorbet	JJ Prüm Graacher Himmelreich Riesling Spätlese, Mosel, Germany ($30)
Lemon Pound Cake	JJ Prüm Graacher Himmelreich Riesling Auslese, Mosel, Germany ($45)
Lemon Cheesecake	Giovanni Allegrini Recioto della Valpolicella Classico, Veneto, Italy ($70)
Apple	
Green Apple Mousse	Château Soucherie Coteaux du Layon, Loire, France ($25)
Apple Fritters	Standing Stone Vineyards Vidal Ice Wine, Finger Lakes, New York, USA ($25)
Apple Tarte Tatin	Maculan Torcolato, Veneto, Italy ($40)
Strawberry	
Strawberries with Champagne Sabayon	Banfi Rosa Regale Brachetto d'Acqui, Piedmont, Italy ($13)
Strawberry Shortcake	Moët et Chandon Nectar Imperial Demi-Sec, Champagne, France ($44)
Strawberry and Blueberry Crisp	Royal Tokaji 5 Puttonyos, Tokaj-Hegyalja, Hungary ($56)
Chocolate	
Chocolate Soufflé with Orange Crème Anglaise	Pommery Brut Rosé, Champagne, France ($14)
Chocolate Mousse with Strawberries	Fonseca Bin. 27 Ruby Port, Duoro, Portugal ($16)
Flourless Hazelnut Chocolate Cake with Raspberry Sauce	NV Osborne Sherry Pedro Ximenez 1827, Jerez, Spain ($22)

Lemon Sorbet

LEMON

Lemons have been cultivated for over 3,000 years and are thought to have originated in Asia. Christopher Columbus is credited with carrying lemon seeds to the New World. Florida and California are responsible for the largest share of the US crop. Select lemons that have bright yellow skin that is firm and those that are heavy for their weight.

LEMON SORBET

Yield: 1 quart

Ingredients	Amounts - US	Volume	Metric
Water	12 fl. oz.	1 ½ cups	360 ml
Sugar, granulated	12 oz.	1 ½ cups	340 grams
Lemon rind, no pith	1 ¾ oz.	4 ea. lemons	50 grams
Lemon juice	16 fl. oz.	2 cups	500 ml

Lemon Sorbet

1. Combine the water, sugar, and lemon rind in a saucepan; bring to a simmer and cook gently until the sugar is dissolved, turn off the heat, and steep for 15 minutes.
2. Strain the syrup and cool to room temperature.
3. Combine the lemon juice and the syrup.
4. The brix (sugar content) can be tested with a refractometer or an egg. The brix should be 28–32%. If using an egg, you are assessing the density: place a clean egg (in the shell) in the sorbet base once it has been mixed; the egg should float and an area the size of a nickel should be above the surface. If the area is too small, add additional syrup; if the area is too large, add more lemon juice or water. Taste to determine the flavor and balance. Chill the sorbet base under refrigeration.
5. Process the sorbet in an ice cream machine as per the manufacturer's instructions.
6. Freeze the sorbet for 2–4 hours before use.

This is a classic recipe for sorbet and doesn't contain any stabilizers, thus it is best used within 24 hours or it will become very dense.

WINE SELECTED with Lemon Sorbet

Wine: JJ Prüm Graacher Himmelreich Riesling Spätlese ($30)
Origin: Graacher Himmelreich, Mosel, Germany

Taste and Texture Comparisons

Dish: Light, Refreshing, Cold, Acidic, Crisp Lemon Flavor
Wine: Delicate, Lightly Sweet, High Acidity, Moderately Low Alcohol, Citrus, Slight Floral and Botrytis Notes

Spätlese means "late harvest" in German. Sometimes the grapes are infected by botrytis and sometimes not. This is what gives the wine dried fruit and marzipan-like notes. These wines generally have less sugar and are a little higher in alcohol than an Auslese (this wine is 45 g/l residual sugar and under 9% abv).

Why This Is a Good Pairing

- ***Matching*** – The dish and the wine have a lightness to them that prevents one from overpowering the other. They also match in terms of sweetness and acidity.
- ***Complementing*** – There is a strong complementary connection between the lemon flavors in the sorbet and the citrus notes in the Riesling.
- ***Contrasting*** – The Riesling also has a floral element, which contrasts nicely with the lemon in the dish. This floral-citrus dance seems to elongate the flavors on your palate.
- ***Cleansing*** – There is no question that the dish and the wine together are refreshing. Although the dish and the wine are quite high in acidity, this does not compound. The sweetness is balanced.

Wines That Didn't Work

Brut Champagne – Unlike the Demi-Sec, there is no perceived sweetness in the Brut to offset its high acidity. The high acidity in the champagne creates an acid compounding effect with the sorbet. If you are an acid freak you may like this aspect. However, the sugar in the sorbet is much sweeter than the dry champagne, which makes the champagne taste sour.

Dry Rosé – We tried a few dry rosés because strawberry and lemon tend to pair well. However, in this recipe they clash and the wine's crisp acidity compounds with the acid in the dish. Additionally, the sorbet's sweetness makes the dry wine taste sour.

Alternative: Demi-Sec Champagne—The light sweetness of the Demi-Sec (which can be anywhere from 35–50 g/l residual sugar) complemented the sweetness in the sorbet. There is also a bridge in the lemony/citrus character between the two. The pure flavors of the sorbet also bring out some of the autolytic notes and the slight crème brulée character in the Demi-Sec as the freshness of the fruit contrasts with it.

SUMMARY	Riesling Spätlese	Demi-Sec Champagne	Brut Champagne	Dry Rosé
Matching	+	+	(–)	(–)
Complementing	+	+		
Contrasting	+	+		
Compounding			(–)	
Complexing				
Cleansing	+			
Covering				
Clashing				(–)

Lemon Pound Cake

LEMON POUND CAKE

Yield: 10 portions

Ingredients	Amounts - US	Volume	Metric
For the Lemon Pound Cake			
Cake flour	6 ½ oz.	1 ½ cups	184 grams
Baking powder		1 tsp.	
Butter, unsalted, cubed, room temperature	8 oz.	16 Tbl.	228 grams
Sugar, granulated	7 oz.	1 cup	198 grams
Lemon zest	¼ oz.	1 ½ Tbl.	6 grams
Salt, kosher		¼ tsp.	
Eggs, large, whisked	7 oz.	4 each	198 grams
Lemon juice, fresh	2 fl. oz.	¼ cup	60 ml
Vanilla extract		1 tsp.	
For the Chantilly Cream			
Heavy cream	8 fl. oz.	1 cup	240 ml
Sugar, granulated	¾ oz.	1 ½ Tbl.	20 grams

Chantilly Cream

1. Whip the cream until a soft peak forms.
2. Add the sugar and continue whipping until a stiff peak has formed.
3. Reserve under refrigeration until needed.

Lemon Pound Cake

1. Prepare a loaf pan, 1 lb. (8 ½ x 4 ½ x 2 ¾), by lining the bottom with parchment paper and lightly coating it with butter.
2. Preheat the oven to 325 F (162 C) degrees; have a rack positioned in the center of the oven for even baking.
3. Sift the cake flour and the baking powder.
4. Using a stand mixer with a paddle attachment on medium speed, cream the butter, sugar, lemon zest, and salt. Scrape down the sides and bottom with a rubber spatula as needed during mixing until the mixture is pale in color, blended evenly and smooth, approximately 5–6 minutes.
5. Combine the eggs, lemon juice, and vanilla extract; whisk to combine thoroughly.
6. While mixing on low speed, add the egg mixture in 3 additions, scraping the sides and bottom with a rubber spatula as needed to evenly incorporate. *In between the additions add 1–2 Tbl. of the sifted dry ingredients as needed so that the mixture doesn't separate; this can occur because of the amount of fat.*
7. Add the sifted dry ingredients and mix slowly until just combined; scrape down the sides and bottom with a rubber spatula as needed.
8. Pour the batter into the prepared loaf pan. Bake until just set, when an inserted skewer will come out clean, approximately 1 hour.
9. Cool the cake in the pan for 10 minutes and then remove to cool on a wire rack.
10. Slice the cake, plate, and garnish with a quenelle of Chantilly Cream.

When adding the flour, overmixing the batter will develop the gluten and result in a tougher cake.

WINE SELECTED with Lemon Pound Cake

Wine: JJ Prüm Graacher Himmelreich Riesling Auslese ($45)
Origin: Graacher Himmelreich, Mosel, Germany

Taste and Texture Comparisons

Dish: Lemon, Sweet, Rich/Buttery, Soft
Wine: Citrus, Medium Sweetness, Light, High Acidity, Low Alcohol, Honey, and Floral Notes

Mosel Auslese tends to be sweeter, more delicate, higher in acid, and lower in alcohol than other German Rieslings. Auslese means "selected harvest" yet this doesn't mean the grapes are infected with botrytis. This wine is about 80 g/l residual sugar and its high sugar makes it seem delicately sweet.

Why This Is a Good Pairing

- ***Matching*** – The cake and the wine match in sweetness as well as in intensity of flavor.
- ***Complementing*** – The delicate lemony flavors in the pound cake create a bridge to the citrus notes in the wine. This compounds the lemon flavor in a positive way, making it refreshing.
- ***Contrasting*** – The lemon flavor in the cake contrasts with some of the floral notes in the wine, bringing out notes of lavender and acacia.
- ***Cleansing*** – The wine's high acidity is refreshing with the cake. This makes you feel like you are not eating pound cake, which makes some of us feel less guilty for eating dessert!

Wines That Didn't Work

NV Brut Champagne – The wine is too dry for this delicately sweet dessert. It makes the wine taste sour and the lemon in the cake makes the Champagne taste like lemon-scented cleanser.

Riesling Spätlese – Although there are some complementary flavors (similar to the Auslese), the wine is not sweet enough to match the cake and it creates a sweet and sour reaction that makes the wine taste like a lemon/lime sour candy.

Brachetto – The wine is too sweet and intense in its berry flavors and covers the dish's flavors entirely.

SUMMARY	Riesling Auslese	Brut Champagne	Riesling Spätlese	Brachetto
Matching	+	(–)	(–)	
Complementing	+		+	
Contrasting	+			
Compounding				
Complexing				
Cleansing	+			
Covering				(–)
Clashing				

LEMON CHEESECAKE

Yield: 10 portions – 9-inch

Ingredients	Amounts - US	Volume	Metric
For the Crust			
Graham cracker crumbs	6 ½ oz.	1 ½ cups	184 grams
Brown sugar, light	¾ oz.	2 Tbl.	20 grams
Butter, unsalted, room temperature	2 oz.	4 Tbl.	56 grams

(Continues on next page)

Ingredients	Amounts - US	Volume	Metric
For the Filling			
Cream cheese	24 oz.	3 cups	680 grams
Sugar, granulated	8 oz.	1 cup plus 2 Tbl.	226 grams
Lemon zest		2 tsp.	
Salt, kosher		¼ tsp.	
Sour cream	4 ½ oz.	½ cup	128 grams
Lemon juice, fresh	1 ½ fl. oz.	3 Tbl.	45 ml
Vanilla extract		1 ½ tsp.	4 grams
Eggs, large, whisked	5 ⅝ oz.	3 each	160 grams
Egg yolks, large, whisked	½ oz.	1 each	14 grams

Setup and Making the Crust

1. Preheat a conventional oven at 350 F (176 C) degrees.
2. Set up a water bath for baking a 9-inch cake pan.
3. Combine the graham crackers, brown sugar, and butter in a stainless steel bowl and mix well.
4. Line the bottom of the cake pan with parchment and press the graham mixture evenly into the bottom of the pan.
5. Bake until light brown, approximately 8–10 minutes. Cool to room temperature.
6. Reduce the oven temperature to 325 F (162 C) degrees.

Filling

1. Combine the cream cheese, sugar, lemon zest, and salt in the bowl of a stand mixer. Mix on medium speed, with a paddle, until completely smooth, approximately 4 minutes. Scrape down the sides and bottom with a rubber spatula as needed.
2. Add the sour cream, lemon juice, and vanilla; mix until evenly combined.
3. Add the eggs and yolks in 3 additions, scraping down the sides and bottom with a rubber spatula as necessary between additions until evenly combined. Be careful not to overmix while adding the eggs as this can incorporate excess air into the batter.
4. Pour the batter into the pan and gently tap down the pan to remove any air.
5. Bake at 325 F (162 C) degrees in a water bath until the cake has set in the center (there will still be a slight jiggle), approximately 1 hour and 20 minutes.
6. Remove the cake from the oven and cool on a rack until room temperature.
7. Gently run a paring knife around the edge of the pan and then refrigerate until needed.
8. Warm the pan slightly over a burner to release the cake. Place a cardboard cake circle (or plate), covered with plastic wrap, on top of the pan and gently invert to remove the cake. Turn back onto a serving plate or cardboard cake circle.
9. Dip a slicing knife in hit water, wipe dry to slice the cake.

WINE SELECTED with Lemon Cheesecake

Wine: Giovanni Allegrini Recioto della Valpolicella Classico ($70)
Origin: Valpolicella Classico, Veneto, Italy

Taste and Texture Comparisons

Dish: Rich, Dense, Sweet, Creamy, Lemon Flavor, Slight Acidity
Wine: Rich, Medium Sweetness, High Alcohol, Medium Acid

This red dessert wine, Recioto, starts out the same way as Amarone, but the Recioto's fermentation is stopped before all the sugar is turned into alcohol (leaving residual sugar). This is why Recioto is sweet and most Amarone is dry.

Why This Is a Good Pairing

- ***Matching*** – The dish and the wine match in terms of flavor intensity and weight.
- ***Complementing*** – The graham cracker crust in the cheesecake creates a bridge to some of the spice tones from the oak in the wine.
- ***Contrasting*** – Lemon and red berry are a classic match. There is a contrast between the lemon in the cheesecake and the red berry flavors of the wine. The lemon still comes through and the lemon's bright acidity heightens the berry flavors.
- ***Cleansing*** – The acidity of the wine cuts through the richness of the cheesecake without stripping the flavor of the cheesecake.

Wines That Didn't Work

Sauternes – The sweetness intensity matches the dish, but the pure, clean lemon flavors in the cheesecake clash with the more complex flavors in the Sauternes, which makes the wine taste bitter and somewhat like dirty wet leaves.

Moscato d'Asti – The intense floral notes in the wine clash with the cheesecake, making the wine taste like soap.

Alternative: Riesling Ice Wine—There is a strong connection between the lemon flavors in the Riesling and in the cheesecake. The wine's high acidity cuts through the richness of the cheesecake for a cleansing sensation. Additionally, the sweetness level of the wine matches the cheesecake. However, this does make it a very sweet pairing. If you are looking to dial back the sweetness, go with the Recioto.

SUMMARY	Recioto della Valpolicella	Inniskillin Riesling Ice Wine	Sauternes	Moscato d'Asti
Matching	+	+	+	
Complementing	+	+		
Contrasting	+	+		
Compounding				
Complexing				
Cleansing	+	+		
Covering				
Clashing			(–)	(–)

APPLE

Granny Smith apples were discovered in Australia and named after Maria Ann Smith. They made their way to the US in the mid 1900s and are cultivated predominantly in Washington State and California. They are characterized by a thick green skin, firm crisp texture, juicy flesh, and a tart flavor with a hint of sweetness. Their texture and moisture content make them an ideal choice for cooking.

GREEN APPLE MOUSSE WITH APPLE CHIPS

Yield: 10 portions

Ingredients	Amounts - US	Volume	Metric
For the Apple Chips			
Granny Smith apples, sliced paper thin		10 each	
Simple syrup, 50/50		as needed	

Ingredients	Amounts - US	Volume	Metric
For the Green Apple Mousse			
Water	2 fl. oz.	¼ cup	60 ml
Calvados	1 fl. oz.	2 Tbl.	30 ml
Gelatin, powdered	¼ oz.	2 ½ tsp.	8 grams
Heavy cream	8 fl. oz.	1 cup	240 ml
Green apple puree	8 oz.	1 cup	226 grams
Egg yolks, large	2 ¾ oz.	8 each	78 grams
Sugar	5 oz.	¾ cup	142 grams

Apple Chips

1. Preheat an oven to 200 F (94 C) degrees.
2. Peel and slice the apples paper thin on a mandolin; place them immediately in the warm simple syrup.
3. Remove the apple slices from the syrup and wipe the excess syrup gently on the pan or bowl.
4. Place the slices on a sheet pan lined with a nonstick baking mat. Bake until crisp, approximately 3 hours, and carefully remove from the mat while the chips are warm to prevent cracking. Store in an airtight container until needed.

Green Apple Mousse

1. Prepare the molds for the mousse; line the molds with acetate if using a ring-style mold.
2. Set up a double boiler (see note on page 101).
3. Combine the Calvados and the water in a stainless steel bowl, and slowly sprinkle the gelatin over the surface of the liquid until it is evenly absorbed. Set aside to bloom.
4. Whip the heavy cream to a medium peak and reserve.
5. Melt the gelatin mixture in the stainless steel bowl over a gently simmering water bath (ensure that water doesn't touch the bottom of the bowl) until completely liquid; set aside and keep warm.
6. Combine the apple puree, egg yolks, and the sugar and place over the water bath. Whisk constantly until it begins to thicken and forms a ribbon. Be careful not to overheat/cook the eggs; heat to approximately 160 F (71 C) degrees. Whip until cool; this can be done on a small stand mixer for best results.
7. Whisk the gelatin into the apple mixture until fully incorporated.
8. Working in three stages, fold the whipped cream into the apple mixture until evenly incorporated. (Use a whisk when folding to keep the mousse as light as possible.)

There are three main components to a mousse: base, binder and aerator. In this recipe the apple puree is the base, gelatin is the binder, and the heavy cream is the aerator.

Green apple puree can be purchased in 16-oz. containers. Alternatively you can also gently poach the apples in a slightly acidulated simple syrup, drain well, and purée until very smooth. The shelf life of the apple chips will vary according to the humidity in the air.

WINE SELECTED with Green Apple Mousse with Apple Chips

Wine: Château Soucherie Coteaux du Layon ($25)

Origin: Coteaux du Layon, Loire, France

Taste and Texture Comparisons

Dish: Apple, Sweet, Creamy Texture, Fruity, Airy

Wine: Sweet, Fairly Full-Bodied, Notes of Apples, Quince, Honey, Botrytis, Moderate Acidity

Coteaux du Layon is a sweet white wine made from Chenin Blanc in the Loire Valley. It is known for quince, honey, and botrytis notes.

Why This Is a Good Pairing

- ***Matching*** – The sweetness and acidity level in the mousse and the wine match.
- ***Complementing*** – Chenin Blanc in the Loire has some apple flavors that make it a complementing wine for this mousse.
- ***Contrasting*** – The apple flavor of the mousse contrasts with some of the honeyed tones in the wine, which creates a pleasant *complexing* wherein you taste layers of flavors throughout the mousse and the wine (green apple, hint of citrus, honey, minerals, etc.).

Wines That Didn't Work

Moscato d'Asti – There is a clash between the floral notes and the fruit in the mousse. Additionally, the low acid of the wine does not allow the flavors of the apple to come through. In fact, the wine covers the dish.

Vidal Ice Wine – The wine is too viscous and sweet for this dish and quite overpowering.

Demi-Sec Champagne – The wine matches in lightness and sweetness (and has a *complementing* bridge of flavors of apple), but its high acidity strips the flavor and the wine and the dish seem to cancel each other out.

SUMMARY	Coteaux du Layon	Moscato d'Asti	Vidal Ice Wine	Demi-Sec Champagne
Matching	+		(–)	+
Complementing	+			+
Contrasting	+			
Compounding				
Complexing	+			
Cleansing				(–)
Covering		(–)	(–)	
Clashing		(–)		

Apple Fritters

APPLE FRITTERS

Yield: 10 portions

Ingredients	Amounts - US	Volume	Metric
For the Dry Ingredients			
Flour, all-purpose, unbleached	5 oz.	1 cup	144 grams
Sugar, granulated	¾ oz.	2 Tbl.	20 grams
Baking powder	¼ oz.	2 tsp.	8 grams
Lemon zest		1 ½ tsp.	
Salt		¼ tsp.	
For the Wet Ingredients			
Ricotta cheese, drained well	1 lb.	2 ½ cups	456 grams
Granny Smith apples, grated	12 oz.	2 ½ cups	336 grams
Eggs, large, whisked	5 ½ oz.	3 each	160 grams
Apple cider	1 ½ fl. oz.	3 Tbl.	45 ml
Amaretto	1 fl. oz.	2 Tbl.	30 ml
For the Garnish			
Powdered sugar		as needed	

Apple Fritters

1. Combine the dry ingredients and mix well.
2. Combine the wet ingredients and mix well.
3. Add the dry to the wet ingredients and mix until evenly combined.
4. Cover and refrigerate for 1 hour.
5. Preheat a fryer to 350 F (176 C) degrees.
6. Using two serving spoons, form quenelles and carefully slide them into the oil. Test one fritter to ensure the batter is the proper consistency, adjust with flour as needed. Fry the fritters for approximately 5–6 minutes until golden brown and hot in the center; turn carefully during cooking to ensure even browning and cooking.
7. Drain well onto absorbent towels.
8. Plate and dust with powdered sugar.

Apples can oxidize quickly. To prevent this, scale and mix the wet ingredients before peeling and grating the apples. Once the wet base ingredients are mixed, grate the apples and mix them in immediately. Ensure that the fryer oil is clean and fresh for the fritters as they are delicate and can pick up any "off" flavors from the oil. An extra virgin olive oil blend or pure olive oil is a good choice for this recipe.

WINE SELECTED with Apple Fritters

Wine: Standing Stone Vineyards Vidal Ice Wine ($25)
Origin: Finger Lakes, New York, USA

Taste and Texture Comparisons

Dish: Sweet, Fruity, Creamy, Airy, Toasted
Wine: Sweet, Full-Bodied, Stone Fruit, Dried Fruit, Honey

Vidal is a French–American grape hybrid. It was created to withstand the cold of the US Northeast and Canada. Ice wines made from Vidal can be as elegant and as long-lived as Riesling ice wines. However, Vidal has lower acidity, a denser concentration, and a fuller body.

Why This Is a Good Pairing

- ***Matching*** – The richness of the fritters is matched by the richness and weight of the wine. The intensity of flavor is also equally matched. Additionally, the sweetness and acidity level of the wine and the fritters are very well balanced.
- ***Complementing*** – Vidal can have more of a tree-fruit flavor (e.g., apples, pear, quince, etc.) than, say, Riesling Ice Wine (whose flavors are more in the citrus family), and so there is a bridge between the flavors in the dish and the wine.
- ***Contrasting*** – The toasty flavors of the fried dough contrast with the fruit in the fritter and in the wine, making both stand out more.

Wines That Didn't Work

Brut Champagne – Although there is a bridge between the toastiness in the fried dough and the toasty autolytic notes in the Champagne, the sweetness of the dish clashes, making the wine taste sour.

Riesling Spätlese – The sweetness is appropriate, but the high acidity of the wine is a bit too cleansing and you lose the flavor of the fritters.

Tokaji 5 Puttonyos – The wine's high acidity is too cleansing. Additionally, the dried apricot notes in the Tokaji and the apple flavor in the dish clash (making the fruits in both the wine and the dish taste overripe).

SUMMARY	Vidal Ice Wine	Brut Champagne	Riesling Spätlese	Tokaji 5 Puttonyos
Matching	+	(–)	+	
Complementing	+	+		
Contrasting	+			
Compounding				
Complexing				
Cleansing			(–)	(–)
Covering				
Clashing		(–)		(–)

APPLE TARTE TATIN

Yield: 10 portions

Ingredients	Amounts - US	Volume	Metric
For the Dough			
Flour, all-purpose, unbleached	8 ½ oz.	1 ½ cups	240 grams
Salt, kosher		½ tsp.	
Butter, unsalted, diced, chilled	5 oz.	10 Tbl.	140 grams
Water, ice cold	2–3 fl. oz.	4–6 Tbl.	60–90 ml
For the Apples			
Granny Smith apples		8 each	
Sugar, light brown	1 ¾ oz.	6 Tbl.	52 grams
Cinnamon, ground		1 ½ tsp.	
Nutmeg, ground		½ tsp.	
Sugar, granulated	2 ¾ oz.	5 Tbl.	76 grams
Butter, unsalted	2 ½ oz.	5 Tbl.	72 grams

Dough

1. Combine the flour and the salt; cut the butter in until the pieces are approximately the size of a pea. Work quickly as to not warm the butter.
2. Slowly add enough ice water, while gently working the dough, until it just comes together. Carefully shape the dough into a circle approximately ½-inch thick. Wrap the dough and refrigerate it for a minimum of 1 hour or until needed.

Preparing the Tarte Tatin

1. Preheat oven to 425 F (218 C) degrees.
2. Peel the apples, cut into quarters, and remove the core. Combine the apples with the brown sugar, cinnamon, and nutmeg; mix well to coat evenly.
3. Place the granulated sugar in a 10-inch sauté pan and caramelize over medium-low heat. Turn off the heat. Add the butter and mix to incorporate.
4. Begin placing the apples around the outside of the pan with the skin side down; slightly overlap each piece. Fill in the center and then place the remaining apples on top to create a level surface. *Alternately, use a tarte tatin pan by pouring the caramel in the bottom and proceed as above.*
5. Working on a lightly floured surface, roll out the dough, from the center towards the ends, until it is ¼-inch thick; ensure that the dough is even in thickness (the dough can also be rolled out in advance and stored flat on an appropriate pan and refrigerated until needed).
6. Place the dough on top of the apples. It should just come to the ends on the pan; trim if necessary. Using a paring knife, cut 4–5 small-vent slits in the top of the dough.
7. Place the pan on a half-sheet pan and bake for 20 minutes or until the dough begins to brown.
8. Turn the oven down to 350 F (176 C) degrees and continue baking until the apples are tender, approximately 20 minutes. Use a skewer or the tip of a paring knife to check the apples.
9. Remove from the oven to cool.
10. Once the tart is cool, invert onto a plate or pan for portioning. If the tart has set in the pan, gently warm it over a burner to release before inverting.

WINE SELECTED with Apple Tarte Tatin

Wine: Maculan Torcolato ($40)
Origin: Veneto, Italy

Taste and Texture Comparisons

Dish: Apple, Sweet, Cooked Fruit, Caramelization, Biscuity, Spice, Nutty
Wine: Sweet, Dried Fruit, Rich, Full-Bodied, Honey, Caramel, Nutty

Torcolato means "twisted" in Italian. This dessert wine is made from grapes (85% Vespaiolo, 10% Tocai, and 5% Garganega) left to dry on giant, corkscrew-shaped strands hung from attic ceilings for 4–5 months. It is also aged in French oak barrels (one-third new oak) for a year. All of these characteristics create the wine's unique flavor.

Why This Is a Good Pairing

- ***Matching*** – The tarte and the wine are equally intense in terms of sweetness and flavor.
- ***Complementing*** – The dried fruit character in the wine strongly connects with the cooked apples and the caramel/brown sugar notes in the tarte.
- ***Contrasting*** – The wine and the tarte have caramel/spice and fruit that contrast nicely.

Wines That Didn't Work

Tawny Port – Lots of complementing between the caramel in the dish and the caramel and nut in the wine, but the flavor of the apple is lost. It is not entirely unpleasant (and if you like lots of nutty flavors, this is for you), but the compounding of the caramel and nut flavors covers the rest of the dish.

Alsatian Gewürztraminer – We tested two Alsatian Gewürztraminers: a dry one and a Vendage Tardive, which is a bit sweet. There is a compounding of the spiciness in the wine and the brown spices in the dish, which covers the flavors of the apple and the fruit in the wine.

Alternative: Recioto della Valpolicella—This sweet cousin of Amarone creates quite the *complexing* reaction. The spice in the tarte also creates a bridge to some of the spice notes in the wine. There are many layers of flavors to taste: berry notes in the wine, caramelization in the apples, and pie crust.

SUMMARY	Maculan Torcolato	Recioto della Valpolicella	Tawny Port	Alsatian Gewürztraminer
Matching	+			
Complementing	+	+		
Contrasting	+	+		
Compounding			(–)	(–)
Complexing		+		
Cleansing				
Covering			(–)	(–)
Clashing				

Strawberries with Champagne Sabayon

STRAWBERRY

Strawberries are available year-round in the United States with California and Florida producing the majority of the crop. Mexico also accounts for a portion of the fruit on the market today. It is important to always taste strawberries and to evaluate flavor prior to use as color isn't a great indicator of a strawberry's taste. When possible, source a local berry in season for the best flavor and quality.

STRAWBERRIES WITH CHAMPAGNE SABAYON

Yield: 10 portions

Ingredients	Amounts - US	Volume	Metric
Strawberries, washed, hulled, sliced ¼"	30 oz.	5 ¾ cups	840 grams
Egg yolks, large	3 ¾ oz.	6 each	102 grams
Sugar, granulated	2 ⅝ oz.	⅓ cup	72 grams
Champagne, brut	6 fl. oz.	¾ cup	180 ml
Vanilla extract		¾ tsp.	

Strawberries with Champagne Sabayon

1. Set up a double boiler (see note on page 101).
2. Place the strawberries into serving glasses and set aside.
3. Combine the yolks and the sugar in the bowl and whisk well; add the Champagne and vanilla extract and whisk to evenly incorporate.
4. Place the yolk mixture over the water bath and whisk constantly until it begins to thicken and forms a ribbon; be careful not to overheat/cook the eggs.
5. Pour over the strawberries and serve immediately.

WINE SELECTED with Strawberries with Champagne Sabayon

Wine: Banfi Rosa Regale Brachetto d'Acqui ($13)
Origin: Piedmont, Italy

Taste and Texture Comparisons

Dish: Lightly Sweet, Fresh, Acidic, Slight Frothy Creamy Texture, Vanilla
Wine: Sweet, Red Berry Flavor, Moderate Acidity, Low Alcohol, Lightly Effervescent

This wine is made from 100% Brachetto grapes from one of Italy's smallest quality regions. It generally has raspberry flavors with some soft effervescence.

Why This Is a Good Pairing

- ***Matching*** – The wine and the dish match in terms of flavor intensity. There is also a connection between the light effervescence of the wine and the frothiness from the Sabayon made with sparkling wine.
- ***Complementing*** – There is a definite bridge between the berry flavors in the wine and the strawberries in the dish.
- ***Contrasting*** – The Sabayon with its vanilla flavor contrasts nicely with the berry flavors, making the fruit in the dish and the wine pop.
- ***Compounding*** – There is a very pleasant reaction with the intense berry fruitiness of the wine compounding with the fresh fruitiness of the strawberries.

Wines That Didn't Work

Demi-Sec Champagne – The wine is too cleansing for the dish, the flavors are stripped away.

Moscato d'Asti – The wine is a bit too sweet and overpowers the flavors of the dish and the wine wins.

Alternative: Muscat Vin doux Natural—This sweet Vin doux Natural from Minervois has hints of orange blossom and slight orange notes that contrast and dance well with the strawberries. There also is an excellent balance between all of the elements (sweetness, alcohol, acid, body, flavors, etc.).

Legend has it that Julius Caesar and Marc Antony presented Cleopatra with several gourds of Brachetto. She then had her lovers drink the wine to unleash their passion.

SUMMARY	Banfi Rosa Regale Brachetto	Muscat Vin doux Natural	Demi-Sec Champagne	Moscato d'Asti
Matching	+	+		
Complementing	+			
Contrasting	+	+		
Compounding	+			
Complexing				
Cleansing			(–)	
Covering				(–)
Clashing				

STRAWBERRY SHORTCAKE

Yield: 10 portions

Ingredients	Amounts - US	Volume	Metric
For the Shortcake			
Flour, all-purpose, unbleached	20 oz.	4 ½ cups	568 grams
Sugar, granulated	5 ¼ oz.	¾ cup	150 grams
Baking powder	½ oz.	1 Tbl.	14 grams
Salt, kosher		¼ tsp.	
Butter, unsalted, diced, chilled	4 ½ oz.	9 Tbl.	128 grams
Eggs, large	5 ¼ oz.	3 each	150 grams
Heavy cream	7 ½ fl. oz.	¾ cup plus 3 Tbl.	225 ml

Ingredients	Amounts - US	Volume	Metric
Milk, whole		as needed	
Sugar, granulated		as needed	
For the Chantilly Cream			
Heavy cream	8 fl. oz.	1 cup	240 ml
Sugar, granulated	¾ oz.	1 ½ Tbl.	20 grams
For the Strawberry Sauce			
Strawberries, washed, hulled	8 oz.	1 ½ cups	228 grams
Simple syrup, 50/50	2 fl. oz.	¼ cup	60 ml
Honey	½ fl. oz.	1 Tbl.	15 ml
Strawberries, washed, hulled, sliced	1 ¾ lbs.	5 ½ cups	794 grams

Chantilly Cream

1. Whip the cream until a soft peak forms.
2. Add the sugar and continue whipping until a stiff peak has formed.
3. Reserve under refrigeration until needed.

Shortcake

1. Combine the dry ingredients and mix well.
2. Cut the butter into the dry ingredients and smear until the pieces are very small.
3. Whisk the eggs and combine with the cream. Slowly add the cream mixture to the dry ingredients and gently work until the dough just forms.
4. Shape the dough into a square, cover, and refrigerate for 30 minutes.
5. Preheat oven to 375 F (190 C) degrees.
6. Roll out the dough on a lightly floured surface until it is 1-inch thick and cut with a 2 ½-inch round biscuit cutter.
7. Place the shortcakes on a parchment-lined double sheet pan (if a single pan is used, the shortcake may darken too much on the bottom). Brush the tops lightly with milk and sprinkle with a pinch of sugar.
8. Bake for 25 minutes or until light golden brown. Cool on a rack.

Strawberry Sauce

1. Puree the 8 oz. of strawberries, simple syrup, and honey until a sauce consistency; add more simple syrup if necessary.
2. Combine the sliced strawberries with the sauce.
3. Slice the shortcakes in half with a serrated knife.
4. Spoon ½ cup of the strawberries onto the bottom of the biscuit.
5. Place the top biscuit offset and spoon the whipped cream on top of the strawberries.

WINE SELECTED with Strawberry Shortcake

Wine: Moët et Chandon Nectar Imperial Demi-Sec ($44)
Origin: Champagne, France

Taste and Texture Comparisons

Dish: Strawberry, Lightly Sweet, Biscuity, Fresh, Mixture of Weights and Textures, Creamy

Wine: Lightly Sweet, Sparkling, Slight Autolytic Character, High Acidity, Hint of Cream

This is a semi-sweet Champagne. Demi-Sec Champagnes range from 35–50g/l, yet their sweetness is slightly offset by the high level of acidity in the Champagne.

Why This Is a Good Pairing

- ***Matching*** – The dish and the wine are lightly sweet and match quite well.
- ***Complementing*** – The biscuity, toasty autolytic character in the Champagne brings out the flavors of the shortcake. This also works because the biscuit is not too sweet.
- ***Contrasting*** – There is a lovely contrast between the light green apple and lemon flavors of the Champagne and the strawberries. The combination makes both come alive.
- ***Cleansing*** – The high acidity in the Champagne creates a refreshing, cleansing sensation.

Wines That Didn't Work

Dry Rosé Champagne – The flavors complement one another very well, but the sweet tones of the dish are too sweet for the Champagne, making the wine taste sour.

Lightly Sweet Rosé – We tried a couple of slightly sweet rosés from California and Australia. There is some nice complementing of the berry flavors with the dish, but the wines were not sweet enough to match the intensity of the dish.

Late Harvest Botrytized Semillon – The wine is too intense in flavor and sweetness and overpowers the dish.

SUMMARY	Champagne Moët et Chandon Nectar Imperial	Dry Rosé Champagne	Lightly Sweet Rosé	Late Harvest Botrytized Semillon
Matching	+	(–)	(–)	
Complementing	+	+		
Contrasting	+			
Compounding				
Complexing				
Cleansing	+			
Covering				(–)
Clashing		(–)	(–)	

Strawberry and Blueberry Crisp

STRAWBERRY AND BLUEBERRY CRISP

Yield: 10 portions

Ingredients	Amounts - US	Volume	Metric
For the Berries			
Strawberries, washed, hulled, sliced ¼"	3 lbs.	9 cups	1360 grams
Blueberries, washed	1 ½ lbs.	4 ½ cups	680 grams
Cornstarch	¾ oz.	3 Tbl.	21 grams
Honey	2 fl. oz.	¼ cup	60 ml
Butter, unsalted, room temperature		as needed	
For the Crisp Topping			
Oats, quick cook	3 ¼ oz.	1 cup	92 grams
Flour, all-purpose, unbleached	2 ½ oz.	½ cup	72 grams
Almonds, sliced, toasted, chopped	4 oz.	1 cup	112 grams
Sugar, light brown	3 oz.	½ cup	84 grams
Cinnamon		2 tsp.	
Nutmeg		1 tsp.	
Salt, kosher		½ tsp.	
Butter, unsalted, room temperature	5 oz.	10 Tbl.	144 grams

Crisp Topping

1. Combine all ingredients, except for the butter; mix well until evenly incorporated.
2. Add the butter and blend into the mixture until crumbly and the butter pieces are not larger than a pea. Reserve until needed.

Strawberries and Blueberries

1. Lightly coat 8-oz. ramekins with butter and set aside until needed.
2. Preheat an oven to 375 F (190 C) degrees.
3. Combine the strawberries, blueberries, cornstarch, and honey; mix well to combine evenly. Ensure that there are no lumps of cornstarch.
4. Place the berry mixture into the ramekins and top with approximately 2 ½ Tbl. crisp topping (the amount will vary with the size of the ramekin).
5. Place the ramekins on a sheet pan and bake until golden brown and the fruit is bubbling, approximately 20 minutes.

The butter for the crisp topping should be pliable but not too soft. This can also be baked in a large earthenware container if desired.

WINE SELECTED with Strawberry and Blueberry Crisp

Wine: Royal Tokaji 5 Puttonyos ($56)
Origin: Tokaj-Hegyalja Hungary

Taste and Texture Comparisons

Dish: Cooked Strawberry, Sweet, Spice, Earthy, Caramelization
Wine: Sweet, Dried Apricots, Orange Peel, Spice, Honey, High Acidity, Moderate Alcohol

Tokaji is a sweet wine from the Tokaj-Hegyalja region in Hungary made from botrytis-infected grapes. They have a distinctly high acidity and have a taste reminiscent of dried apricots, orange peel, and honey. The Puttonyos connotes the level of sweetness in the wine.

Why This Is a Good Pairing

- ***Matching*** – The dish and the wine match in intensity of sweetness. Neither the dish nor the wine overpowers the other.
- ***Complementing*** – There is a connection between the cooked fruit character in the dish and the dried fruit character in the wine. Additionally, the oxidative character (dried fruit, spice) in the wine from its oak aging creates a bridge to the almonds and the spice in the dish.
- ***Contrasting*** – A wonderful contrast between the orange peel notes in the wine and the strawberries and the blueberries in the dish.
- ***Complexing*** – There are so many reactions occurring that one can taste all the layers of flavors. The pairing makes the dish and the wine taste more complex.
- ***Cleansing*** – The high acidity from the Tokaji makes the dish and the wine seem less sweet. This creates a nice balance and elongates the finish.

Wines That Didn't Work

Demi-Sec Champagne – Although the almonds and oats in the dish are complemented by some of the biscuity notes in the wine, the dish is much sweeter than the wine, which makes the wine taste sour.

Brachetto – The berry fruitiness in the wine is definitely brought out by the dish, however, the oats and almonds are a bit overpowering. The pairing thins the wine, making it seem one-dimensional.

Alternative: Moscato d'Asti—This sparkler softens the intensity of flavors of the dish. The slight orange blossom flavors also contrast nicely. It works and makes the dish taste fresh, but is not as complex as the Tokaji.

SUMMARY	Royal Tokaji 5 Puttonyos	Moscato d'Asti	Demi-Sec Champagne	Brachetto
Matching	+	+	(–)	
Complementing	+		+	+
Contrasting	+	+		
Compounding				
Complexing	+			(–)
Cleansing	+			
Covering			(–)	
Clashing				

Chocolate Soufflé with Orange Crème Anglaise

CHOCOLATE

Chocolate enjoys a long and glamorous history, which can be traced back over 2000 years to Central America and the Mayan people. Cocoa beans were originally used to produce a beverage mixed with spices such as; chili, vanilla, annnatto, cinnamon, and honey. This prized bean was also used as a form of currency in the early days and known as a food of the gods. Once the cocoa bean is harvested it is fermented, dried, roasted, and then the shell is removed. The resulting cocoa nib is then ground into cocoa mass which is liquefied to yield cocoa liquor. The two main components of this liquor are cocoa solids and cocoa butter. The solids are what dictate the percentage of cocoa (for example, 64%) and interestingly white chocolate only contains cocoa butter and no cocoa solids.

CHOCOLATE SOUFFLÉ WITH ORANGE CRÈME ANGLAISE

Yield: 10 each

Ingredients	Amounts - US	Volume	Metric
For the Chocolate Soufflé			
Dark chocolate, 64%, chopped	5 oz.	1 ¼ cups	140 grams
Milk, whole, room temperature	6 fl. oz.	¾ cup	180 ml
Sugar, granulated	1 ¾ oz.	¼ cup	48 grams
Butter, unsalted	1 ½ oz.	3 Tbl.	44 grams
All-purpose flour	1 oz.	4 Tbl.	28 grams
Egg yolks, large	2 ¾ oz.	5 each	78 grams
Egg whites, large	12 ½ oz.	10 each	350 grams
Cream of tartar		1 tsp.	
For the Orange Crème Anglaise			
Milk, whole	8 fl. oz.	1 cup	240 ml
Heavy cream	8 fl. oz.	1 cup	240 ml
Sugar, granulated	4 oz.	½ cup	114 grams
Egg yolks, large	3 ½ oz.	6 each	102 grams
Vanilla bean, split		½ each	
Orange zest, blanched		½ tsp.	
Salt, kosher		pinch	
Grand Marnier		1 tsp.	
Preparing the Soufflé Molds			
Butter, unsalted, room temperature		as needed	
Sugar, granulated		as needed	

Traditional soufflés are based on either a roux/bechamel or pastry cream and these are the most stable. Some recipes call for simply chocolate, butter, egg yolks/whites, and cream of tartar; these will typically be more delicate and fragile.

(Continues on next page)

Orange Crème Anglaise

1. Prepare an ice bath for the final sauce. This should include a clean stainless steel bowl or bain marie, clean chinois, and a rubber spatula.
2. Place the milk, cream, half of the sugar, vanilla bean, orange zest, and salt in a heavy-bottomed saucepan. Bring to a simmer, reduce the heat to low. Taste the mixture and adjust the amount of zest if necessary—the potency of the zest can vary greatly.
3. Combine the yolks and remaining sugar in a stainless steel bowl and whisk well. *Do not combine the sugar and yolks until you are ready for this step or the sugar will "burn" the yolks and the sauce will become grainy.*
4. Temper the yolks by adding 2 oz. of the hot milk/cream mixture and stirring well. Repeat this step 1 more time.
5. Then pour the tempered egg mixture into the saucepan, over low heat. Stir this with a wooden spoon until a light nappe is achieved, you can also check with a thermometer at 140 F (60 C) degrees.
6. Remove from the heat immediately and strain through a chinois into a stainless steel bowl or bain marie in an ice bath. Stir with a clean wooden spoon or a rubber spatula until cool.
7. Add the Grand Marnier and mix well.
8. Refrigerate until needed.

It can be difficult to make a crème anglaise in small batches because the base gets hot quickly and the yolks can scramble easily. It is critical to monitor the temperature very closely.

Chocolate Soufflé

1. Prepare 6-oz. soufflé cups by coating lightly and evenly with butter. Place a tablespoon of sugar in the cup and turn gently to coat, turn out the excess sugar into another cup and repeat. Clean the top edge of the soufflé cups with a paper towel so that the soufflé will rise evenly and not trail over the edge. Store in a cool part of the kitchen.
2. Preheat the oven to 400 F (204 C) degrees. Ensure that the rack is in the center of the oven.
3. Place the chocolate in a stainless steel bowl, set over a gently simmering double boiler and stir until melted. Hold at room temperature.
4. Scald the milk and half of the sugar, set aside at room temperature.
5. Melt the butter in a saucepan over medium heat.
6. Add the flour and stir with a wooden spoon until the roux is the consistency of wet sand. Cook gently while stirring over low heat for 3–4 minutes.
7. Add the scalded milk while whisking constantly to ensure that there are no lumps. Bring this mixture to a boil and remove from the heat.
8. Add the egg yolks one at a time, mixing well to incorporate.
9. Combine the chocolate and the egg yolk mixture.
10. Whisk the whites until they begin to form a peak, add the remaining sugar and the cream of tartar; whisk until a medium peak.
11. Working in three stages, fold the egg whites into the chocolate mixture. Using a whisk will help maintain the air that has been incorporated into the whites. Use a rubber spatula to ensure that you have "cleaned" the bottom and sides of the bowl.
12. Carefully pour the soufflé mixture into the prepared cups almost to the top and bake for approximately 14 minutes or until the soufflés have risen well above the rim and are just set.
13. Serve immediately. At tableside, use the tip of a spoon to gently open the top of the soufflé and carefully pour the orange crème anglaise in the center.

If you whisk the whites to a stiff peak the soufflé will have trouble expanding and holding its shape. Take caution when coating the molds with butter; too much butter on the sides will cause a soufflé to rise unevenly.

WINE SELECTED with Chocolate Soufflé with Orange Crème Anglaise

Wine: Pommery Brut Rosé ($14 per 187 ml)
Origin: Champagne, France

Taste and Texture Comparisons

Dish: Airy Texture, Semi-Sweet, Delicate Citrus, Chocolaty
Wine: Effervescent, Dry, Crisp, Delicately Fruity (Hint of Strawberries)

This Champagne is made with two black grapes and one white grape: Pinot Noir (for berry fruit, structure), Pinot Meunier (generally berry and floral notes), and Chardonnay (for acidic backbone and citrus notes).

Why This Is a Good Pairing

- ***Matching Texture*** – The soufflé has an airy texture and the wine has bubbles. Both have an airiness about them.
- ***Contrasting*** – The dessert is sweet, however, not so sweet that it makes the Champagne taste sour (which is what usually happens with dry Champagne and desserts). Additionally, the fruit flavors (light strawberry notes in the rosé Champagne and orange in the sauce) contrast and thereby lift up the chocolate flavors.
- ***Complementing*** – The orange sauce creates a bridge to the rosé Champagne as even rosé Champagne has some slight citrus notes (focusing on the Chardonnay in the blend).
- ***Complexing*** – There is a layering effect that happens wherein you taste the berries in the rosé Champagne, chocolate from the soufflé, and the orange sauce. You taste every layer.
- ***Cleansing*** – There is a slight cleansing here in a positive way. The high acidity adds a "lift" to the dish, adding refreshment.

Wines That Didn't Work

Tokaji – This sweet wine from Hungary is known for flavors of dried apricots drizzled with honey and orange peel. However, when paired with this dish, a compounding takes place. Orange in the sauce + orange notes in the wine = way too much orange (orange^2).

Pedro Ximenez (PX) – PX is quite sweet and has flavors of molasses, nuts, and dates. With this dish, the sweetness is compounded and Sugar + Sugar = Sugar^2. It is too overpowering for this dish.

Alternatives: Banyuls and Port work as well. Their rich berry flavors contrast nicely with the chocolate and Orange Crème Anglaise.

SUMMARY	Pommery Rosé Champagne	Banyuls and Ruby Port	Tokaji 5 Puttonyos	Pedro Ximenez
Matching	+	+		
Complementing	+	+		
Contrasting	+	+		
Compounding			(–)	(–)
Complexing	+			
Cleansing	+	+		
Covering			(–)	(–)
Clashing				

Chocolate Mousse with Strawberries

CHOCOLATE MOUSSE WITH STRAWBERRIES

Yield: 10 portions

Ingredients	Amounts - US	Volume	Metric
Strawberries, washed, hulled, small dice	1 lb.	2 cups	454 grams
Heavy cream	16 fl. oz.	2 cups	500 ml
Dark chocolate, 64%, chopped	9 oz.	2 ¼ cups	254 grams
Eggs, large	7 oz.	4 each	200 grams
Sugar, granulated	2 ½ oz.	¼ cup plus 1 Tbl.	70 grams

Chocolate Mousse

1. Clean the molds for the mousse. Prepare a piping bag with a straight tip.
2. Whip the cream to a stiff peak, not grainy, and reserve at room temperature.
3. Set up a double boiler (see note on page 101). Place the chocolate in a stainless steel bowl over a gently simmering water bath (ensure that water doesn't touch the bottom of the bowl), and stir until melted. Remove from the heat but keep in a warm location.
4. Combine the eggs and the sugar in a stainless steel bowl and whisk over a double boiler (ensure that water doesn't touch the bottom of the bowl) until 140 F (60 C) degrees. The egg mixture will thicken slightly. Once you have reached 140 F (60 C) degrees, remove from the heat and whisk until it is cool and leaves a ribbon.
5. Combine the chocolate and the egg mixture; mix well to blend thoroughly.
6. Working in three stages, fold the whipped cream into the chocolate mixture; use a whisk to keep the air in the mousse. You will need a rubber spatula to "clean" the sides and bottom of the bowl.
7. Fill the piping bag with the chocolate mousse.
8. Place 1 tablespoon of strawberries in the base of each cup and then pipe the mousse to fill the cup halfway.
9. Spread an additional tablespoon of strawberries on top of the mousse.
10. Continue piping and fill the molds three-quarters of the way, cover, and place in the refrigerator.
11. Place another tablespoon of strawberries on top of the mousse just before serving.

You must work cleanly and quickly with mousse as it is time and temperature sensitive. If the mixtures are too hot, the mousse will lose volume; if you take too long, the base will begin to set up before you are ready to fill the molds. In this recipe chocolate acts as the base and binder for the mousse.

WINE SELECTED with the Chocolate Mousse with Strawberries

Wine: Fonseca Bin. 27 Ruby Port ($16)
Origin: Duoro Valley, Portugal

Taste and Texture Comparisons

Dish: Sweet, Soft, Fruity, Chocolaty (Flavor and Texture), Creamy

Wine: Sweet, Soft Texture, Fruity, Balanced Acidity, High Alcohol

A ruby-style Port with rich red and blackberry fruit with about 20% level of alcohol and 100 g/l residual sugar.

Why This Is a Good Pairing

- ***Matching Intensity and Texture*** – The intensity of the sweetness is evenly matched. The Chocolate Mousse has a soft creamy texture, yet you can feel some of the tactile texture of the cocoa. Similarly, in the Ruby Port there is a soft, slight chocolaty texture. There is a bridge here in terms of texture that matches.
- ***Complementing*** – There is a bridge between the strawberries and the red berry fruit in the Port, making both stand out. The strawberries add a freshness and "lift" to the red fruit in the Port.
- ***Contrasting*** – Raspberry, black cherry, and other black fruit of the Port contrast with the chocolate, making both stand out more.
- ***Dance*** – The richness of the cream in the mousse is not cut too much by the acidity in the Port (and the sweetness of both match in intensity), and the fat carries the flavors on the palate for a long dance.

Wines That Didn't Work

Rosé Champagne – Although the Champagne's flavor of berry fruit builds a bridge to the strawberries in the dish, the dry Champagne clashes with the sweetness of the mousse. The high acidity and effervescence of the Champagne cleanse, and almost neutralize, the flavors of the mousse.

Tawny Port and Pedro Ximenez – Both wines overpower the dish and the nutty, oxidized flavors clash with the freshness of the strawberries and cream.

Alternative: Banyuls is a sweet, red fortified wine from southern France. It can vary in its sweetness and tannin levels from producer to producer. The one we tried works because its sweetness, tannin, and acid structure are very similar to that of the Ruby Port.

SUMMARY	Fonseca Bin. 27 Ruby Port	Rosé Champagne	Tawny Port	Pedro Ximenez
Matching	+			
Complementing	+	+		
Contrasting	+			
Compounding				
Complexing				
Cleansing		(–)		
Covering			(–)	(–)
Clashing			(–)	(–)

FLOURLESS HAZELNUT CHOCOLATE CAKE WITH RASPBERRY SAUCE

Yield: 10 portions

Ingredients	Amounts - US	Volume	Metric
For the Cake			
Extra virgin olive oil		as needed	
Hazelnuts, lightly roasted	5 oz.	1 cup	144 grams
Sugar, granulated	5 oz.	¾ cup	144 grams
Extra virgin olive oil	1 fl. oz.	2 Tbl.	30 ml
Butter, unsalted, cubed	5 oz.	10 Tbl.	142 grams
Cayenne pepper		¼ tsp.	
Heavy cream	4 fl. oz.	½ cup	120 ml
Chocolate, dark, 64%, chopped	16 oz.	4 cups	454 grams
Egg yolks, large	3 ⅜ oz.	6 each	106 grams
Egg whites, large	6 ⅜ oz.	6 each	182 grams
For the Chantilly Cream			
Heavy cream	8 fl. oz.	1 cup	240 ml
Sugar, granulated	¾ oz.	1 ½ Tbl.	20 grams
For the Raspberry Sauce Yield: 2 cups			
Raspberries, fresh	12 oz.	3 cups	340 grams
Honey	1 fl. oz.	2 Tbl.	30 ml
Chambord	1 fl. oz.	2 Tbl.	30 ml
Lemon-lime soda	½ fl. oz.	1 Tbl.	15 ml

Chantilly Cream

1. Whip the cream until a soft peak forms.
2. Add the sugar and continue whipping until a stiff peak has formed.
3. Reserve under refrigeration until needed.

Raspberry Sauce

1. Puree the raspberries in a blender until smooth; strain through a chinois or hand-held strainer.
2. Combine the raspberries and the honey in a small saucepan and bring to a gentle simmer. Add the Chambord and remove from the heat; cool to room temperature.
3. Add the lemon-lime soda and mix well to combine. Refrigerate until needed.

Flourless Hazelnut Chocolate Cake

1. Line a 9-inch cake pan with a parchment paper circle. Lightly coat with olive oil. Reserve until needed.
2. Using a food processor, grind half of the nuts and half of the sugar until fine and evenly ground. Grind the remaining nuts with the olive oil to a smooth paste.
3. Place the chocolate in a stainless steel bowl. Bring the cream and butter to a simmer and pour over the chocolate. Stir until the chocolate is completely melted. Cool to room temperature.
4. Combine the chocolate, cayenne, and both nut mixtures and stir until evenly incorporated.
5. Using a stand mixer, whisk the egg yolks until pale and they form a ribbon. Stir the yolks into the chocolate-hazelnut mixture.
6. Whisk the egg whites until they begin to rise, add the remaining sugar, and whisk until a medium peak.
7. Working in stages, fold three even additions of egg whites into the chocolate-hazelnut mixture. Using a whisk will help to maintain the air that has been incorporated into the whites. Use a rubber spatula to ensure that you have "cleaned" the bottom and sides of the bowl.
8. Pour the mixture into the prepared pan; there should be at least 1 inch of space in the top of the pan to allow for rising.
9. Bake at 275 F (135 C) degrees convection for 50–60 minutes or until the cake has set. Check the center of the cake with a thin skewer; it should be slightly wet.
10. Allow the cake to cool before unmolding and slicing.
11. Serve with the raspberry sauce and chantilly cream.

Because the sweetness and moisture of raspberries can vary greatly, it may be necessary to add a small amount of simple syrup while pureeing the raspberries. Always taste and adjust the sweetness as needed.

WINE SELECTED with Flourless Hazelnut Chocolate Cake with Raspberry Sauce

Wine: NV Osborne Sherry Pedro Ximenez 1827 ($22)
Origin: Jerez, Spain

Taste and Texture Comparisons

Dish: Chocolaty, Nutty, Sweet, Rich
Wine: Sweet, Viscous, Intense Nut/Molasses/ Raisin Flavors, Slight Earth Note, Fortified Alcohol, Low Acidity

Pedro Ximenez (or PX) is a white grape. These grapes are dried in the sun, then fermented and fortified to create this wine. It is typically used to sweeten Oloroso, or in this case, made into a raisiny-sweet fortified varietal wine.

Why This Is a Good Pairing

PX is not the first wine most people think of to pair with chocolate. It is very sweet while the flourless chocolate cake is not as sweet. However, nuts and chocolate are a classic pairing and the PX has lots of nutty flavors.

- ***Matching Density and Intensity*** – The cake and the wine are both quite dense, rich, and intense.
- ***Complementing*** – Hazelnuts in the cake create a bridge to the nuttiness in the PX, making it shine.
- ***Contrasting*** – The raspberry fruit contrasts with the chocolate flavors. It also contrasts with the earthy notes in the PX and makes all of the flavors pop, creating a *complexing* effect.
- ***Complexing*** – You taste all the layers in this dish: chocolate, hazelnuts, raspberry, dried fruit, molasses, and a touch of earthiness that is alluring.

Wines That Didn't Work

Brut Rosé Champagne – Although there is a complementing between the berry notes in the Champagne and the raspberry sauce, the richness of the dish overpowers the wine.

Napa Cabernet Sauvignon – The raspberry notes in the sauce bridge the black currant notes in Cabernet, but the sweetness of the raspberry sauce makes the wine a bit sour. Additionally, the firm gripping tannin in the Cabernet combines with the slight bitterness in the cocoa, compounding it.

Alternatives: Banyuls, Ruby Port, and Tawny Port also work. This dish demonstrates the upper range of viscous, sweet wines with which chocolate dishes can pair very well.

If you love Napa Cabernet and chocolate, chances are you love them together. This isn't wrong. Personal preferences have an impact on perception and you will likely gravitate towards them. Even though we believe it's not the best pairing here, there are flavors that work between the wine and the chocolate cake. If you do this pairing, be aware that it can be polarizing. The reaction from your guests may be divided.

SUMMARY	Osborne Sherry Pedro Ximenez 1827	Banyuls, Ruby Port, Tawny Port	Brut Rosé Champagne	Napa Cabernet Sauvignon
Matching	+	+		(–)
Complementing	+	+	+	+
Contrasting	+	+		
Compounding				(–)
Complexing	+			
Cleansing			(–)	
Covering				
Clashing				

DESSERTS PAIRING SUMMARY AND CONCLUSIONS

Lemon

Dish	Method	Wine
Lemon Sorbet		Riesling Spätlese, JJ Prüm Graacher Himmelreich
Lemon Pound Cake	Bake	Riesling Auslese, JJ Prüm Graacher Himmelreich
Lemon Cheesecake	Bake	Recioto della Valpolicella Classico Giovanni Allegrini

- ***Main ingredient tendencies:*** Lemon is light and has high acidity which allows it to pair well with sweet white and red wines. It can be a challenge to pair with dry wines based on body, sweetness, and acidity.

- ***Specific techniques that changed the pairing:*** Sorbet is the lightest of the three recipes, which calls for a light sweet wine.

- ***Specific ingredients that changed the pairing:*** There is a strong complementary connection between the lemon and the citrus notes in Riesling. The varying body/acid/sweetness balance between the sorbet and pound cake matches two Rieslings at different sweetness levels. The cheesecake was the richest, which allows for it to pair with a red sweet wine. Red berry fruit in the Recioto contrasts well with the lemon in the cheesecake.

Apple

Dish	Method	Wine
Green Apple Mousse	Sabayon	Chenin Blanc, Côteaux du Layon, Château Soucherie
Apple Fritters	Deep-Fry	Vidal Ice Wine, Standing Stone Vineyards
Apple Tarte Tatin	Bake	Torcolato, Maculan

- ***Main ingredient tendencies:*** Green apples have tart acidity, yet a softer acidity than lemon, and have perceptible sweetness.

- ***Specific techniques that changed the pairing:*** Baking the apples in the Tatin creates cooked fruit and caramelized flavors, which complement the dried fruit, caramel, and nutty tones in the Torcolato.

- ***Specific ingredients that changed the pairing:*** The Green Apple Mousse's flavor complements the bruised apple notes in the Chenin Blanc. The apples in the fritter meet the purity of the fruit flavor in the ice wine. Additionally, the richness from the ricotta matches the weight in richness of the ice wine.

Strawberry

Dish	Method	Wine
Strawberries with Champagne Sabayon	Raw/Sabayon	Brachetto d'Acqui, Banfi Rosa Regale
Strawberry Shortcake	Bake	Demi-Sec, Champagne Moët et Chandon Nectar
Strawberry and Blueberry Crisp	Bake	Tokaj 5 Puttonyos, Royal Tokaji

- ***Main ingredient tendencies:*** Strawberries have a pure flavor, an inherent sweetness, and high moisture content. Strawberries tend to contrast and pair well with lemon and orange flavors.

- ***Specific techniques that changed the pairing:*** The purity of the strawberry sauce with the shortcake contrasts well with the freshness of the citrus notes in the Demi-Sec Champagne. Baking creates more intense flavor and changes the nature of the strawberries, which paired well with the dried fruit notes in the Tokaji.

- ***Specific ingredients that changed the pairing:*** The sabayon contrasts well with the red berry notes in the Brachetto (which complement the strawberries), yet the champagne's high acidity strips this dish's flavor. The shortcake itself complements the champagne's autolytic character. The baked strawberries in the crisp contrast well with the orange peel notes in the Tokaji.

Chocolate

Dish	Method	Wine
Chocolate Soufflé with Orange Crème Anglaise	Soufflé	Rosé Champagne, Pommery
Chocolate Mousse with Strawberries	Mousse	Ruby Port, Fonseca Bin. 27
Flourless Hazelnut Chocolate Cake with Raspberry Sauce	Bake	Pedro Ximenez Sherry, Osborne

- ***Main ingredient tendencies:*** Chocolate desserts are in general more rich and dense than fruit-based desserts. This extends the range of pairings generally to the full-bodied and fortified end of the spectrum.

- ***Specific techniques that changed the pairing:*** The airiness of the soufflé complements the lightness and effervescence of the champagne. The density of the flourless chocolate cake allows for a rich, dense sweet wine.

- ***Specific ingredients that changed the pairing:*** The Orange Crème Anglaise contrasts well with the red berry notes in the Rosé Champagne (which also contrasted well with the chocolate). The strawberries in the mousse create a connection to the berry notes in the ruby port. Chocolate in general matches in weight with ruby port and contrasts very well with its rich red fruit. The hazelnuts in the flourless chocolate cake bridge to the nutty notes of the Pedro Ximenez and contrast with the raspberry sauce so that all the flavors pop.

10
Conclusions and Observations

In order to approach food and wine pairing successfully, it is incredibly important to understand the flavors and aroma of a food as well as the attributes of a wine and how they will react together. We have laid the groundwork for the dynamics of food and wine pairing and its drivers (main ingredient, techniques, and additional ingredients). You will be able to effectively apply these principles to create magical food and wine pairings.

OVERALL CONCLUSIONS

Throughout our food and wine pairing exploration, we identified that the most successful pairings have several elements in common: balance, complementing and contrasting components and length of pleasing flavors on the palate.

Balance

Balance is one of the main reasons why a pairing works or doesn't work. The key factors that need to be in balance are: sweetness, acidity, bitterness, salt, umami, and flavor. Additionally, great pairings must also balance in terms of weight and texture.

Complementing and Contrasting Elements

The presence of *complementing* and *contrasting* elements is another key to great pairings. Some pairings create multiple layers of flavors where a complexing reaction occurs. When this happens, the food and the wine both taste more sophisticated and this enriches and enhances the entire experience.

Long Length

On several occasions we refer to something we call "the dance." The best pairings are those that create an extended finish on your palate. Most often this occurs because there is a rich flavor in the food that is carried by the wine on your palate without the acid in the wine stripping that richness away.

ADDITIONAL OBSERVATIONS

In addition to the three key elements discussed above, we make a few additional observations about great pairings.

Great Pairings Occur at All Price Points

Great pairings can happen at any place within the price range spectrum. In fact, 71% of the recipes we tested pair well with wines under $25 (36% are under $15; 11%, under $10).

General Rules Are Guidelines

The general rules are merely starting points (e.g., "white wine with fish; red wine with red meat"); you should feel free to experiment. Many of the successful pairings in this book are outside the lines of the general rules. For example, over 40% of the beef recipes in this book pair well with white wine.

Wine Knowledge Is Key

Even though wines made from the same grape share similar characteristics, there are differences that will impact a pairing (terroir and winemaking).

Knowledge of a grape variety's characteristics, terroir, and production techniques is key to understanding why one wine pairs over another of the same variety and/or region. It can also help you predict and narrow the field for suitable pairings before ever opening a bottle to taste.

Delicate Line between Complementing and Compounding

Complementing creates a bridge between the flavors in a dish and a wine. This is a delicate balance. Just a touch of grassy notes in a Sancerre may complement Grilled Salmon with Dill Butter, but a South African Sauvignon Blanc with stronger herbal tones compounds with this dish in a negative way.

Delicate Line between Cleansing and Stripping

Acid in a wine can be cleansing and refreshing for a dish. However, acid can quickly cross the line and strip the flavor of a dish. In general, this happens between high-acid wines and mild-flavored dishes that don't have enough fat or richness to balance the pairing. We experienced this when we tested a dry sparkling wine with the Hot Smoked Chicken Breast with Creole Mustard Sauce.

However, some high-acid wines pair well with dishes with high acid and with little richness or fat. An example of this is the Vinho Verde or the Eden Valley Riesling with Shrimp and Scallop Ceviche. This is because there are other elements and flavors that tie the pairing together.

Creating Pairings for a Wide Range of Palates

We recognize people's preferences for their favorite wines. People have different palates and, as we mention in Chapter 1, it is natural for you to gravitate towards those things you enjoy. For example, chocolate and Cabernet Sauvignon represented a challenge during our testing. The pairing didn't always work. However, some people love Cabernet Sauvignon with chocolate. If it works for you, enjoy the pairing.

Through this book we have meticulously outlined the taste and texture comparisons between the dish and the wine and the dynamics that happen as a result of each pairing. It is our hope that by focusing your palate on these attributes and reactions you will become more objective and improve your skills in creating pairings that are magical for a wide range of palates.

HOW TO MAKE A DISH MORE WINE-FRIENDLY

Adjusting a recipe can enhance the pairing. Once the wine is chosen, the only place to make "tweaks" is the dish.

- ***Reduce the amount of spice to balance heat.*** The majority of table wine produced and paired with food is dry and 12% abv or higher. Spices that yield heat, such as black pepper, cayenne, serrano chilis (or any within the capsicum family that have the chemical capsaicin) emphasize the heat of the alcohol and compound with tannins in a wine. Reducing the spice in a dish can provide more balance.
- ***Create a bridge.*** Select ingredients that will complement the flavors in the wine. For example, if a wine has an herbaceous note, you can complement it by adding an element of herbs to the dish.
- ***Contrast by introducing a savory element.*** In many cases, a savory component can contrast with the fruit in a wine, enhancing the flavor of the fruit. Savory elements we see in this book that bring out a wine's fruit are fennel, sage, prosciutto, and basil.

- ***Balance sweetness.*** Sweetness in a dish can make a dry wine taste sour. In order to avoid this you may have to reduce sweetening elements which not only include things like sugar and honey, but also fruits and some vegetables that are sweet (such as red peppers and onions).
- ***Balance bitter elements.*** Dishes with bitter elements can particularly compound the bitterness with tannins in red wine. Some ingredients are known for bitterness (e.g., broccoli rabe). By balancing these elements, you also reduce the risk of clashing with the tannins in a red wine (or the bitterness sometimes caused by elevated alcohol in a wine).

HOW TO CHOOSE A WINE THAT IS MORE FOOD-FRIENDLY

In some cases, the dish may be set and you have the freedom to choose different wines. This book is full of suggestions (refer to the Appendices for a list of recipes by wine and wines by recipe), but here are a few to make your wine choice more food-friendly:

- ***Choose wines with low or moderate alcohol.*** Wines with low or moderate alcohol (generally 12–13.5% abv) have less risk of exacerbating spice in a dish.
- ***Choose a wine that creates a bridge.*** Choose a wine that has some flavors complementary to the dish. For example, proteins with a Maillard reaction tend to complement wines with some toasty notes from their oak treatment. (You can find a list of typical wine flavors in Chapter 3.)
- ***Choose a wine moderate in fruit intensity.*** Wines with strong fruit intensity sometimes overpower or cover up the flavors of the dish. By choosing a wine with moderate fruit intensity, you reduce the risk of overpowering a dish (particularly a mild-flavored dish).
- ***Choose a wine with moderate weight.*** Unless you know the dish is quite rich and bold (or very delicate), choose a wine that is more moderate in its weight. This prevents the wine from overpowering the dish. (For wines with light, medium, or full body, see Chapter 3.)
- ***Choose a wine with a touch of sweetness.*** Specifically for dishes that have intense spice or flavor, this can add balance. (For wines with sweetness, see Chapter 3.)
- ***Choose a wine with modest tannins.*** Obviously this depends on the dish. Generally, wines with high tannins pair well with a more limited range of dishes than those with more moderate tannins. If there is any spice or element of bitterness to the dish, the tannins will exacerbate the bitterness. So, by choosing a wine that is more modest in its tannins, you reduce the risk of this happening. (For a list of wines with low, medium, or high tannins, see Chapter 3.)

TASTE AND LEARN

With more than 280 combinations in this book, there are numerous examples from which to learn how to create the best food and wine pairings. We encourage you to have an open mind and to taste different combinations on your own for your best pairings.

WHEN ONE NEEDS TO OUTSHINE THE OTHER

There may be situations where you want the dish to stand out more than the wine or the wine to stand out more than the dish. For example, you may have a special bottle of wine that you've been saving or there may be an ingredient in season that you want to highlight.

Wine over Dish

In order to make a wine the star of the pairing, choose one that is more powerful than the dish in its fruit, flavors, and structure. Another option is to construct the dish so that it amplifies a specific complementary aspect of the wine.

Dish over Wine

To make a dish stand out more than the wine, choose techniques and ingredients that are stronger, more powerful, and more flavorful than the wine. Choose wines that have balance but do not have obvious flavors that will clash with the dish.

INTERESTING FACTS

- 47% of the recipes paired well with white wine
- 32% of the recipes paired well with red wine
- 11% of the recipes paired well with sparkling wine (half of which paired with shellfish and fish)
- 6% of the recipes paired well with sweet/dessert wine
- 4% of the recipes paired well with rosé wine
- A small number of wines crossed the boundary between sweet and savory (meaning some sweet wines paired well with savory dishes and some dry wines paired with desserts)
- 47% of the beef recipes paired well with white wine
- 14% of the shellfish and fish recipes paired well with red wine
- Chardonnay and Pinot Noir are the two grape varieties with the most versatility; they paired well with 20% of the recipes in the entire book

CLOSING THOUGHTS

The exploration into food and wine pairing is exciting, with discovery at every turn. We both learned a great deal more about food and wine pairing as a result of this book. Our work and experience revealed to us that if you truly focus on the reactions between food and wine, you can create magic.

FOUNDED 1987

Appendix A
Recipes by Wine

GRAPE/BLEND	WINE	MAIN PROTEIN/ INGREDIENT	RECIPE TITLE	PAGE
Sparkling	Agrapart & Fils 7 Crus	Lobster	Lobster Thermidor	74
Sparkling	Charles Heidsieck Brut Réserve	Ravioli	Shrimp Ravioli with Tomato Coulis	223
Sparkling	Domaine Carneros Sparkling Rosé	Crab	Jumbo Lump Crab with Cocktail Sauce	37
Sparkling	Moët et Chandon Nectar Imperial Demi-Sec	Strawberry	Strawberry Shortcake	282
Sparkling	Piper-Heidsieck Brut	Shrimp	Shrimp Tempura with Soy Dipping Sauce	53
Sparkling	Pommery Brut Rosé	Chocolate	Chocolate Soufflé	290
Sparkling	Veuve Clicquot Yellow Label Brut	Salmon	Gravlax	98
Albariño	Burgans Albariño	Ravioli	Cheese Ravioli with Asparagus	215
Arneis	Valdinera Roero Arneis	Halibut	Poached Halibut with Fennel and Orange Slaw	82
Chardonnay	Au Bon Climat Chardonnay	Beef Tenderloin	Beef Tartare	158
Chardonnay	Chateau St. Jean Chardonnay	Mezze Rigatoni	Mezze Rigatoni Salad with Roasted Butternut Squash	239
Chardonnay	Christian Moreau Chablis	Chicken Legs	Buttermilk Fried Chicken	122
Chardonnay	Gloria Ferrer Chardonnay	Chicken Breast	Chicken Breast Stuffed with Spinach and Gruyère	119
Chardonnay	Olivier Leflaive Puligny-Montrachet	Lobster	Lobster Bisque	71
Chardonnay	Penfolds Bin 311 Chardonnay	Shrimp	Shrimp Scampi	56
Chardonnay	Sequoia Grove Chardonnay	Scallops	Sautéed Sea Scallops with Truffle Goat Cheese Sauce	62
Chenin Blanc	Château Soucherie Côteaux du Layon	Apple	Green Apple Mousse	270
Chenin Blanc	Ken Forrester "Petit" Chenin Blanc	Pork	Sous Vide Pork Tenderloin with Spicy Pineapple Salsa	145

GRAPE/BLEND	WINE	MAIN PROTEIN/ INGREDIENT	RECIPE TITLE	PAGE
Garganega	Tedeschi Soave Classico	Mezze Rigatoni	Mezze Rigatoni with Broccoli Rabe and Sausage	236
Gewürztraminer	Willm Gewürztraminer	Tuna	Seared Tuna with Sesame and Coriander	92
Gewürztraminer	Willm Gewürztraminer	Chicken Legs	Chicken Cacciatore	125
Grüner Veltliner	Domaine Wachau Grüner Veltliner	Pork	Grilled Pork Tenderloin with Caramelized Apple Compote	151
Grüner Veltliner	Domaine Wachau Grüner Veltliner	Pizza	Fennel Sausage and Porcini Mushroom Pizza	250
Moscato/Muscat	Nivole Moscato d'Asti	Beef Shank	Thai Beef with Massaman Curry	186
Moscato/Muscat	Trimbach Muscat	Halibut	Sautéed Halibut with Tomatoes and Capers	85
Pedro Ximenez	Osborne Pedro Ximenez	Chocolate	Flourless Hazelnut Chocolate Cake with Raspberry Sauce	296
Pinot Gris/Grigio	Caposaldo Pinot Grigio	Lobster	Steamed Lobster	67
Pinot Gris/Grigio	Ponzi Pinot Gris	Beef Flank Steak	Beef and Broccoli Stir-Fry	168
Riesling	Dr. Konstantin Frank Semi-Dry Riesling	Beef Shank	BBQ Pulled Beef	179
Riesling	Dr. Loosen Erdener Treppchen Riesling Kabinett	Duck	Smoked Duck Salad	138
Riesling	JJ Prüm Graacher Himmelreich Riesling Auslese	Lemon	Lemon Pound Cake	264
Riesling	JJ Prüm Graacher Himmelreich Riesling Spätlese	Lemon	Lemon Sorbet	260
Riesling	Pewsey Vale Dry Riesling	Salmon	Poached Salmon with Sauce Hollandaise	102
Riesling	Selbach-Oster Zeltinger Schlossberg Spätlese Riesling	Crab	Crab Cake with Spicy Chipotle Sauce	45
Sauvignon Blanc	Craggy Range Sauvignon Blanc	Beef Flank Steak	Grilled Flank Steak with Chimichurri Sauce	171
Sauvignon Blanc	Michel Redde La Moynerie Pouilly-Fumé	Scallops	Grilled Sea Scallops	59

GRAPE/BLEND	WINE	MAIN PROTEIN/ INGREDIENT	RECIPE TITLE	PAGE
Sauvignon Blanc	Nederberg Sauvignon Blanc	Spaghetti	Spaghetti con le Vongole (Clam Sauce)	227
Sauvignon Blanc	Vincent Gaudry Sancerre	Salmon	Grilled Salmon with Dill Butter	104
Terbbiano	Ruffino Orvieto Classico	Halibut	Halibut Wrapped in Phyllo	88
Vernaccia	Azienda Agraria Le Rote Vernaccia di San Gimignano	Spaghetti	Spaghetti alla Puttanesca	233
Vinho Verde Blend	Fâmega Vinho Verde	Shrimp	Shrimp and Scallop Ceviche	49
Viognier	Guigal Côtes du Rhône Blanc	Tuna	Tuna Poke	90
Viognier	Guigal Côtes du Rhône Blanc	Lamb	Rosemary Roasted Rack of Lamb	189
Tokaji Blend	Royal Tokaji 5 Puttonyos	Strawberry	Strawberry and Blueberry Crisp	285
Vespaiolo, Tocai and Garganega	Maculan Torcolato	Apple	Apple Tarte Tatin	276
Vidal	Standing Stone Vineyards Vidal Ice Wine	Apple	Apple Fritters	273
Rosé	Banfi Rosa Regale Brachetto d'Acqui	Strawberry	Strawberries with Champagne Sabayon	279
Rosé	Château de Campuget Costières de Nimes Rosé	Ravioli	Meat Ravioli in Brodo	219
Rosé	Domaine Pélaquié Tavel Rosé	Chicken Breast	Chicken Salad	111
Aglianico	Cantravelli Taurasi Riserva	Lamb	Grilled Lamb Chops with Mint Emulsion	192
Amarone Blend	Giovanni Allegrini Recioto della Valpolicella Classico	Lemon	Lemon Cheesecake	267
Amarone Blend	Masi Costasera Amarone della Valpolicella	Spaghetti	Spaghetti alla Carbonara	230
Cabernet Sauvignon	Motes Alpha Cabernet Sauvignon	Venison	Roasted Venison with Sauce Grand Veneur	201
Carmenere	Root 1 Carmenère	Beef Flank Steak	Grilled Flank Steak Sandwich	175
Garnacha	Atteca Old Vines Garnacha	Lamb	Chinese Five Spice Sautéed Lamb Chops	195
Grenache	Guigal Côtes du Rhône Rouge	Duck	Sous Vide Duck Breast	133
Malbec	Agua de Piedra Gran Reserva Malbec	Beef Tenderloin	Sautéed Beef with Cognac Peppercorn Sauce	161
Merlot	Château La Bienfaisance St. Emilion	Beef Tenderloin	Gorgonzola Dolcelatte Topped Beef Tournedos	164

GRAPE/BLEND	WINE	MAIN PROTEIN/ INGREDIENT	RECIPE TITLE	PAGE
Petite Sirah	Bogle Petite Sirah	Venison	Venison Chili	204
Pinot Noir	Bearboat Pinot Noir	Pizza	Margherita Pizza	247
Pinot Noir	Benton Lane Pinot Noir	Scallops	Prosciutto-Wrapped Sea Scallops	65
Pinot Noir	Bodega Chacra Barda Pinot Noir	Beef Shank	Beef Bourguignon	183
Pinot Noir	Craggy Range Pinot Noir	Pork	Pork Schnitzel	148
Pinot Noir	Louis Jadot Beaune Clos des Ursules	Crab	Crab and Avocado Salad	41
Pinot Noir	Yabby Lake Pinot Noir	Chicken Breast	Hot Smoked Chicken Breast	115
Pinot Noir	Yerring Station Pinot Noir	Tuna	Grilled Tuna Skewers	95
Pinotage	Wildekrans Pinotage	Duck	Sautéed Duck Breast with Sun-Dried Cherry Sauce	141
Port Blend	Fonseca Bin. 27 Ruby Port	Chocolate	Chocolate Mousse	293
Sangiovese	Barone Ricasoli Brolio Chianti Classico	Pizza	Ricotta, Taleggio, and Arugula Pizza	253
Shiraz/Syrah	Brokenwood Shiraz	Chicken Legs	Tandoori Chicken	129
Tempranillo	Bodegas Alejandro Fernandez Tinto Pesquera	Venison	Venison Burgers	198
Zinfandel	St. Francis Old Vines Zinfandel	Mezze Rigatoni	Mezze Rigatoni alla Sauce Bolognese	242

Appendix B
Wines by Recipe

RECIPE TITLE	GRAPE/BLEND	WINE	PAGE
Crab			
Jumbo Lump Crab with Cocktail	Sparkling	Domaine Carneros Sparkling Brut Rosé	35–37
Crab and Avocado Salad	Pinot Noir	Louis Jadot Beaune Clos des Ursules	38–41
Crab Cake with Spicy Chipotle Sauce	Riesling	Selbach-Oster Zeltinger Schlossberg Spätlese Riesling	42–45
Shrimp			
Shrimp and Scallop Ceviche	Vinho Verde Blend	Fâmega Vinho Verde	46–49
Shrimp Tempura	Sparkling	Piper-Heidsieck Brut	50–53
Shrimp Scampi	Chardonnay	Penfolds Bin 311 Chardonnay	54–56
Scallops			
Grilled Sea Scallops	Sauvignon Blanc	Michel Redde La Moynerie Pouilly-Fumé	57–59
Sautéed Sea Scallops with Truffle Goat Cheese Sauce	Chardonnay	Sequoia Grove Chardonnay	60–62
Prosciutto-Wrapped Sea Scallops	Pinot Noir	Benton Lane Pinot Noir	63–65
Lobster			
Steamed Lobster	Pinot Gris/Grigio	Caposaldo Pinot Grigio	66–67
Lobster Bisque	Chardonnay	Olivier Leflaive Puligny-Montrachet	68–71
Lobster Thermidor	Sparkling	Agrapart & Fils 7 Crus	72–74
Halibut			
Poached Halibut with Fennel and Orange Slaw	Arneis	Valdinera Roero Arneis	79–82
Sautéed Halibut with Tomatoes and Capers	Moscato/Muscat	Trimbach Muscat	83–85
Halibut Wrapped in Phyllo	Terbbiano	Ruffino Orvieto Classico	86–88
Tuna			
Tuna Poke	Viognier	Guigal Côtes du Rhône Blanc	89–90
Seared Tuna with Sesame and Coriander	Gewürztraminer	Willm Gewürztraminer	91–92
Grilled Tuna Skewers	Pinot Noir	Yerring Station Pinot Noir	93–95

RECIPE TITLE	GRAPE/BLEND	WINE	PAGE
Salmon			
Gravlax	Sparkling	Veuve Clicquot Yellow Label Brut	96–98
Poached Salmon with Sauce Hollandaise	Riesling	Pewsey Vale Dry Riesling	99–102
Grilled Salmon with Dill Butter	Sauvignon Blanc	Vincent Gaudry Sancerre	103–104
Chicken Breast			
Chicken Salad	Rosé	Domaine Pélaquié Tavel Rosé	109–111
Hot Smoked Chicken Breast	Pinot Noir	Yabby Lake Pinot Noir	112–115
Chicken Breast Stuffed with Spinach and Gruyère	Chardonnay	Gloria Ferrer Chardonnay	116–119
Chicken Legs			
Buttermilk Fried Chicken	Chardonnay	Christian Moreau Chablis	120–122
Chicken Cacciatore	Gewürztraminer	Willm Gewürztraminer	123–125
Tandoori Chicken	Shiraz/Syrah	Brokenwood Shiraz	126-129
Duck			
Sous Vide Duck Breast	Grenache	Guigal Côtes du Rhône Rouge	130–133
Smoked Duck Salad	Riesling	Dr. Loosen Erdener Treppchen Riesling Kabinett	134–138
Sautéed Duck Breast with Sun-Dried Cherry Sauce	Pinotage	Wildekrans Pinotage	139–141
Pork			
Sous Vide Pork Tenderloin with Spicy Pineapple Salsa	Chenin Blanc	Ken Forrester "Petit" Chenin Blanc	142–145
Pork Schnitzel with Lemon	Pinot Noir	Craggy Range Pinot Noir	146–148
Grilled Pork Tenderloin with Caramelized Apple Compote	Grüner Veltliner	Domaine Wachau Grüner Veltliner	149–151
Beef Tenderloin			
Beef Tartare	Chardonnay	Au Bon Climat Chardonnay	156–158
Sautéed Beef with Cognac Peppercorn Sauce	Malbec	Agua de Piedra Gran Reserva Malbec	159–161
Gorgonzola Dolcelatte Topped Beef Tournedos	Merlot	Château La Bienfaisance St. Emilion	162–164

RECIPE TITLE	GRAPE/BLEND	WINE	PAGE
Beef Flank Steak			
Beef and Broccoli Stir-Fry	Pinot Gris/Grigio	Ponzi Pinot Gris	165–168
Grilled Flank Steak with Chimichurri Sauce	Sauvignon Blanc	Craggy Range Sauvignon Blanc	169–171
Grilled Flank Steak Sandwich	Carmenere	Root 1 Carmenère	172–175
Beef Shank			
BBQ Pulled Beef	Riesling	Dr. Konstantin Frank Semi-Dry Riesling	176–179
Beef Bourguignon	Pinot Noir	Bodega Chacra Barda Pinot Noir	180–183
Thai Beef with Massaman Curry	Moscato/Muscat	Nivole Moscato d'Asti	184–186
Lamb			
Rosemary Roasted Rack of Lamb	Viognier	Guigal Côtes du Rhône Blanc	187–189
Grilled Lamb Chops with Mint Emulsion	Aglianico	Cantravelli Taurasi Riserva	190–192
Chinese Five Spice Sautéed Lamb Chops	Garnacha	Atteca Old Vines Garnacha	193–195
Venison			
Venison Burgers	Tempranillo	Bodegas Alejandro Fernandez Tinto Pesquera	196–198
Roasted Venison with Sauce Grand Veneur	Cabernet Sauvignon	Motes Alpha Cabernet Sauvignon	199–201
Venison Chili	Petite Sirah	Bogle Petite Sirah	202–204
Ravioli			
Cheese Ravioli with Asparagus	Albariño	Burgans Albariño	211–215
Meat Ravioli in Brodo	Rosé	Château de Campuget Costières de Nimes Rosé	216–219
Shrimp Ravioli with Tomato Coulis	Sparkling	Charles Heidsieck Brut Réserve	220–223
Spaghetti			
Spaghetti con le Vongole (Clam Sauce)	Sauvignon Blanc	Nederberg Sauvignon Blanc	224–227
Spaghetti alla Carbonara	Amarone Blend	Masi Costasera Amarone della Valpolicella	228–230
Spaghetti alla Puttanesca	Vernaccia	Azienda Agraria Le Rote Vernaccia di San Gimignano	231–233

RECIPE TITLE	GRAPE/BLEND	WINE	PAGE
Mezze Rigatoni			
Mezze Rigatoni with Broccoli Rabe and Sausage	Garganega	Tedeschi Soave Classico	234–236
Mezze Rigatoni Salad with Roasted Butternut Squash	Chardonnay	Chateau St. Jean Chardonnay	237–239
Mezze Rigatoni alla Sauce Bolognese	Zinfandel	St. Francis Old Vines Zinfandel	240–242
Pizza			
Margherita Pizza	Pinot Noir	Bearboat Pinot Noir	245–247
Fennel Sausage and Porcini Mushroom Pizza	Grüner Veltliner	Domaine Wachau Grüner Veltliner	248–250
Ricotta, Taleggio, and Arugula Pizza	Sangiovese	Barone Ricasoli Brolio Chianti Classico	251–253
Lemon			
Lemon Sorbet	Riesling	JJ Prüm Graacher Himmelreich Riesling Spätlese	258–260
Lemon Pound Cake	Riesling	JJ Prüm Graacher Himmelreich Riesling Auslese	261–264
Lemon Cheesecake	Amarone Blend	Giovanni Allegrini Recioto della Valpolicella Classico	265–267
Apple			
Green Apple Mousse	Chenin Blanc	Château Soucherie Côteaux du Layon	268–270
Apple Fritters	Vidal	Standing Stone Vineyards Vidal Ice Wine	271–273
Apple Tarte Tatin	Vespaiolo, Tocai and Garganega	Maculan Torcolato	274–276
Strawberry			
Strawberries with Champagne Sabayon	Rosé	Banfi Rosa Regale Brachetto d'Acqui	277–279
Strawberry Shortcake	Sparkling	Moët et Chandon Nectar Imperial Demi-Sec	280–282
Strawberry and Blueberry Crisp	Tokaji Blend	Royal Tokaji 5 Puttonyos	283–285
Chocolate			
Chocolate Soufflé	Sparkling	Pommery Brut Rosé	286–290
Chocolate Mousse	Port Blend	Fonseca Bin. 27 Ruby Port	291–293
Flourless Hazelnut Chocolate Cake with Raspberry Sauce	Pedro Ximenez	Osborne Pedro Ximenez	294–296

Glossary

abv Alcohol by volume.

Al dente "To the tooth." This refers to the doneness of pasta/rice, meaning there is a slight bite.

Amarone A dry red wine style made in Valpolicella, Italy. Amarone is made with dried grapes and is fermented to dryness. Because the grapes are dried, the sugar concentration increases and results in wines that are more concentrated and generally above 15% abv (*see also* Recioto).

Auslese "Selected harvest."

Autolytic A wine descriptor associated with the process of autolysis, a process of yeast cells dying as a result of being eaten by their own enzymes. This process results in the toasty, biscuity, yeasty flavors that one sees in Champagne and wines aged on lees for extended periods of time.

Bain marie A cylindrical container, usually made of stainless steel.

Bâtonnage The French term for "lees stirring." Wines that go through prolonged lees stirring are generally richer in body and sometimes have yeasty, biscuity tones (particularly white wines).

Beurre noisette Brown butter.

Blood line The dark flesh on a fish, most identifiable in salmon, that runs down the center of a filet on the skin side. It has a very oily strong flavor and if the skin is being removed, the blood line should also be carefully removed. It is considered a delicacy in many Asian countries.

Botrytis Also called "noble rot." Botrytis cinerea is a fungus that lies on the surface of the grape and allows the grape's water to evaporate through the skin. This concentrates the grape's sugars, acids, and flavor without adversely affecting the grape (unlike its cousin, black rot or gray rot). Botrytized grapes are used in the production of sweet wines.

Botrytis notes An aromatic descriptor for wine. Wines with "botrytis notes" or "botrytic notes" show signs that the grapes have seen botrytis. The aroma is sometimes be described as marzipan-like.

Broad Wine descriptor that refers to a wine's mouthfeel structure. Wines that are broad are generally those that have rich fruit concentration particularly in combination with a full body (and, with red wines, dense tannins). Opposite of lean.

Brut Champagne term that refers to level of sweetness. By regulation, Brut can be anything under 15 g/l residual sugar. While 5 g/l is the normal human threshold for sugar, the acidity in Champagne is so high that it can seem dry up to 15 g/l.

Caper The berry of the caper plant that is typically brined or salt-packed.

Celeriac A root vegetable that has a prominent celery flavor.

Chapitalized Adding sugar before wine fermentation is complete which increases the wine's body and alcohol level.

Chinois A conical fine-meshed strainer typically used to strain stocks and sauces.

Chipotle pepper A smoked jalapeño pepper, most often canned.

Ciabatta An Italian-style roll that means "slipper."

Classico A term seen on Italian wines (e.g., Chianti Classico, Soave Classico) that means the grapes used to make the wine come from a specified region within the original, historic defined boundaries of the region.

Combination heat A cooking method that combines more than one type of heat, for example, moist and dry.

Complexity Used to describe the many layers of flavors in a dish or a wine. Wines that have more flavor categories (fruit, minerals, vanilla, toast, etc.) are said to be more complex or have more complexity. Complexity is one of the parameters used to determine quality in wine. Wines that are more complex, in general, are higher in quality.

Court bouillon Cooking liquid often flavored with mirepoix, typically used for deep poaching.

Cream of tartar A powdered acid that is typically used in baking and in whipping egg whites to maintain a peak.

Creole mustard A spicy grain mustard that is often used in Cajun/Creole cuisine.

Crisp Wine descriptor that refers to a high level of acidity in a wine. Wines with high acidity are perceived as crisp, the opposite of "flabby" (*see* Flabby and Racy).

Cuisson The liquid resulting from a shallow poach that is turned into a sauce.

Cutlets A tender portion cut of protein that is pounded thin.

Dance A term used to refer to the positive and harmonious interaction between food and wine. If the reaction happens for a long time, we say it is a "long" dance. The dance can vary in intensity and reactions, just as real dances do. For example, a waltz is elegant and harmonious, while a jive has high energy and is popping. Food and wine pairings can interact with one another in a similar way.

Darne A cross-cut, portion size, from a whole fish that includes the skin and bone.

Deglaze The process of capturing the fond from a pan, typically with stock or wine.

Demi-glace A classic brown sauce made from a brown veal stock that is thickened with roux.

Demi-sec A term that translates to "semi-dry," but can mean varying levels of residual sugar in wines. In Champagne, demi-sec is reserved for those with sugar levels between 35 and 50 g/l.

Diacetyl A chemical by-product that results from some malolactic fermentations. It is a compound that is reminiscent of butter. White wines that go through malolactic fermentation and create diacetyl will have a buttery taste.

Dredge To dip an item in flour and shake off the excess.

Dry Wine term that refers to no perceptible sweetness in the wine (less than 5 g/l for still table wine).

Earthy An aromatic descriptor for wine referring to aromas in wines that are reminiscent of fresh, upturned soil.

Egg wash Whisked whole eggs that may contain a small amount of milk or water.

Federspiel A term used to describe Austrian wines from the region of Wachau that have an alcohol level between 11% and 12.5% abv. They are generally medium-bodied and are more concentrated than the Steinfeder style, yet not quite as rich as the Smaragd style (*see* Steinfeder and Smaragd).

Fennel fronds The feathery herb that is attached to the stalks of a fennel bulb.

Fennel pollen A dried spice that is harvested from the fennel plant; it has an intense flavor and is relatively expensive.

Filet A tender boneless portion cut of beef, poultry, or fish.

Filtering A winemaking process used to clarify wine. Although techinques vary, generally wine is pumped through a filter where solid particles are suspended in the filter, thereby clarifying the wine.

Finesse A descriptor of a wine related to its texture. A wine with finesse has a fine (as opposed to coarse) texture. For white wines, finesse is related to a combination of characteristics including lighter body, higher acidity, and greater balance. For red wines, it is related to a combination of fine tannin texture, lighter body, and greater balance.

Fining A winemaking process to clarify wine. This process reduces suspended particles or colloids in a wine, preventing them from forming a haze. It is also used to polymerize tannins to make them more fine and less astringent. Fining is carried out using compounds such as egg whites, milk, fish bladders, and bentonite clay.

Finish A wine term that refers to the flavors that linger on the palate after a wine has been tasted.

Flabby (Flabbiness) A wine term used to describe a wine of low acidity in relation to its other elements and is generally mentioned when a wine is out of balance; the opposite of crisp (*see* Crisp).

Flinty An aromatic descriptor of wine with strong mineral notes reminiscent of gunflint.

Fond The drippings that remain in the bottom of a pan after certain cooking methods, such as sauté and roasting. Also the French name for stock.

Fork tender A sign of tenderness referring to a braised/stewed item where a fork is inserted and comes out with little resistance. It can also refer to tenderness in roasted vegetables such as beets.

Forward fruit (fruit forward) Used to describe a wine whose fruit characteristics are upfront, obvious, and pronounced.

Ghee Clarified browned butter that is traditionally used in Indian cuisine.

Gorgonzola dolcelatte A sweet cow's milk blue cheese from Italy.

Grand Cru (Burgundy) A term that refers to the classification system in Burgundy. Grand Cru is the quality level assigned to the vineyard the grapes come from and is the highest quality level attained in Burgundy (*see also* Village-Level and Premier Cru).

Grassy An aromatic/flavor descriptor for wines such as Sauvignon Blanc. It describes the scent associated with the wine and is reminiscent of fresh-cut grass.

Growth (Bordeaux) Classification of wines in Bordeaux that made the cut to be classified within the 1855 classification in Bordeaux. This can refer to any of the levels: first, second, third, fourth, or fifth growth levels.

Guanciale Cured pig cheeks.

Hot A wine descriptor that refers to the impression of alcohol intensity in a wine. When one says a wine is "hot" one refers to the thermal reaction that is experienced on the back palate from an intense level of alcohol.

Ice wine A dessert wine made with frozen grapes. Ice wine grapes are generally picked frozen on the vine. The water in the grape is ice and when the grapes are pressed, the ice crystals separate from the concentrated sugary nectar that is left to ferment. Generally, the yeast cannot complete fermentation and leaves a fair amount of residual sugar (which makes the wine sweet).

Interventionist winemaking The opposite of minimalist winemaking where the winemaker has no issue with intervening at several points during the winemaking process to protect, enhance, or improve the wine.

Intramuscular fat The internal fat found in the muscle that is often referred to as "marbling".

Jus lie A sauce traditionally derived from a roasted item that is thickened with a slurry.

Lard Rendered pork fat.

Lardons A classic term referring to a cut of pork fat or bacon, 1" × ¼" × ¼". A larding needle can be used to insert pork lardons into a roast prior to cooking.

Lean Wine descriptor that refers to a wine's mouthfeel structure. Wines that are lean are generally those with low fruit concentration, particularly in combination with crisp/racy acidity and light body; the opposite of Broad.

Lees The sediment, resulting from the winemaking process, at the bottom of wine fermentation tanks or vessels. It includes dead yeast cells, grape seeds, pulp, stem and skin fragments, and insoluble tartrates.

Length Refers to how long the flavor lasts on the palate after it has been tasted.

Maillard reaction The browning of a carbohydrate chain, specifically referring to protein, cocoa, and wheat.

Malolactic fermentation A reaction that occurs during the winemaking process. Malic acid (an acid associated with green apples) turns into lactic acid (an acid associated with milk). This happens naturally after fermentation and is desired in almost all red wines, and in some whites.

Medallion A small round tender portion cut of protein (e.g., beef, veal, pork, venison etc.).

Mince To finely chop.

Minerality An aromatic descriptor for wine that refers to aromas reminiscent of minerals, wet stone, sidewalk pavement, etc. Many wines from the Old World (*see* Old World) tend to have these types of aromas, particularly those from grapes grown in limestone soils.

Minimalist A winemaking term used to describe wines made with as little intervention as possible from the winemaker.

Mise en place French term that translates to "everything is in place", referring to: ingredients, equipment, mental preparedness, etc...

Modern A wine style term that can mean reductive winemaking and/or presence of new oak characteristics and/or interventionist winemaking (*see* Reductive and Interventionist).

Monopole A French term used primarily in Burgundy to refer to a wholly owned vineyard or climat.

Mount To incorporate butter into a sauce or soup while whisking.

Nappe Refers to the consistency of a sauce, it should coat the back of a spoon.

New World A term used to describe a wine region outside of Europe. Wines from the New World generally tend to be more focused on forward fruit.

Non-reactive pan A non-porous pan that does not react with acidic ingredients and impart a flavor on foods. Stainless steel, glass, plastic, and ceramic are nonreactive, while aluminum is reactive.

Oaked A term used to describe wine that has been influenced by oak during the winemaking process (whether via fermentation in barrels, aging in barrels, or the presence of oak staves or chips).

Old World Term used to describe a wine region within the winemaking countries of Europe. In comparison to New World wines (*see* New World), Old World wines are generally less upfront or forward in their fruit and feature more mineral, terroir notes.

One dimensional Term used to describe a wine that has only one dimension to its flavor (usually it is solely fruit-based). One-dimensional wines lack complexity (*see* Complexity).

One-way pairing When the dish makes the wine taste better OR the wine makes the dish taste better. Not both.

Opulent Descriptor for wine associated with the wine's body and fruit concentration. Wines that are full-bodied with a high concentration of fruit (and many times forward fruit), are said to be opulent.

Organic Descriptor for foods that are not genetically modified or irradiated and have not been exposed to pesticides, chemicals, or additives.

Oxidative Wine aroma descriptor that describes characteristics present in wine as a result of oxidation. As wines age in barrels (or other vessels that allow oxygen to get to the wine), aromas change from fresh and fruity to more dried fruit and spice (the color also turns towards the orange, tawny, and brown hues). These characteristics are referred to as oxidative as they are a result of the process of oxidation.

Pan gravy A sauce derived from a roasted item; the natural fat is used to make a roux and then stock is added to create the sauce.

Pellicle A term that refers to the "tacky" exterior of a protein that has been brined and then dried. This texture helps the smoke adhere and flavor the item.

Perfume (Perfumy) Descriptor related to a wine's pronounced aromatic intensity. Perfumed wines are intensely aromatic and often feature elements found in perfume (flowers, spice, etc.).

Pimenton Spanish smoked paprika.

Premier Cru (Burgundy) A term that refers to the classification system in Burgundy. Premier Cru wines are those whose grapes come from Premier Cru quality level designated vineyards. According to Burgundy's quality hierarchy, Premier Cru wines are between the village-level classification and Grand Cru (*see also* Village-Level and Grand Cru).

Prime beef Top grade of beef from the United States Department of Agriculture (USDA) that should result in a tender, juicy, full-flavored cut.

Primi piatti The first course of an Italian meal, served after the antipasti.

Quenelle A shape formed by spoons. It can refer to a mousseline, whipped cream, sorbet, etc.

Racy A wine descriptor associated with a wine's structure, particularly its acidity. Wines that are racy tend to be very high in acidity and are generally combined with light body.

Raft A term used to describe the clarification ingredients used to make a consommé once the protein has coagulated. Typically, these are egg whites, ground protein, ground mirepoix, tomato, and a small amount of acid.

Recioto Sweet red wines from the region of Valpolicella in the Veneto, Italy. They are made similarly to Amarone but are not fermented to dryness. Their fermentation either stops naturally or is intentionally stopped for some residual sugar.

Reductive Characteristics that result from winemaking with as little exposure to oxygen as possible (the opposite of oxidative winemaking). The purpose of reductive winemaking is to preserve fruit character and to prevent faults.

Reserve (Champagne) Refers to a process of making non-vintage Champagnes, whereby a portion of wine from a previous vintage(s) that has been aged is blended in for added richness and complexity. These aged wines that are blended in are referred to as reserve wines.

Reserve (General) A wine term that is applied differently around the world. In some regions it has a legal definition where the wine has spent a specified time in the barrel (e.g., Riserva in Italy or Reserva in Spain). In the New World, there are fewer to no legal parameters to using the term. Some New World producers use it as a term to refer to the highest-quality wine in their portfolio.

Ribbon stage Refers to the consistency of an item (e.g., egg yolks and sugar) that has been whisked while cooking over a double boiler. The flow of eggs will form a ribbon in the bowl as it falls.

Ricotta Impastata A fresh dry ricotta cheese.

Rondeau A large cooking pan with high, straight sides.

Round A descriptor of the mouthfeel of a wine. Wines that are more "round" in their mouthfeel are more soft and have a more mouth-filling texture (the opposite of round is linear or austere).

Sachet A small pouch of dried thyme, parsley stems, black peppercorns, bay leaf, and clove that is wrapped in cheesecloth. It is best to tie the sachet with butcher's twine and secure to the handle of the pot for easy removal.

Sauté A dry-heat method of cooking for tender portion cuts.

Sautoir A straight-sided sauté pan.

Scald A term that typically refers to milk brought to just below a boil before using in a recipe.

Schnitzel A thin cutlet of pork or veal that is breaded and pan-fried.

Score To slice into the skin/fat (e.g., duck breast skin), without cutting into the muscle. This helps render fat and self-baste.

Short cut A term that refers to a very thin cut of chives.

Slurry A mixture of cornstarch or arrowroot and water or stock that is used to thicken a sauce. The mixture should be blended by hand until smooth, the consistency of heavy cream, and be added to a simmering liquid while whisking constantly.

Smaragd A term used to describe Austrian wines from the region of Wachau that have an alcohol level over 12.5% abv. These are highly prized wines as they show more concentration and richness (given that the grapes are riper) than the Steinfeder or Federspiel styles (*see* Steinfeder and Federspiel).

Spätlese Means "late harvest" in German. Sometimes the grapes are infected by botrytis and sometimes they are not. This gives it dried-fruit and marzipan-like notes. They are generally lower in sweetness and slightly higher in alcohol than an Auslese.

Steinfeder A term used to describe Austrian wines from the region of Wachau that have an alcohol level below 11% abv. They are generally lighter in style than Federspiel and known to have a slight effervescent prickle to them (*see* Federspiel).

Sweat This cooking technique usually refers to onions, shallots, and garlic. The pan is preheated over medium-low heat, oil is added, then the aromatics and a lid is placed on top. The aromatics should cook until tender and translucent without color.

TCM Tinted cure mixture is a curing salt that contains sodium nitrate. Traditionally, TCM is used in charcuterie and garde manger for curing sausages, patés, and terrines. It keeps the cooked product pink throughout.

Temper To slowly incorporate a cold- or room-temperature item into a hot item.

Tenderloin A tender muscle that runs along the spine of an animal; this is usually one of the most expensive cuts.

Terroir A French term that refers to all of the natural elements that influence a wine's flavor, texture, structure, or weight. Among other things, soil, sunlight exposure, topography, and climate are elements included in terroir.

Three-way pairing A two-way pairing (*see* Two-way pairing) with something extra that adds an element not found in either the dish or the wine alone.

Tomalley The soft green liver and pancreas found inside lobster and crab, sometimes used to thicken sauces.

Tournedo A small round, thin, tender portion cut of protein (e.g., beef, veal, pork, venison, etc.)

Traditional A wine style term that can mean separately or together oxidative winemaking and/or minimalist winemaking (*see* Oxidative and Minimalist).

Train wreck A term we use to refer to food and wine pairings that taste dreadful; the opposite of a magical pairing.

Two-way pairing Occurs when the dish makes the wine taste better and the wine makes the dish taste better.

Umami Japanese for "good flavor" or "good taste." Refers to a basic taste sensation. It has been described as the fifth perceived taste alongside sweet, sour, bitter, and salty. Foods that are high in umami are meat, cheese, broth, stock, and other protein-heavy foods. However, there is still some mystery as to how the tongue perceives umami.

Unfiltered Wines that have not gone through the filtering process. They tend to be more dense and less visually clear. Winemakers who do not filter suggest that filtering strips a wine of its flavor (*see* Filtering).

Unfined Wines that have not gone through the process of fining (*see* Fining).

Unoaked Wine that has seen no influence of oak during the winemaking process.

Upfront fruit A term used to describe wine whose fruit characteristics are obvious and pronounced (*see also* Forward fruit).

Velouté A mother sauce that consists of chicken stock that is thickened with roux.

Vielles Vignes French term for "Old Vines." Generally refers to vines more than 25 years old, although there is no universal global law on how old the vines must be to be called old vines.

Village-Level (Burgundy) A term that refers to the classification system in Burgundy. Village-level wines are those labeled with the name of the village the grapes come from. According to Burgundy's quality hierarchy, Village-level wines in Burgundy are between the regional classification (Bourgogne) and Premier Cru, which is named after a specific vineyard (*see also* Premier Cru and Grand Cru).

Index

Bold page numbers indicate the definition in the Glossary.